The BBC Proms Guide to Great Concertos

Nicholas Kenyon has been Director of the BBC Proms since 1996. He was a music critic for *The New Yorker*, *The Times*, and the *Observer*, and was Controller, BBC Radio 3, from 1992 to 1998, responsible for the award-winning Radio 3 seasons 'Fairest Isle' and 'Sounding the Century'. He wrote the history of the BBC Symphony Orchestra and edited the influential volume *Authenticity and Early Music*. In 2001 he wrote a new edition of his biography of Simon Rattle. He is now Controller, BBC Proms, Live Events and Television Classical Music, and was appointed a CBE in 2001.

THE BBC PROMS GUIDE TO
Great Concertos

edited by Nicholas Kenyon

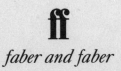

faber and faber

First published in 2003
by Faber and Faber Limited
3 Queen Square London WC1N 3AU

Typeset by Faber and Faber Limited
Printed in England by Bookmarque Ltd, Croydon

A CIP record for this book
is available from the British Library

ISBN 0–571–22331–1

10 9 8 7 6 5 4 3 2 1

Contents

List of Contributors

Andrew Achenbach 15
Julian Anderson 117
Nicholas Anderson 10, 13
Brendan Beales 60
Meirion Bowen 279
Susan Bradshaw 221
Anthony Burton 26, 28, 31, 51, 53, 63
Piers Burton-Page 68, 89, 93
Anthony Bye 24
David Cairns 37, 142
Philip Clark 1
Andrew Clements 18, 131, 133
Rob Cowan 19
David Cox 114
David Fanning 235
Noël Goodwin 35, 247
Rodney Greenberg 97
David Gutman 181, 185, 188, 234
Paul Hamburger 21
Malcolm Hayes 293
Ivan Hewett 119
Arthur Hutchings 156
Andrew Huth 65, 122, 127, 171, 183, 190, 198, 200,
    204, 241, 254, 259, 266, 269, 272, 275
Adrian Jack 84, 194, 196, 207, 209, 226, 256
Stephen Johnson 229, 238
Lindsay Kemp 7, 12, 100, 145, 153, 154, 158, 160,
    165, 168, 287
Michael Kennedy 86
Tess Knighton 58
Richard Langham Smith 176
Malcolm MacDonald 39, 45, 48, 111, 212
Hugh Macdonald 42

Introduction

Some musical forms seem immortal. They stand the test of time, and in spite of the most radical changes in taste, repertory and style, reinvent themselves to flourish in new musical worlds. Who would have thought that the idea of a single violin playing in dialogue with an orchestra, heard in the first half of the eighteenth century in nature painting by Vivaldi, would have come full circle through the huge nineteenth-century virtuoso masterpieces of Brahms and Tchaikovsky, the world-weary beauty of Berg, through the post-war originality of Lutosławski and Ligeti, to flourish already in the new twenty-first century with a gem-like concerto by Oliver Knussen?

The concerto, pitting a single virtuoso soloist (or sometimes more than one) against the might of the symphony orchestra, has been one of the most enduring forms in Western classical music. This book provides an authoritative and up-to-date guide to the greatest concertos in the repertory, works which have proved their continual power to engage and move listeners – whether in concerts, recordings, or broadcasts. If you want to know more about what inspired the great concertos, and what to listen out for as you encounter these thrilling pieces, this book is the place to start.

The notion of a concerto as inevitably a contest between a virtuoso and an orchestra is, of course, simplistic. In the beginning the term 'concerto' signified no more than that musicians were 'performing together' – whether in a madrigal (Monteverdi used the term for his seventh book of madrigals) or a church piece (the *concerti ecclesiastici* of the late sixteenth century). Even J. S. Bach, who wrote several of what we would now recognise as concertos, also used the term to describe some of his church cantatas, simply because there various performers played and sang together. There has always been a fruitful tension between the meaning of concerto as 'working together' and that of 'dispute, debate, contend'.

It was not a coincidence that it was the violin that became the favoured solo instrument of the new concerto; it had been emancipated from its role as a provider of popular but definitely downmarket dance music, and turned into a vehicle of the highest, most sophisticated art. As with the creation of opera at the start of the seventeenth century, the language of Baroque music depended on the replacement of the equal-voiced discourse of the Renaissance with a soloistic, professionalised leading voice (whether in operatic aria or concerto solo) which was accompanied and supported by the *basso continuo* of keyboard and bass instruments that gave harmonic support to the soloist.

Thus the concerto took root, was admirably suited to the demonstrative temper of the musical times, and was speedily developed. Vivaldi wrote for a variety of different solo instruments which were played by his female Venetian virtuosi, but not the keyboard: it was J. S. Bach who took the formal inventions of Vivaldi (and in some cases Vivaldi's music as well) and made them into concertos for himself and his sons and pupils to play on keyboard instruments. (The dazzling effects of his concertos for three and four harpsichords remains to be surpassed by later composers.)

The eighteenth century saw the composition of literally thousands of now forgotten concertos, for an increasing number of public and court concerts, often amiably superficial and uninventive works which are now justly ignored except by musicologists. The virtuoso tradition continued in quirkily original pieces such as the violin concertos of the Chevalier de Saint-Georges, but it was Mozart, as so often, who subsumed the fashions of the time into something profoundly original and musical. It is a shock to realise how recently most of Mozart's marvellous piano concertos entered the regular repertory. As with his symphonies, only a couple were known and played regularly before the recent revival, a point which the BBC Proms repertory demonstrates clearly. By contrast, the Baroque concerto, represented by Bach's single and double violin concertos, was always in evidence in the Proms repertory, but who could have predicted the extraordinary revival of Vivaldi's music?

When comparing this book with the first volume of this series of programme notes, on great symphonies, it is noticeable that the eleven decades of the BBC Proms have seen rather fewer fluctuations of taste where concertos are concerned. The great favourites, especially Beethoven's later piano concertos and violin concerto, remain central, as do the violin concertos of Brahms, Mendelssohn and Tchaikovsky. There have been over a hundred performances each of Beethoven's Fourth and Fifth Piano Concertos; even more, surprisingly, of Schumann's. No single Mozart concerto has been as popular as these, though his concertos as a whole have had over four hundred performances. The roll-call of soloists who have performed these works most often at the BBC Proms is a history of performance in our time: among pianists there have been Myra Hess (the most popular soloist at the Proms, who played at ninety-one Prom seasons between 1908 and 1961), Benno Moiseiwitsch (eighty-eight Prom seasons) and Clifford Curzon (sixty-eight Prom seasons from 1924 to 1981), and more recently Alfred Brendel and Martha Argerich.

Then there are those concertos which are, by some alchemy, by far the greatest symphonic works of their composers: Bruch's Violin Concerto No. 1 and Grieg's Piano Concerto, absolute audience-winners and poll-toppers, whose inclusion in programmes even today is likely to produce reliable results at the box office. Looking back at the early years of Henry Wood's Proms, most of the concertos that have vanished are pretty insignificant, though the piano concertos of Mendelssohn and Saint-Saëns arguably deserve better from today's programmers. Then there are particular works which have fallen out of fashion: one especial Proms favourite was the John Ireland Piano Concerto, played every year after its composition for many years, but now infrequently heard at the Proms or indeed elsewhere.

Previous histories of the concerto tended to view the evolution of the form in a straight line. An amusing qualification was offered by J. Raymond Tobin in his introduction to Ralph Hill's Penguin symposium, *The Concerto* (a standard work, first published half a century ago). He compared the question 'what is a concerto' to the question 'what is a house?' – 'The story of the house stretches from the meanness of the mud hut to the magnificence of the mansion, while the most recent chapter, the pre-fab of today, is a reminder that . . . even austerity does not rule out some advance and advantage.' Where that left some austere concertos of the post-war years was not entirely clear.

As an introduction to the importance of the concerto, it is still difficult to better the display of learning and understanding in Donald Tovey's early essay 'The Classical Concerto', written in 1903 (exactly a century before the publication of the present volume): it is most handily reprinted in volume 3 of Tovey's *Essays in Musical Analysis* (OUP). Tovey wanted to give the concerto a weight and significance that the symphony naturally possessed, but which in many empty virtuoso vehicles the concerto lacked. 'The idea that the professed purpose of the form is technical display has been actually maintained by musicians who yield to none in their reverence and love for the great concertos of Beethoven and Mozart.' Yet technical display has been, and remains, a key element of the concerto, and that does inevitably lead some composers to an idiom which can be regarded as flamboyant: we perhaps take a less moral tone towards this today than did Tovey the Scot, determined to improve our musical fibre.

The concerto today shows every sign of maintaining its inventiveness. This book concentrates on those that have already found a secure place in the repertory, and comes up to date with Ligeti's piercingly original Violin Concerto, but there are many other innovative works – the concertos of Thea Musgrave which, like the recent Horn Concerto by Colin Matthews, makes use of movement by players around the stage, the Oboe Concerto commissioned for the Proms from John Woolrich, with its 'echo chamber' of oboists behind the principal soloist.

The BBC Proms has had a long tradition of providing the best possible programme notes for all its concerts, and we have felt for some time that the excellent material produced for audiences in the Royal Albert Hall should be able to reach a far greater number of music lovers. We were therefore delighted when Faber and Faber was responsive to the idea of a collection of programme notes for some of the central works in the repertory. A first volume on symphonies is appearing concurrently with this volume, and we hope more will follow.

Each note is designed to be consulted and read separately, so there is some inevitable repetition between different notes.

Acknowledgements

Our first thanks go to the many outstanding authors who have allowed their work to be reprinted in this new format. The notes were originally commissioned by BBC Proms Publications, under the editorial guidance first of George Hall and more recently of Mark Pappenheim, whose expert hands have made an important contribution to the consistency and shape of the notes. Many thanks to them, and especially to Edward Bhesania who has contributed all the new composer biographies and helped with the selection and editing of the material for this volume. Sarah Breeden, who now runs BBC Proms Publications, has overseen the project for the BBC, and her assistant Hannah Rowley has been tireless in her help. At Faber, Belinda Matthews and her team have been supportive and patient as this book has taken shape alongside the many other pressing deadlines of the BBC Proms season. My thanks to them all.

Nicholas Kenyon
Director, BBC Proms

John Adams (b. 1947)

John Adams has been described as the composer who gave minimalism a human face, and he has developed a popular appeal beyond that of many of his contemporaries, absorbing a wide range of eclectic musical influences. Even as a Harvard undergraduate in the 1960s, Adams had embraced jazz and rock for their directness of expression. On moving to California he experimented with electronic music. In the late 1970s he produced his first important works incorporating minimalist processes – *Phrygian Gates* (1978) and the string septet *Shaker Loops* (1978, later revised for string orchestra). An association with the San Francisco Symphony (1978–85) led to large-scale orchestral works, including *Harmonium* (1980–1), with choir, setting texts by Donne and Dickinson; *Grand Pianola Music* (1982) featuring two piano soloists, and *Harmonielehre* (1984–5). His two full-scale operas, *Nixon in China* (1987) and *The Death of Klinghoffer* (1991), took scenarios from current affairs, and Adams's engagement with world events continued with his rock-oriented 'songplay' *I Was Looking at the Ceiling and then I Saw the Sky* (based on the LA earthquake in 1994), and *On the Transmigration of Souls*, commissioned by the New Philharmonic to mark the first anniversary, in 2002, of the September 11 terrorist attacks.

∾ Violin Concerto (1993)

1 ♩ = 78 –
2 Chaconne: Body through which the dream flows
3 Toccare

'Adams didn't take many risks in this piece,' John Adams mocked himself when grilled by an interviewer about his Violin Concerto, 'he bought it off the rack!' From the composer who wrote *Gnarly Buttons*, *Hoodoo Zephyr* and *Lollapalooza* the generic title of this work may indeed seem disappointingly prosaic and akin to reinventing the wheel. But Adams goes even further in this self-criticism, claiming that the title reflects his timidness in inventing a structure of his own – it's a concerto that behaves like a concerto. The fast–slow–fast shape allows space for a flashy cadenza at the end of the first movement, where tradition would dictate it should be, and a toccata-like finale draws the threads of the piece together. Moreover, the explicit stylistic clashes that colour nearly everything else Adams has written are jettisoned in favour of the dialectic tension between soloist and orchestra that is a time-honoured feature of the genre.

Adams approached writing his first concerto with trepidation. The principle of a solo instrument battling it out against an orchestral mass ran contrary to the monolithic architecture and dense orchestration of his earlier works. In this respect the more lyrical and obviously melodic language which Adams created for his second opera, *The Death of Klinghoffer* (1991), became a turning point, and the soloist continually 'sings' throughout the half-hour duration of the Violin Concerto. Adams describes the violinist's material as a 'hyper-melody' and, notwithstanding the off-the-peg structure, this melody line is etched with Adams's familiar triadic and modal melodic cells. Like Charlie Parker stripping away the content of 'How High the Moon' and using its shell to create 'Ornithology', Adams's Violin Concerto borrows a pre-existing structure as a vehicle for fluid invention.

Another analogy – that of an Escher staircase – describes the regenerative loops that permeate the first movement. The violinist enters over a series of airily orchestrated rising triads in the strings and synthesiser. At first he moves without much rhythmic fuss but then accumulates more notes and friskier syncopations. As a plateau of complexity is reached, the violinist doubles back and returns to rhythmically simpler material which kick-starts the process again. With the soloist and strings acting as a unit, Adams casts the woodwind as a delayed echo. A solo clarinet appears after twelve bars with a version of the violinist's opening gesture as the violinist himself has already moved on to more complex material. Later, scampering flutes and clarinets latch on to the runs of semiquavers in the violin part and offer flowing embellishment. A break in the violinist's frenetic activity gives the woodwind room to paraphrase the string triads that opened the work, and later an oboe seems rudely to interrupt the solo line.

With the exuberance of the first movement spent, the violinist embarks on a cadenza which seamlessly melts into the slow movement. Adams took the title 'Body through which the dream flows' from a poem by Robert Haas which accurately reflects the way he contracts and expands the repeated bass line of a chaconne. A portentous tubular bell and eerie synthesiser parts give a supernatural atmosphere and Adams describes the violinist as 'floating like a disembodied spirit above the orchestral tissue'.

The moto perpetuo finale relates back to the pulse and graduated accelerations of *Shaker Loops* (1978). Although the music is notated in rapid groups of semiquavers in four, a recurring violin figuration pushes against this prevailing pulse, as do spiky flute and piccolo stabs. Eventually, in a reflection of both Ives and Nancarrow, Adams has the entire woodwind section walking in five against the prevailing metre of four. But it's not long before we are firmly back in four and careering towards an end-point that finds violin and orchestra topping one another's heights.

Philip Clark © BBC

Malcolm Arnold (b. 1921)

Drawn to the trumpet as a child through jazz (he was an especial fan of Louis Armstrong), Arnold entered the Royal College of Music as a trumpeter and composer, and later became principal trumpet of the London Philharmonic Orchestra in 1943. His reputation grew quickly after his comic overture *Beckus the Dandipratt* was recorded by the LPO in 1948. His melodic invention (often influenced by British folk song and dances), rhythmic vitality, and brilliance as an orchestrator are partnered with a gift for fluency, which sustained his prodigious output of over a hundred film scores, including the Oscar-winning music for *The Bridge on the River Kwai* (1957). His output includes nine symphonies, five ballets, two operas and over a dozen concertos (including those written for Larry Adler, Julian Bream, James Galway, Benny Goodman and Yehudi Menuhin). His jazzy *Concerto for Two Pianos (Three Hands)*, written for the husband-and-wife team Cyril Smith and Phyllis Sellick, was premiered at the Proms in 1969.

∾ Clarinet Concerto No. 2, Op. 115 (1974)

1 Allegro vivace
2 Lento
3 The Pre-Goodman Rag: Allegro non troppo –
  Prestissimo

Giving genuine pleasure to a wide audience is often not a high priority among contemporary composers. Sir Malcolm Arnold is an exception. Blessed with a natural and spontaneous gift for melody, allied to a fluent technique, and a willingness to cross the Great Divide which separates 'popular' from 'serious' music, Arnold suffered particularly badly at a time when the only British composers to be taken seriously were those who flirted – with varying degrees of failure – with the avant-garde. According to received critical opinion, Arnold was a musical lightweight, a traditionalist who wrote tuneful, tonal music, a jester – and even worse, a composer who actually *made money* out of his work, and was proud to acknowledge his award-winning film scores, such as *Bridge on the River Kwai*, rather than keeping them anonymous.

Under William Glock's regime, Arnold did not fare too badly in his relationship with the BBC: Glock commissioned both the Fourth Symphony, and the *Fantasy for Audience and Orchestra*, performed on the Last Night of the Proms in 1970. But after Glock's retirement in 1973, Arnold fell into total disfavour: together with other unfashionable British symphonists, his large-scale works were hardly ever performed at the Proms, and BBC commissions dried up. But the pendulum swings back: in recent years, 'New Romanticism' has brought rehabilitation and official recognition, and Arnold was knighted in the 1993 New Year's Honours List.

In the early 1970s, in despair at establishment neglect and critical sniping, Arnold took himself and his family off to Dublin for five years. There, in a more congenial and convivial atmosphere, he completed his Seventh Symphony, a Second String Quartet, the *Fantasy on a Theme of John Field* and a Second Clarinet Concerto (the First, for clarinet and strings, had been written around a quarter of a century earlier, during Arnold's first burst of creativity). The Second Concerto was dedicated to Benny Goodman, who gave the first performance in Denver, Colorado, in August 1974.

Just as Mozart or Handel moulded solo works to fit the exact individual requirements of their exponents, Arnold the consummate craftsman took Goodman's strengths and limitations into account. Jazz clarinettists come into their own in the upper register, and this concerto skilfully exploits a wide range of dynamics within a fairly limited tessitura. Arnold also considerably bore in mind his soloist's relatively advanced age – sixty – keeping the piece short and giving him plenty of rests! Towards the end of the first movement,

Arnold reverts to traditional practice, encouraging the soloist to improvise a cadenza 'as jazzy and way-out as you please, based on the concerto's themes'. At the British premiere, Goodman apparently ignored the composer's advice and went off into inspired improvisatory realms of his own, leaving the fabric of the piece far behind!

The second movement is a lyrical rhapsody, opening with a tender and reflective dialogue for clarinet and oboe. In complete contrast, the riotous finale – Arnold in his most unbuttoned mood – is headed 'The Pre-Goodman Rag'. The clarinet exploits its shrill upper register for all it's worth, abetted by shrieking brass and an extrovert range of noises from the 'kitchen' department.

© Wendy Thompson

Johann Sebastian Bach (1685–1750)

Born in the German town of Eisenach, Bach was a chorister then violinist before taking his first organist post at Arnstadt while still a teenager. It was in Weimar, as court organist from 1708, that Bach began to produce cantatas regularly, and wrote many of his great organ works, as well as organ transcriptions of concertos by Vivaldi. In 1717 Prince Leopold offered him the position of Kapellmeister at Cöthen, where he wrote the 'Brandenburg' Concertos, the Four Orchestral Suites and the violin concertos, and married his second wife Anna Magdalena, who bore him thirteen children. Bach's heavy duties in his final job, as Kantor of the Thomasschule in Leipzig from 1723 until his death, involved for some years the writing of a new cantata each week, as well as teaching Latin and music, choir training, and directing the music for church services. In later years he drew his art together in such major works as the Mass in B minor, the *Art of Fugue*, the *Musical Offering* and the *Goldberg Variations*. His densely contrapuntal idiom became unfashionable soon after his death until the early nineteenth century, when a revival of interest in his music began that has lasted to the present.

❧ Harpsichord Concerto in D minor, BWV 1052 (*c.* 1730)

1 Allegro
2 Adagio
3 Allegro

Of the twenty-or-so concertos by Bach which survive, fewer than half – the Concerto for Two Violins in D minor, the solo violin concertos in E major and A minor, and the six 'Brandenburgs' – are still in their likely original scoring. The remainder are arrangements for one or more harpsichords and orchestra of existing concertos, 'new' works fashioned for performance at the gathering of the Leipzig Collegium Musicum, the pro-amateur concert society of which he assumed the directorship in 1729.

These keyboard concertos occupy a seminal position in the history of the genre. Not only are they probably the first compositions of their type, but their level of influence was almost certainly boosted by the subsequent cultivation and dissemination of the keyboard concerto by Bach's sons Wilhelm Friedemann, Carl Philipp Emanuel and Johann Christian (the first two of whom would presumably have joined their father in performances of the concertos for two, three and four harpsichords before they left home in the mid-1730s).

It is conceivable, however, that Bach had no specific notion of creating something new. Quite possibly he simply found these concertos a quick and convenient way of furnishing material for the Collegium, a supposition that might make it easier to understand why he limited himself to the recasting of existing works (though the autograph manuscripts do show that he took considerable pains over his transcriptions, and that the solo parts often underwent substantial revision). Whatever his intentions, the fact is that the keyboard concerto, non-existent in 1700, had become a firmly established genre by the time of his death fifty years later.

The models for Bach's keyboard concertos are sometimes clear enough – the violin concertos and the Fourth 'Brandenburg' all exist in harpsichord arrangements – but for most of them the identity of the original solo instrument can only be conjectured. Such a work is the longesst of them, the D minor Concerto, BWV1052. The keyboard version which survives today is possibly the second or third reworking of the original, generally thought to have been a violin concerto composed during Bach's time as Kapellmeister to Prince Leopold of Anhalt-Cöthen between 1717 and 1723. Versions of all three movements appear in cantatas of 1728:

the first two, this time with organ solo (and, in the case of the Adagio, four-part chorus as well) appear in Cantata No. 146, while the last movement turns up (also with organ) in Cantata No. 188. Uncertainties remain, however: it has been suggested that a still-earlier version, possibly for viola d'amore, may have been written during the composer's pre-Cöthen years in Weimar; while doubts have even been voiced concerning Bach's authorship of the original work at all.

This last proposition seems the hardest to swallow. If the concerto did start life as the work of someone else, the original must be well submerged here, for the evidence of one's ears points to just one possible author. This is noble and powerful music, conceived on a scale that surely betrays Bach's hand. Equally characteristic is the way in which the Vivaldian structural model of recurring orchestral sections (or ritornellos) and freer solo passages is adapted by deliberately blurring the thematic distinction between the two with a wealth of contrapuntal and accompanimental detail.

The D minor has long been the most commonly performed of the Bach harpsichord concertos, thanks no doubt to its relative difficulty, its robust keyboard textures and an undemonstrative but persistently demonic quality whose appeal to a later age was bound to be strong. And just as it was the first of them to have been accepted on the piano (Moscheles played it in public during the first Bach revival of the 1830s), so in the new age of the harpsichord it would appear to be the last, enjoying a continuing tradition not only at the hands of committed Bach pianists, but also among a younger generation of piano virtuosi as well. It is a tradition that seems likely to survive as long as its elemental strength continues to be appreciated.

© Lindsay Kemp

❧ Violin Concerto in A minor, BWV 1041
(1730)

1   Allegro
2   Andante
3   Allegro assai

Although only three of Bach's violin concertos (BWV 1041–3) have been preserved in their original form, there were evidently a great many more. Several have survived in later versions as harpsichord concertos, while individual movements from lost concertos are almost certainly contained within the body of Bach's cantatas. Most of these works have generally been considered to date from the mainly happy years in Bach's life when he served Prince Leopold as Kapellmeister at the court of Anhalt-Cöthen (1717–23). Yet there is little or no conclusive evidence to support the theory. Bach's autograph scores of the three well-known violin concertos – those in A minor, E major, and D minor for two violins – have been lost, and these works are known only by surviving parts, some of them in Bach's hand, and by the composer's own adaptation of them as harpsichord concertos during the 1730s.

It was during his Weimar period (1708–17) that Bach first encountered concertos by his Italian contemporaries, among whom were Albinoni, Alessandro Marcello and, above all, Vivaldi. Whereas Rome had been the leading centre of concerto production during the closing years of the seventeenth century, the focus had now turned to Venice, and it was the 'avant-garde' concertos of the Venetians that made such a powerful impact on the young Bach. Concertos by Vivaldi, and doubtless by others too, were circulating in European courts and other centres of musical activity well before their publication.

At Weimar Bach was doubly fortunate, since not only were concertos especially cultivated but, in Johann Ernst, the youthful and artistically talented nephew of his employer,

Grand-Duke Wilhelm Ernst of Saxe-Weimar, he seems to have had an ally. Johann Ernst may well have brought back with him from his studies in Holland all sorts of concertos, in both manuscript and printed copies – Amsterdam was one of the leading cities for music publishing at this time. In Bach's own concertos the formal layout of three movements, the basic ritornello structure of an alternating pattern of solo and tutti (ensemble) episodes, and the harmonic concept (notably spacious in his hands), all stem from Venetian models, especially those provided by Vivaldi. We think of Bach first and foremost as a keyboard player, but he was also an accomplished violinist, as his second musically gifted son, Carl Philipp Emanuel, attests. 'In his youth and until the approach of old age', C. P. E. Bach recalled, '[father] played the violin cleanly and resonantly.'

The surviving parts of the Violin Concerto in A minor, most of which are in Bach's hand, date from 1730, when he probably introduced the piece to the concerts of the Collegium Musicum whose directorship he had assumed the previous year. This was one of two such musical societies in Leipzig, made up mainly of students but including professional musicians.

In its organisation of tutti and solo episodes the opening movement of the A minor Violin Concerto closely follows Vivaldi's method. The manner in which Bach treats these episodes, however, and the brilliant way in which he interrelates them, far transcends the techniques of his contemporaries.

A more distinctly Bachian invention is present in the lyrical slow movement. Here the diverse, often playful solo figurations are contained within the Baroque discipline of an ostinato-like bass motif, which stalks, at intervals, through the entire movement. (Some of the telling effect that Bach creates by combining these strikingly well-contrasted elements is, however, lost if the tempo is regarded as more of an Adagio than an Andante.)

The concluding movement is a dance in an almost uninterrupted 9/8 metre in the style of a gigue. Bach, of course, is not merely content to leave it as such, endowing the piece with a subtly contrapuntal character. The main theme is introduced by the first violins, followed by the seconds, the basses and finally the violas.

© Nicholas Anderson

✍ Violin Concerto in E major, BWV 1042
(c. 1717–23)

1   Allegro
2   Adagio
3   Allegro assai

It is sobering to think that Bach's twenty-or-so surviving orchestral concertos for various instruments present a far from complete picture of his total output in the genre. Many concertos have been lost or were recast as instrumental (or even choral) movements for cantatas, while of those we do have, only a handful are in their original scorings. Happily, these include the two concertos for solo violin and orchestra which have come to be numbered among their composer's most popular and frequently performed works.

It is generally agreed that Bach composed most of his concertos during his time as Kapellmeister to the Prince of Anhalt-Cöthen between 1717 and 1723, a happy period for him during which he enjoyed both the support of a musically appreciative employer and the luxury of regularly directing a proficient medium-sized orchestra. After he left Cöthen for Leipzig, opportunities to compose and perform concertos were fewer, however, until in 1729 he took up the directorship of a concert society known as the Collegium Musicum, in which musicians from city and university came together once a week to perform. For these meetings Bach revised much of his earlier orchestral music and arranged some of his concertos – those for violin included – for one or more harpsichords and strings. It is usually assumed, therefore, that he led these performances from the keyboard, but the possibility that he also performed his own violin concertos in Leipzig should not be discounted. His son Carl Philipp Emanuel once recalled that his father was happier directing an orchestra from the violin than from the harpsichord.

Most of Bach's concertos follow the example set by Vivaldi and other Venetian composers, that of three movements in the pattern fast–slow–fast. Vivaldi's habit was to ensure that soloist and orchestra had clearly differentiated melodic material, but Bach preferred to blur this distinction with a wealth of contrapuntal and accompanimental detail, as he does in the first movement of the E major concerto, also cast in the three-part, A–B–A shape reminiscent of a Baroque aria. The slow central movement is a noble soliloquy for the soloist over a sturdily repetitive bass, and the concerto ends, unusually for Bach, with a rondo-like movement in which the orchestra's five statements of the main theme are separated by short but exuberantly inventive interludes for the soloist.

© Lindsay Kemp

∾ Concerto for Two Violins in D minor, BWV 1043 (before 1723)

1 Vivace
2 Largo, ma non tanto
3 Allegro

The court orchestra at Bach's disposal during his period as Kapellmeister at Cöthen (1717–23) was made up of talented players – many of them hand-picked by the Prince himself from the disbanded musicians of the Berlin royal household.

Italian techniques in concerto writing were quickly disseminated throughout Europe, playing a fundamental part in all such works by foreign composers. In his earlier employment at Weimar (1708–17) Bach had made a special study of the Italian concertos of the time and, in particular, those of his Venetian contemporary Vivaldi. The three-movement formal layout, the basic alternating pattern of solo and tutti episodes, and the notably spacious harmonic concept of Bach's own concertos all stem from Venetian (specifically Vivaldian) models. Fugal and canonic devices, on the other hand, and – above all in this Double Concerto – the dialogue and imitative ideas of the solo parts, bear closer affinity with the Roman concerto grosso style of Corelli.

The first movement of the Double Concerto in D minor is a tautly constructed fugal exposition unique among Bach's opening concerto movements. The alternating solo and tutti sections are treated with considerable freedom, and are altogether less clear-cut than those of his Italian contemporaries.

The lyrically sustained Largo is justly regarded as among Bach's most poetic statements. Its song-like melody for the two solo violins lies above a gentle 12/8 string accompaniment, and develops so engagingly that complexities in the writing itself are easily overlooked.

The finale contains dance elements, often hidden beneath a profusion of imitative or canonic conceits. The initial statement is particularly arresting both for the unconventional manner in which the melody is contained solely within the two strands, and for the contrasts in 'affect' which it provides throughout with the restless tutti interjections.

© Nicholas Anderson

Samuel Barber (1910–81)

Among the leading twentieth-century American composers, Samuel Barber, in spite of his European outlook, wrote in a largely conservative idiom. At fourteen, Barber began studies at the Curtis Institute, Philadelphia, producing notable early works such as the song cycle *Dover Beach* and the Cello Sonata. He then travelled to Vienna and Rome (while his compatriots Copland and Carter gravitated to Paris) and secured his reputation as a composer with his First String Quartet and First Symphony. The Adagio for Strings (1938), arranged from his First String Quartet, has become an enduring symbol of American music. He taught at the Curtis Institute from 1939 to 1942 before returning to Europe, where he wrote the Cello Concerto and the nostalgic *Knoxville: Summer of 1915*. His Pulitzer prize-winning opera *Vanessa* (1958) was followed by the less successful *Antony and Cleopatra* (1966), written for opening of the Metropolitan Opera's new house in Lincoln Center.

❧ Violin Concerto, Op. 14 (1939–40)

1　Allegro
2　Andante
3　Presto in moto perpetuo

It was during the summer of 1939 that Samuel Barber – not yet thirty and still basking in the extraordinary popular success of his Adagio for Strings, which Toscanini had premiered the previous year – set to work on a violin concerto for the Odessa-born Iso Briselli, a pupil of the legendary Carl Flesch and (like Barber) a graduate of Philadelphia's Curtis Institute of Music.

Briselli was the adopted son of a wealthy Philadelphia soap manufacturer by the name of Samuel Fels, with whom Barber had agreed a fee of $1,000 for the new concerto (half of it payable in advance). When Barber subsequently presented Briselli with the first two movements, the twenty-seven-year-old virtuoso declared them 'too simple and not brilliant enough for a concerto', whereupon Barber was able to reassure him that the finale would serve up 'ample opportunity to display the artist's technical powers'. However, when Briselli saw the first couple of pages of the finale, he complained that it was too difficult – and Fels promptly demanded his $500 back!

In an extraordinary sequence of events, a 'trial' performance was quickly arranged to prove that Barber's music was indeed playable. At two hours' notice, Herbert Baumel (a gifted student at the Curtis Institute who possessed formidable sight-reading skills) learnt part of the finale and triumphantly demonstrated the masterly practicability of Barber's exhilarating, helter-skelter passagework.

Barber had been vindicated, and Fels not only handed over the rest of his payment but also relinquished the rights to the concerto's first performance. Baumel in fact went on to perform the work with the symphony orchestra of the Curtis Institute (under the baton of Fritz Reiner, no less), but it was left to Albert Spalding and the Philadelphia Orchestra under Eugene Ormandy to give the concerto its official, critically acclaimed premiere on 7 February 1941, since when its irresistible combination of lyrical ardour and jaw-dropping bravura has secured it a place in the hearts of great virtuosos and audiences the world over.

Beautifully laid out for modest forces (Barber asks for double woodwind and just a pair of horns and trumpets – listen out, too, for a deliciously subtle contribution from the piano), the concerto's red-blooded melodic impulse is immediately exemplified by the soloist's sublimely expansive G major tune heard at the very outset. The smiling second subject (first heard on the clarinet) has more than a hint of a Scotch snap about it, and there's a notably impassioned climax before the brief (accompanied) cadenza, but the first movement's abiding mood is one of songful serenity.

If anything, the central Andante in E major merely intensifies this generously lyrical vein, boasting as it does yet another gloriously long-breathed main theme (the principal oboe the lucky recipient this time). The reappearance of this theme following the more agitated central section (with the soloist playing on the G string) must be one of the most lusciously Romantic passages in any concerto.

By contrast, the A minor finale is a veritable tour de force, a giddy 'perpetual motion' of blistering virtuosity, culminating in a headlong dash to the tape, leaving everyone breathless with excitement.

Andrew Achenbach © BBC

Béla Bartók (1881–1945)

Bartók, along with his contemporary Kodály, built up a Hungarian national art music that drew heavily on the country's rich folk tradition. After studying piano and composition at the Budapest Academy he embarked with Kodály on a series of tours to collect folk song: they recorded, transcribed and classified music from Hungary, Transylvania, North Africa and Turkey. Folk and folk-like material became central to his style, though Liszt and Strauss had been early influences, as, later, had Debussy; but it was the ballets of Stravinsky that led Bartók to his own ballets, *The Wooden Prince* (1914–17), and *The Miraculous Mandarin* (1917). From 1907 to 1934 Bartók taught piano at the Budapest Academy, during which time he developed a major career as a pianist, performing regularly in Hungary and abroad. Following investigations into Bartók's Aryanism under Horthy's pro-Nazi regime, he fled to the USA in 1940. Here, suffering from financial and health problems, he wrote his *Concerto for Orchestra*, the sonata for solo violin and the (incomplete) Third Piano Concerto and Viola Concerto.

∾ Piano Concerto No. 1 (1926)

1   Allegro moderato – Allegro
2   Andante –
3   Allegro molto

More than twenty years separate Bartók's First Piano Concerto from his earliest essays in combining piano and orchestra, the Rhapsody, Op. 1, and the Scherzo, Op. 2, both probably composed in 1904, which reveal the high Romantic influences of Liszt and Richard Strauss respectively. The First Concerto belongs with the substantial body of music for piano that Bartók wrote in 1926 and which also included the suite *Out of Doors* and the Piano Sonata, as well as the first pieces of the collection *Mikrokosmos*. Bartók's career as a concert pianist was then at its height, and obviously a concerto of his own to take on tour was a highly marketable proposition.

The concerto shares with the suite and the sonata an approach to writing for the piano that is essentially percussive; ostinatos abound in the solo part, tightly packed tone clusters take on a purely colouristic function. The thematic content of the outer movements is appropriately short-breathed; there is no room for grand rhetorical statements as the constant insistence of the rhythmic pulse presses the music ever onward.

Despite such expressionist trappings, the structure of both outer movements corresponds more or less to classical forms. The first movement is roughly a sonata form, though its tonal connections are sometimes tenuous: after a slower introduction there is a well-defined exposition, and later a varied reprise, while the development changes tack at bewildering speed. The finale is a highly episodic rondo, if anything even more propulsive. Between them Bartók places an Andante, which, despite its prominent use of the orchestral percussion, goes as far as admitting a hint of lyricism into the piano lines. The first section is given entirely to the soloist and the percussion; in the second the woodwind enters to weave a polyphonic web around the piano's persistent ostinato. The return of the opening material serves at length to introduce the finale via vivid trombone glissandos that instantly dispel any lingering reveries.

© Andrew Clements

⌇ Piano Concerto No. 2 (1930–1)

1 Allegro
2 Adagio – Presto – Adagio
3 Allegro molto

Bartók's 1931 Second Piano Concerto is the work of a redblooded fifty-year-old. Viewed chronologically, it falls midway between the emotionally charged stage masterpieces (*Duke Bluebeard's Castle* and *The Miraculous Mandarin*) and the troubled lyricism of the Fifth String Quartet and *Music for Strings, Percussion and Celesta*. It is an unequivocally triumphant statement, less experimental than the hammering First Concerto of five years earlier and tougher-grained than the mostly peaceful Third Concerto. The Second is more post-Baroque than modernist, a sparring tour de force fuelled by an energy level that subsides only for parts of the nocturnal middle movement.

Bartók thought well of his First Concerto, but he intended his Second to present 'fewer difficulties for the orchestra and more pleasant themes'. This 'pleasantness' strikes us more as confidence, even cockiness, especially at the outset of the piece, with its manic solo trills and brash fanfares. The first themes are angular and optimistic, and much of what follows grows from them. There are no strings in the first movement, just woodwinds, brass, percussion and a bustling barrage of counterpoint. Bartók thrives on the rigours of sonata form (where material is displayed, developed and recapitulated) and his rhythmic writing has the stamp of indigenous Hungarian dance music – at times, even of jazz.

There are plenty of surprises, too – not least the softened transformation of the principal idea that breezes in roughly halfway through the opening Allegro and the perky woodwinds that brighten the mood just before the movement ends. Time and again the brass rally round in an attempt to bring the soloist to heel, until he (or she) finally calls their bluff, then fires off on a spectacular solo cadenza. Like the finale, the first movement climaxes with infectious high spirits.

The second movement opens to mysterious string chords before the soloist and timpanist take over. One might perhaps think in terms of a dialogue between a lonely shepherd and distant thunder (could Bartók have had Berlioz's *Symphonie fantastique* in mind?). This is a telling example of Bartók's 'night music', the sort of writing that crops up time and again in his solo piano music and string quartets. The dialogue gradually intensifies before relative peace returns and quiet strings take over. But not for long. Suddenly, the strings rush for cover while the pianist launches a flurry of repeated notes and the winds respond with flustered chatter. Bartók's nocturnal wildlife seems startled, hyperactive and clearly visible under a bright moon. Gossip crescendos with a vengeance before a piercing cry sends the entire community packing and the strings return with a nervous tremor. The movement ends with a variation of its opening sequence, except that this time the strings play a more prominent role.

The concerto's finale opens with a hefty wallop on the bass drum, before the soloist thrashes an upward flourish and an accelerating timpani part underpins the warlike first theme. Thereafter, the musical material mirrors – by Bartók's own admission – most of what we heard in the first movement. The fanfares return, and so do the chattering woodwinds and the occasional beam of light, though the central argument is a knotted mass of sweat and sinew. The big drums kick out in protest, but to no avail. Again, Bartók has a surprise up his sleeve, and he closes his concerto in a naively jubilant mood, as if it had all been no more – or less – than a mischievous game.

Rob Cowan © BBC

✦ Piano Concerto No. 3 (1945)

1 Allegretto
2 Adagio religioso –
3 Allegro vivace

In 1940 Bartók left his native Hungary for good, as his fierce patriotism was bringing him increasingly into conflict with the ruling pro-Nazi regime. On arrival in the United States, he and his pianist wife, Ditta Pásztory, were the recipients of many honours but found little employment, and their situation during the remaining five years of Bartók's life remained precarious.

Unlike his fellow exile Arnold Schoenberg, Bartók refused to teach composition, feeling that to do so would interfere with his own creative work. Apart from occasional concerts in which the Bartóks usually played the Sonata for Two Pianos and Percussion, their main source of income was Bartók's associate professorship at Columbia University, which enabled him to continue his lifelong study of Eastern European folk music; the result was a scholarly work on Serbo-Croat folk song which appeared in 1951, six years after Bartók's death.

Four works date from these years in America: the Concerto for Orchestra, commissioned by the Koussevitzky Foundation; the solo violin sonata, written for Yehudi Menuhin; the sketches of a Viola Concerto for William Primrose, completed posthumously by Bartók's friend Tibor Sérly; and the Third Piano Concerto. This last work was not a commission, and it may be assumed that the ailing composer wrote it as a legacy for his wife. Gradually succumbing to leukaemia, Bartók was yet able to complete the work, except for the final seventeen bars. These, in the form of a short score, he wrote out in bed during his last days, and this small fragment, like the sketches for the Viola Concerto, was deciphered and orchestrated by the faithful Sérly.

Compared with the preceding concertos of 1926 and 1930–1, which upset audiences with their aggressiveness and percussiveness – though they have long since been accepted as modern classics – the Third Concerto is a much mellower work. Without loss of individuality, Bartók here enters into the succession of classical and Romantic concerto writing; in particular, he returns to the interplay between orchestra and soloist, and to the concertante sonata and rondo form which he had largely abandoned in the astringent, uncompromising works of his middle period. Like the *Concerto for Orchestra*, the Third Piano Concerto is more immediately accessible to the listener than Bartók's works of the 1920s and 1930s; indeed, Bartók has been reproached by some 'modernists' for lowering his standards and courting popularity in the works he wrote in his American exile. Yet in the half-century and more since his death, it has become increasingly clear that the Third Piano Concerto as well as the *Concerto for Orchestra* is a genuine product of a late style: while the surface gets simpler and the apparatus is reduced, the message becomes more concentrated, embracing the artistic experience of a lifetime in formulations of definitive validity.

The concerto's first movement is utterly lucid in structure and tonality, spare in orchestration to the point of tenuousness, and has considerable – though lightly worn – rhythmic finesse. Its basic mood of reticence and tenderness is at times overwhelmed by sweeping 'Hungarian' tunes, entering with a flourish and exiting with stealth.

The word 'religioso' in the title of the slow movement, appearing here for the first time in Bartók's music, does not denote a religious intention as such, but describes the character of the first theme – a chorale given out by the piano in sustained legato chords. On its recurrence after the central section, the chorale is taken up by the orchestra, while the pianist embroiders upon it. The central section itself is Bartókian 'nature music': bird calls and insect noises in a magical scoring for woodwind, muted brass, xylophone and scuttling piano runs.

In the lively finale, much play is made with the invigorating contrast between a chordally harmonised Hungarian dance tune, forming the principal idea, and several finely elaborated fugues forming the episodes of this rondo form. In an exhilarating coda, the homophonic and polyphonic elements begin to jostle one another, until they fall in a heap during the last bars.

© Paul Hamburger

✑ Violin Concerto No. 2 (1937–8)

1   Allegro non troppo
2   Andante tranquillo – Lento – Allegro scherzando –
    Tempo 1
3   Allegro molto – Risoluto

It is one of the many mysteries and miracles of the creative process that only rarely can anything be inferred about the personal circumstances of the creator from the mood or intent of the finished work. Many are the works of heroic optimism nurtured in situations of appalling deprivation, and many too are the works of unrelenting bleakness, the products of apparent contentment. Such was the case with Bartók, whose most uncompromising music, the Fourth String Quartet and *The Miraculous Mandarin*, for example, was composed at – for him – times of relatively good fortune.

The period when Bartók worked on his Second Violin Concerto, however, was darkened by considerable political unrest. This included the annexation of Austria by the Nazis, one consequence of which was the closure of Bartók's publisher, Universal Edition. In Nazi eyes this was a breeding ground of degeneracy and racial imperfection: not surprisingly, the 'purity' of Bartók's own ancestry came under suspicion. Even worse was the horrific and ever-growing possibility of Hungary's own capitulation to Nazi domination, an occurrence which finally resulted in Bartók's emigration to the USA. Yet his music from this period bears little trace of this unstable background: the Second Violin Concerto is one of Bartók's sunniest compositions, and initiated a series of masterpieces, such as *Music for Strings, Percussion and Celesta*, the *Divertimento* and the Third Piano Concerto, in which the techniques and innovations explored with obsessive thoroughness earlier in his career are put to the service of music of utter unselfconsciousness and prodigious generosity of spirit.

When Bartók received the commission to compose a violin concerto from the leader of the Hungarian Quartet, Zoltán Székely, he was no stranger to writing for solo violin. In addition to the two sonatas for violin and piano and two rhapsodies for violin and orchestra, he had composed a violin concerto exactly thirty years earlier. The offspring of a close emotional attachment, it came to dissatisfy Bartók and he withdrew it (it wasn't played until after his death). The Second Concerto was begun in August 1937, but work on it was interrupted by the composition of *Contrasts* for clarinet, violin and piano. The concerto was eventually finished on 31 December 1938 and first performed in Amsterdam by the Concertgebouw Orchestra under Willem Mengelberg with Székely as soloist. Bartók himself was not present at the premiere, but declared himself well satisfied when he finally did hear the piece nearly five years later, in New York, with Yehudi Menuhin as soloist.

Székely had requested a concerto in the grand manner, a worthy successor to the Beethoven and Brahms, and Bartók's initial suggestion that it might take the rather modest form of a set of variations was received unfavourably. Bartók, however, remained undeflected from his initial purpose and adopted the ingenious plan of fusing the principle of variation with the received forms of the Austro-German tradition, to which he had always been committed, despite his present understandable antipathy to things German. Not only is the central slow movement a disarmingly straightforward set of variations on a theme stated at the outset, but the entire material of the sonata-form last movement is clearly a variation of the material of the sonata-form first movement, a sleight of hand accomplished without any feeling of marking time or retracing old ground.

© Antony Bye

Ludwig van Beethoven (1770–1827)

Beethoven left his native Bonn in his early twenties for Vienna, where he became established in fashionable circles as a composer, piano virtuoso and improviser of considerable ability. His 'early' works developed the classical models of Haydn and Mozart. As early as 1796, he recognised signs of his impending deafness, and his subsequent suffering and alienation, as well as his creative resolve, were disclosed in his 'Heiligenstadt Testament' of 1802. His 'middle period' was characterised by a broadening of form and an extension of harmonic language which reflects his proto-Romantic expressive tendencies; this period produced the Symphonies Nos 2 to 8, notable piano sonatas, several string quartets and his only opera, *Fidelio*. From 1812 to 1818 he produced little music, but his last years saw the mould-breaking 'Choral' Symphony, and an exploration of increasing profundity in the more intimate genres of the string quartet and piano sonata.

∾ Piano Concerto No. 1 in C major, Op. 15
(1795; rev. 1800–1)

1 Allegro con brio
2 Largo
3 Rondo: Allegro scherzando

The Piano Concerto which Beethoven published as No. 1 is not in fact his first. It was preceded by the work we now know as No. 2; and there was an even earlier Concerto in E flat (No. 0), written when he was fourteen, which has survived only in a short score. The C major Concerto was probably composed in 1795, and performed by Beethoven in Vienna during that year. He gave another performance on a visit to Prague in 1798. But he seems to have gone on revising the work right up to its publication in 1801.

Beethoven's models for this concerto were quite clearly the late piano concertos of Mozart, and perhaps especially the last of the C major concertos, K503 (No. 25), though it was not published until 1796. The scoring is similarly full, although Beethoven adds two clarinets to Mozart's wind section of flute, oboes, bassoons, horns and trumpets (with timpani); and a good deal of Beethoven's piano passagework stems from Mozart's types of figuration. There are some striking direct echoes of Mozart in Beethoven's first movement: in particular, the military-sounding closing theme of the orchestral exposition, and the unexpectedly offhand entrance of the solo piano shortly afterwards. In more general terms, too, Beethoven's first movement resembles Mozart's in its 'symphonic' handling of the thematic material: the very simple elements of the first subject – just an upward octave in a distinctive rhythm, an upward semiquaver scale and a cadential figure in crotchets – come in for particularly intensive development; the upward octaves even form the starting-point for each of the three cadenzas which Beethoven wrote at various times for this movement.

Another significant feature of this opening Allegro is its regular gravitation to keys on the flat side of C major, notably (and from a surprisingly early stage) to E flat major, which becomes a kind of subsidiary key-centre along with the 'regular' second-subject key of G major. This flatward gravitational pull extends to the expansive Largo, which is in the unusually remote key of A flat major: a key which together with the scoring – clarinets, bassoons and horns only in the wind section – gives this movement its distinctive mood of veiled serenity.

To this the brightness and openness of the final Rondo provide an effective contrast, not least in the central A minor episode with its springing gypsy rhythms. But the closely related first and third episodes once more have a tendency to move to the flat side of the key. The balance is righted only after the cadenza with a brief but telling burst of the extreme sharp key of B major, followed after the last return of the rondo theme by a string of scales and cadences all unshakeably reasserting the home key.

© Anthony Burton

ᔃᔥ Piano Concerto No. 2 in B flat major, Op. 19 (c. 1788–1801)

1   Allegro con brio
2   Adagio
3   Rondo: Molto allegro

This is the earliest of Beethoven's five numbered piano concertos: it follows the so-called 'No. 0' in E flat major, of which only a short score has survived, but precedes the official No. 1 in C major, which was the first to be published. Beethoven began writing the piece during his youth in Bonn, perhaps as early as 1788, and then continued to work on it after moving to Vienna in 1792 to study with Haydn. In the process, he replaced the work's original finale (which is probably the piece published after his death as a separate Rondo in B flat major), and apparently its original slow movement as well. There may well have been performances of an interim version in Vienna in 1795 or 1796, with the composer as soloist; and in 1798 Beethoven wrote out a new orchestral score before performing the concerto (together with No. 1) in Prague. But it was not until 1801 that he fair-copied the piano part (which he must have been playing from memory or from sketches), so that the piece could be published.

Even this does not end the work's long and complex history, because the musicologist Barry Cooper has discovered a batch of revisions which Beethoven wrote into the autograph score of the first movement, but which were not sent to the publisher in time to be printed; the concerto has been recorded with these revisions, but they are not yet included in standard editions. Finally, in 1808, around the time that he stopped playing his own concertos in public with improvised cadenzas, Beethoven wrote out a cadenza for the first movement, presumably for the use of his pupils. It is in his mature middle-period manner, and so hardly a stylistic match for a movement which he had begun some twenty years earlier; but it is such a fine piece of writing that it would be a brave pianist who decided to replace it with something of his own.

The extended gestation of the concerto makes it difficult to assess quite what the influences on it were. For example, it is scored for the same modest orchestra as Mozart's last piano concerto (K595), in the same key, that is flute, two oboes, two bassoons, two horns and strings; and both its finale and its probable original finale are, like that of K595, in rondo form and in 6/8 time. But if the starting-date for the Beethoven of 1788 is anywhere near right, its inception actually pre-dated the completion and first performance of the Mozart. Moreover, very few of Mozart's other late piano concertos were published in his lifetime. However, the young Beethoven might have known a group of Mozart concertos from the early 1780s which was published in Vienna in 1785; and, once in Vienna himself and working on the revisions of his own concerto, he would probably have had access to some of Mozart's later ones. Certainly, while it is harder to find specific Mozartian models for this concerto than for Nos 1 and 3, its piano writing does show the influence of Mozart's piano style. And in more general terms, its simple themes and the way they are treated suggest the influence of Beethoven's teacher Haydn: Roger Fiske, in his BBC Music Guide to Beethoven's concertos and overtures, even calls it 'arguably the most Haydnesque work he ever wrote'.

At the same time, the concerto is not without its Beethovenian fingerprints. The brusque opening phrase of the first movement is, in his usual manner, both a call to attention and the source of a good deal of developmental writing later on. The sudden side-step into D flat major in the course of the orchestral exposition, to introduce a new melodic idea, is the kind of adventurous tonal move which he made throughout his career. His concomitant long-range planning is typified by the fact that the second exposition, with the soloist, also shifts to D flat, but in a different way, while in the development section the side-step gesture recurs in a different tonal context. And the solo part includes passages of great power and brilliance which remind us that, in his early years in Vienna, Beethoven was principally famous not as a composer but as a young lion of the keyboard.

The slow movement is an Adagio in E flat major, with a serene main theme which, as in many of Beethoven's early works with piano, is encrusted with increasing amounts of virtuoso decoration on its later reappearances. Unexpectedly, though, at the point towards the end of the movement where the orchestra pauses for a cadenza, what follows is not more decorative glitter, but a simple unsupported melodic line, marked 'with great expression', which continues in recitative-like dialogue with the strings.

The final rondo has Beethoven's standard concerto-finale ground plan, with the statements of the main theme separated by three episodes, the first recapitulated as the third, the second striking out in different directions. The main theme itself has a distinctive rhythmic pattern, *short*–*long*–*short*–long, with disruptive sforzando markings on the offbeat long notes. Beethoven's sketchbooks reveal that this rhythm emerged during the process of revision, and that the short notes were originally unstressed upbeats. There is a momentary glimpse of this otherwise suppressed version in a brief digression (a tonal digression, too, into G major) towards the end of the third episode, before the rondo theme makes its final fortissimo return.

© Anthony Burton

‿ Piano Concerto No. 3 in C minor, Op. 37
   (1797–1800)

1 Allegro con brio
2 Largo
3 Rondo: Allegro

Beethoven's Third Piano Concerto was written probably between 1797 and 1800, and was first performed by the composer at a concert in Vienna in 1803 – a lengthy affair that also included, among other things, the first performances of the Second Symphony and the oratorio *Christ on the Mount of Olives*. It is the last of Beethoven's concertos to be modelled in its overall proportions on the concertos of Mozart: that is, with each of its three movements a separate entity and carrying roughly equal weight. Subsequently, in the Triple Concerto, the Violin Concerto and the last two piano concertos, the composer adopted a radically different scheme, in which the slow movement is short and leads straight into the finale, and these two movements together balance an expansive opening Allegro.

The C minor Concerto also has some more specifically Mozartian features. It is in the same key as one of Mozart's most dramatic concertos, No. 24 (K491), shares many of its moods, and begins similarly with a quiet, pregnant theme in bare octaves. And, after his first-movement cadenza (not written, incidentally, until around 1808), Beethoven takes the same unusual step that Mozart took in K491 of denying the soloist his customary breather in the coda, and keeping him in action until the end of the movement.

Despite the Mozartian precedent, though, this is actually one of the most characteristically Beethovenian passages in the entire score, with its repeated timpani references to the opening theme, its mysterious atmosphere, and its surging crescendo to the final fortissimo. And it is succeeded by another equally distinctive moment: the start of the Largo, a meditative piano solo in the remote key of E major. The piano writing throughout the movement is extremely ornate, but in the middle section – unexpectedly in G major, approached by a brusque orchestral modulation – the soloist's arpeggios take second place to the melody unfolded as a duet between flute and bassoon.

After the rarefied atmosphere of this slow movement, the main theme of the Rondo finale seems to bring us back to more familiar Mozartian ground; and the beginning of the second of the three episodes sounds remarkably like a bit of a Mozart wind serenade, with clarinet and bassoon taking the melodic lead in the warm key of A flat major. But later in this episode the little developmental fugato, the piano's brief excursion into E major (harking back to the key of the Largo), and the long preparation for the eventual return of the main theme are all Beethoven fingerprints. And there is another moment of quintessential Beethoven at the end of the third episode: fragments of the Rondo theme, three big chords and the simplest of decelerating cadenzas herald a turn simultaneously to C major, 6/8 time and Presto tempo for the coda, in which the Rondo theme makes a final appearance in a completely new guise.

© Anthony Burton

∾ Piano Concerto No. 4 in G major, Op. 58 (1804–6)

1 Allegro moderato
2 Andante con moto –
3 Rondo: Vivace

Many of the compositions of Beethoven's so-called middle period are famously dominated by the notion of heroic struggle, spawning the popular image of the fist-shaking, furrow-browed Titan. But that is far from the whole picture. And in other works, among them the 'Pastoral' Symphony, the Violin Concerto and the Fourth Piano Concerto, the expanded range and scale of Beethoven's symphonic thinking go hand in hand with an unprecedented lyric breadth. In particular, the opening movements of all three works – all, significantly, marked 'Allegro moderato' or 'Allegro ma non troppo' – have a sense of serene spaciousness, with moments of profound reflective stillness, that is in its way no less revolutionary and prophetic than the mighty strivings of the 'Eroica' and Fifth Symphonies.

A sketch for the opening bars of the G major Concerto dates from 1804, and one jettisoned early sketch for the Rondo finale subsequently became the accompaniment to the Act 1 Prisoners' Chorus in his opera *Fidelio*. But Beethoven only turned to the concerto in earnest during 1806, when the Fifth Symphony was also on the stocks; and it is surely no accident that the first movements of each work view the same four-note figure from a drastically different perspective. Tradition has it that Beethoven performed the G major concerto at a private concert in Prince Lobkowitz's palace in Vienna in March 1807, though the evidence is far from watertight.

But we do know that the composer played it in the celebrated gargantuan concert he held in the city's Theater an der Wien on 22 December 1808, which also included the first performances of the 'Pastoral' and Fifth Symphonies, parts of the Mass in C and, as a *bonne bouche*, the hastily written *Choral Fantasy*.

The most famous thing about this concerto is its opening: an exquisitely gentle, questioning theme for the soloist, richly scored in the keyboard's resonant middle register. No previous classical concerto had announced itself with the soloist alone; and none had begun so poetically and speculatively. The orchestra then responds, as if entranced, in a distant, luminous B major, before gliding back to the home key. This immediately establishes the movement's predominant tone of confiding tenderness and prefigures its extraordinarily wide modulatory range (the development reaches as far as C sharp minor, the antipode of G major). Time and again the piano, through reflective understatement, challenges and deflects the orchestra's propensity to assertive action. And one of the movement's characteristic features is the way that prepared climaxes dissolve into lyrical meditation. At the end of the exposition, for instance, a long trill leads us to expect a rousing orchestral tutti. But this is deferred by a magical passage where the soloist muses on a cadential theme first heard in the orchestral introduction. The fortissimo reinterpretation of the main theme at the start of the recapitulation – the logical climax and resolution of the harmonically far-reaching development – is a typical Beethoven ploy. Yet even here the apparent note of triumph quickly yields to ethereal reflection.

The piano also prevails through gentle persuasion, albeit much more theatrically, in the central Andante con moto. It was Beethoven's nineteenth-century biographer A. B. Marx who first compared this movement to Orpheus's taming of the Furies. Yet, unlike many fanciful programmatic interpretations, this one is remarkably true to the content of the music. The movement can also be seen as the confrontation of two musical worlds: Baroque sternness and rigour in the strings' brusque unisons, Romantic pathos in the keyboard's soft harmonised responses. Gradually, the orchestra is appeased by the soloist's increasingly eloquent pleas; and, after an impassioned cadenza-like climax, its harsh dotted rhythms are reduced to a ghostly whisper in the bass.

After the sustained E minor of the Andante, the quiet, faintly military theme of the Rondo, which follows without a break, re-establishes G major via several bars of C major (shades here of Haydn's witty off-key beginnings); this has the knock-on effect of turning the tonic chord, G, into the dominant each time the Rondo theme returns.

For all its swagger and playfulness, this movement shares with the opening Allegro moderato both its elaborate symphonic development and its core of rich, tranquil lyricism: in the dolce second theme, announced by the soloist in two widely spaced contrapuntal lines and expanded by the orchestra in flowing polyphony; and in the beautiful transformation of the main theme towards the end of the movement, first on divided violas (in a remote, dream-like E flat), then, after the cadenza, in canon and, at last, unequivocally in the home key of G major.

Richard Wigmore © BBC

∾ Piano Concerto No. 5 in E flat major, Op. 73, 'Emperor' (1809)

1 Allegro
2 Adagio un poco mosso –
3 Rondo: Allegro

Nobody knows for sure who bestowed the imperial sobriquet on the last and greatest of Beethoven's piano concertos. It was certainly not the composer. Moreover, it is a specifically English nickname, practically never used outside the English-speaking world. Most Beethoven scholars now attribute it to the composer and piano-maker J. B. Cramer (1771–1858), who may once have called it 'an emperor among concertos' – and so in truth it is. It was completed in 1809, following the Fifth and Sixth Symphonies, and was written during the bombardment of Vienna by Napoleon's troops, the noise causing Beethoven much discomfort as he sought refuge with his brother in a house near the city walls. Its first performance did not take place until 1811 in Leipzig, when the soloist was Friedrich Schneider. Vienna first heard it the next year played by Carl Czerny, but the performance seems to have occasioned little comment.

As in the forms of symphony, quartet and sonata, Beethoven's five piano concertos reflect a growth in imagination and scope from the classical models as he found them, to masterworks hitherto unapproached by any other composer. They set a standard and a style that dominated the course of European music for more than a century.

Beethoven had by this time become gradually reconciled to the burden of increasing deafness, and he realised that this would prevent him from performing his Fifth Concerto in public as he had his others. He accordingly broke with the custom of giving the soloist an opportunity for an improvised cadenza, instead writing out exactly what he wanted the pianist to play. The content was also affected by the advance in piano construction that had occurred during the previous twenty-five years. With the keyboard enlarged to six octaves, added resources of pedals and much greater flexibility of action, both piano and orchestral writing could be conceived on an altogether larger scale.

Just how large a scale the 'Emperor' was conceived on becomes evident in the very opening bars when, instead of waiting for the orchestra to present the main themes first, the piano enters immediately with a series of three elaborate flourishes punctuated by orchestral chords. They can be said to represent the pillars of classical tonality, for the first flourish is based on the tonic (E flat, the first note of the scale), the second on the subdominant (A flat, the fourth) and the third on the dominant (B flat, the fifth). These three chords provide the entire harmonic support for the martial first theme, as if to show that vastness of vision can be rooted in basic simplicity. The piano writing is extremely brilliant throughout, fully as demanding on the soloist's technique as any of the showy concertos written by later nineteenth-century composers. The demands here are more severe than in many later examples, however, for the brilliance is an integral part of the musical argument, not merely superimposed on it for decorative effect.

An Adagio in B major forms the central slow movement, with the orchestra proposing a noble, hymn-like main theme on which the piano, reversing the usual procedure, elaborates in a kind of free rhapsodising before simplifying it into its own versions of the theme. At the end of the movement the piano falls silent, while a softly held B on the bassoons drops an enigmatic semitone to B flat on the horns. Quietly the piano suggests an idea, the orchestra catches on, and together they leap into the exuberant finale. The Rondo outline is so closely organised and thoroughly developed that the lighthearted implications of the term are overridden by the music's strength of purpose, demonstrating Beethoven's evident belief that a concerto could be as profound and thoughtful as any symphony.

© Noël Goodwin

❧ Violin Concerto in D major, Op. 61 (1806)

1   Allegro ma non troppo
2   Larghetto –
3   Rondo: Allegro

Among the masterpieces of Beethoven's heroic middle period it is the great conflict works – those that 'seize Fate by the throat' and challenge the musical universe – that have shaped his popular image. But there is another kind of work, no less characteristic and no less powerful, in which the mastery is serene and the composer celebrates the beauties and harmonies of creation, the Almighty's and his own: not least among these is the Violin Concerto that he composed, apparently in a short space of time, towards the end of 1806.

In the manner of the French school of violin concertos that so influenced Beethoven, the writing for the soloist is lyrical. Even in the most brilliant passagework the melodic line is paramount. The two pizzicato notes in the finale stand out startlingly for being in such sharp contrast with the rest of the solo part. At the same time, Beethoven is as masterful in this work as in any of his most dynamic statements.

The huge first movement, propelled by a constant march rhythm (another French influence), achieves a triumphant reconciliation of lyricism and symphonic structure on the largest scale. Its melodic material is of the simplest (often involving rising scales), but it is used with subtlety and ingenuity. Nothing in Beethoven is more mysterious than the modulation which, in the development, takes the music into B minor via a high F natural for the soloist suspended in the void and, far below, the steady notes of the march rhythm entering softly in the bass. The movement also looks forward to later violin concertos in the way the solo part is often integrated into the orchestral texture rather than standing outside it in the relation of melody to accompaniment. The soloist appears after an exceptionally spacious orchestral introduction, and then not with the main theme but with a long, reflective preparation for it. In this movement, too, orchestral colour plays a vital role, from the opening drum taps and the cool sound of the woodwind playing the calm first theme, to the strange pulsation of trumpets and drums in the development section and the bassoon solo which emphasises the mood of deep tranquillity after the cadenza.

The raptly beautiful Larghetto renounces the principle of tonal development dear to Beethoven in favour of a trance-like stillness; the theme is repeated five times in the same key (G), with increasingly delicate and intricate decoration by the solo violin and a wonderful variety of orchestral sonorities: muted violins, plucked chords separated by silence, clarinet and bassoon solos, gently mooing horns.

As often happens in middle-period Beethoven, the movement leads straight to the finale; the music does not conclude so much as break off, interrupted by commanding string chords (violins now unmuted).

The finale is an exuberant Rondo with a disarmingly catchy, strongly rhythmic theme, enclosing a gypsy episode in G minor (naively wistful counterpart of the G minor passage in the first movement) and moments of characteristically Beethovenian humour. It perfectly completes a work that breathes a sense of grand, untroubled power even in its quietest utterances.

© David Cairns

Alban Berg (1885–1935)

Berg was the most lyrical and, to posterity, perhaps the most approachable of the composers who have come to be known as the Second Viennese School. Berg's early works were written under Schoenberg's watchful eye: the Op. 1 Piano Sonata and the *Seven Early Songs*, completed in his early twenties, already pointed to a post-Romantic musical language, and an intense, sensitive character. After his atonal String Quartet (1910) he moved to larger forces in the *Altenberg Lieder* (1912), which caused a riot at its premiere. Following the war he won an international reputation with his first opera *Wozzeck*, while his Chamber Concerto, written for Schoenberg's fiftieth birthday, incorporated serial techniques and ciphers referring to the Schoenberg–Berg–Webern partnership. Berg would continue his use of serialism – though often not as rigorously as Schoenberg and Webern – in the *Lyric Suite* (1925–6) for string quartet, the opera *Lulu* (which remained incomplete on his death and was first performed in a completed version only in 1979), and the Violin Concerto, his most successful work.

ᖫ Violin Concerto (1935)

Part 1
   1 Andante –
   2 Allegretto
Part 2
   3 Allegro –
   4 Adagio

Berg's Violin Concerto was his last finished work, and its composition intervened to prevent the completion of his opera *Lulu* (which, like Mahler's Tenth Symphony, had to wait decades to be finished by another hand). The American violinist Louis Krasner commissioned the concerto in February

1935, and Berg originally planned an abstract piece. But that April he was deeply shaken by the death (from infantile paralysis) of Manon Gropius, the eighteen-year-old daughter of Walter Gropius, the architect, and Mahler's widow Alma, with whom the Bergs had long been on close terms. The Violin Concerto, composed during the summer by the Wörthersee in Carinthia, emerged as a requiem for the gifted and tragic Manon, and is inscribed 'To the memory of an angel'. The premiere took place at the April 1936 International Society for Contemporary Music Festival in Barcelona, with Krasner as soloist, under the baton of Hermann Scherchen (standing in at short notice for Anton Webern, who introduced the work to London in May with the BBC Symphony Orchestra). Berg, however, had died the previous December.

He was already seriously ill by the time he began the finale, but he drove himself to complete it, neglecting food and sleep. Yet the concerto's intricacy of thought and technical mastery are immense, and can hardly be more than hinted at here. According to the composer, the first two of the concerto's four movements are a character portrait of Manon Gropius; the third evokes the horrific illness which overcame and finally destroyed her; while the fourth – variations on the chorale 'Es ist genug! So nimm, Herr, meinen Geist' (It is enough! Take then my spirit, Lord) from Bach's Cantata No. 60 – is a kind of prayer for the repose of her soul. No doubt Manon's early evidence of talent as an actress is reflected, too, in the alternately soulful, lyrical, and sometimes almost skittish demeanour of the solo part.

Recent research, however, has postulated a hidden, autobiographical 'programme' behind the 'official' one. In the finale, Berg's penchant for number symbolism constructs a labyrinth of allusions (largely inaudible) to the numbers twenty-three and ten – the ciphers he had used in his *Lyric Suite* (1925–6) to designate himself and Hanna Fuchs-Robettin, the married woman with whom he was in love. The soloist's amoroso delivery of the chorale melody is doubtless another allusion to their affair in both Romantic and spiritual terms.

The first eight pitches of the twelve-tone row that forms the kernel of the work's melodic ideas and harmonic invention comprise a succession of rising major and minor thirds, beginning with a G minor triad. Hence the familiarly 'tonal' feel of so much of the music. The last four pitches, rising in whole-tones, fit the opening phrase of the Bach chorale. The work's overall structure discloses elements of the arch forms that Berg found so fascinating. Its two parts, of roughly equal length, contain two movements each; the inner ones are scherzos, though of highly contrasting characters, while the outer ones are fairly slow and contemplative. In addition, the work begins with a brief, slow introduction that is recalled at its end, and all four movements themselves display varying degrees of symmetry.

The meditative, soliloquy-like first movement contrasts the brightness of solo violin sonority with rather dark orchestral colours, and gives on to a lively, somewhat 'rustic' scherzo reminiscent in mood of the second movement of Mahler's Fourth Symphony (also dominated by a solo violin). One of the themes invokes the spirit of a Viennese waltz, and this comes more into its own in the two trios, the second of which also introduces a Carinthian Ländler tune. (This has been claimed as another secret allusion: Berg must have known the words that go with this dance tune, in praise of the love-making of one Mizzi, and his earliest affair had been with a Carinthian servant-girl, Mizzi Scheuchl.)

The apparently optimistic ending of Part 1 is immediately contradicted by the second scherzo, whose timpani hammer blows, terrifying chordal structures and stumbling rhythms again recall Mahler (the anguish of his Ninth and Tenth symphonies). From its catastrophe this movement collapses into the soothing harmonies of Bach's chorale; and after two benedictory variations and a transfigured reminiscence of the Carinthian Ländler (the first love reflected in the last?), the concerto closes in regions of ethereal calm.

© Malcolm MacDonald

Hector Berlioz (1803–69)

One of the most imaginative and individual composers of the nineteenth century, Berlioz inherited a French love of instrumental colour and put it at the service of his vivid imagination. Indeed Berlioz encapsulated the essence of the Romantic artist: headstrong, with a turbulent emotional life, he was strongly drawn to literature; his music was inspired by Shakespeare (*Romeo and Juliet*, *Beatrice and Benedict*, as well as his overture *King Lear*), Goethe (*The Damnation of Faust*), and Byron (*Harold in Italy*). His epic opera *The Trojans*, based on Virgil's *Aeneid*, represents the pinnacle of the French grand opera tradition. He was one of the leading conductors of his day and published much vivid musical criticism. Among his writings is a famous and influential treatise on orchestration.

❧ *Harold in Italy*, Op. 16 (1834)

1   Harold in the Mountains. Scenes of melancholy, happiness and joy
2   March of the Pilgrims singing the evening prayer
3   The Abruzzi Highlander's Serenade to his Mistress
4   Brigands' Orgy. Recollections of earlier scenes

Berlioz spent more than a year in Italy in 1831–2, having won the Prix de Rome, instituted by the French government to enable French artists to study in an environment of classical art treasures, whether painting or sculpture. Musicians were loosely thought to need the same benefits, but for Berlioz the price of a few years' state pension was to be exiled from the central sources of his art. He found the cultivation of music in Italy indescribably narrow and parochial, having developed an early distaste for Italian opera of any kind. Operas in Genoa, Florence, Rome and Naples gave him no pleasure. It was in the country, in Tivoli and Subiaco, and on the long walk from Naples to Rome that he really found musical inspiration. 'I long to go to Mount Posilippo,' he wrote, 'to Calabria, or to Capri, and put myself in the service of a brigand chief. That's the life I crave: volcanos, rocks, rich piles of plunder in mountain caves, a concert of shrieks accompanied by an orchestra of pistols and carbines, blood and Lacryma-Christi, a bed of lava rocked by subterranean tremors. "*Allons donc, voilà la vie!*"'

At Alatri, on his return from Naples, Berlioz and his two Swedish travelling companions spent a dreadful night on hard beds, plagued by fleas and the 'young men serenading, going round the village all night singing beneath their mistresses' windows, to the accompaniment of a guitar and a terrible squawking clarinet.' Here, clearly, is the background to the last two movements of *Harold in Italy*. In 1834, two years after his return to Paris, Paganini, in admiration of the *Symphonie fantastique*, asked Berlioz for a work in which he could display his powers on a Stradivarius viola. Berlioz's ideas first centred on Mary Queen of Scots as a suitable subject, but then converged into a four-movement symphony, *Harold in Italy*, incorporating two passages that had actually been composed in Italy: Harold's *idée fixe* (the tune the viola plays first) and another theme in the first movement, both drawn from the overture on *Rob Roy* which Berlioz had recently rejected.

The work was to be a series of Italian souvenirs in a symphonic frame. From Byron's *Childe Harold* Berlioz took the dreamy character of Harold as a spectator of scenes, not a participant in them; he is a Byronic Berlioz. All four movements picture outdoor scenes drawn from the most vivid experiences of his Italian stay. The melancholy of Byron's hero is clearly to be heard at the opening and in the third-movement Serenade, echoes of the spleen vividly described by Berlioz in his *Memoirs*. The pilgrims and tolling bells (deftly scored for horns and harp) in the second movement appeared in any Italian itinerary of the time. Berlioz felt no special sense of identification here as he did with highlanders and brigands, but this makes no difference to the elegant musical design of the piece, nor to its evocative colour. It became a favourite item in Berlioz's concert tours in the 1840s and 1850s, often detached from the rest of the symphony.

The Serenade is an ingenious exercise in creating atmosphere while at the same time combining different rhythms, the more languorous melody on the cor anglais unperturbed by the jaunty piping of the highlander or the stately span of Harold's theme.

The last movement borrows the device of parading previous themes in the manner of Beethoven's Choral Symphony, not for any convincing dramatic reason, but to draw the work together and to pay tribute to the finest symphonic model Berlioz knew. The frenetic vigour of the finale makes a stirring close interrupted only once by distant memories of the pilgrims' march. The solo viola's final phrases in this brief interlude are drowned by the orchestra's savage interruptions, and Harold is heard no more.

Because it is a dramatic and expressive rather than a virtuoso work, the soloist is rarely the protagonist, more often a bystander marking his presence with a recurrent theme. In any case Berlioz did not regard the viola as a virtuoso instrument. Paganini was startled and offended by this; he found the solo part 'too full of rests' and never played it, though he later came to appreciate its worth. The music is full of youthful vitality, tinged with that appealing Romantic sensibility that Berlioz borrowed so fervently from literature. The Italian experience was something to which all his later music, from *Romeo and Juliet* to *The Trojans*, would bear powerful witness.

© Hugh Macdonald

Johannes Brahms (1833–97)

Often seen as a classicist inhabiting the Romantic era, Brahms worked mainly in the established forms – concerto, sonata, symphony – rather than developing new ones, such as the tone poems of Liszt or the grandiose music dramas of Wagner. From an early age Brahms was forced to earn money for his family by playing the piano in Hamburg's seedy sailors' taverns. In 1853 a concert tour brought him famously into contact with Schumann, who publicly declared the young composer a genius. The *German Requiem* (1868) and *Hungarian Dances* (1868–80) advanced his reputation and his *Variations on the St Anthony Chorale* (1873) attracted attention ahead of his First Symphony (1876). He wrote much choral music (he conducted both the Singakademie and the Singverein in Vienna), and led a revival of interest in Renaissance and Baroque music. He also wrote over two hundred songs and much chamber and piano music, but no opera. Late in life he wrote a trio, a quintet and two sonatas inspired by the clarinettist Richard Mühlfeld, which are among his finest achievements in chamber music.

∿ Piano Concerto No. 1 in D minor, Op. 15 (1854–8)

1 Maestoso
2 Adagio
3 Rondo: Allegro non troppo

Brahms was only twenty-five when he completed his First Piano Concerto in 1858. Its gestation had been long and difficult. In March 1854, shortly after Schumann's attempted suicide (by drowning) and subsequent incarceration in a mental asylum, Brahms began a two-piano sonata which soon started to turn into a four-movement symphony. The work was sketched in two-piano score, but the finale was never finished. Virtuoso piano writing kept intruding into the conception, and though Brahms did score the first movement for orchestra, he was still inexperienced in this field and dissatisfied with the result.

Only in 1856, shortly before Schumann's death, did Brahms hit upon the solution of combining the resources of piano and orchestra in a concerto. The symphony's incomplete finale was discarded, as was the slow scherzo in sarabande tempo (years later he used its main theme as the basis of the second movement of the *German Requiem*) and the original slow movement; the first movement was rescored (with the benefit of advice from Joseph Joachim) and united to a new slow movement and finale. The premiere took place in Hanover on 22 January 1859 under Joachim's baton, with Brahms as soloist. Despite its teething troubles, the work emerged with a grandeur and scope that no concerto had attained since Beethoven's 'Emperor', and accordingly its public reception was puzzled and cautious – indeed a second performance in Leipzig was a critical disaster. But performances continued, and within Brahms's own lifetime the concerto was recognised for its true worth.

The huge first movement is nearly the biggest, probably the most dramatic and certainly the finest sonata design since Beethoven. The terse yet stormy opening theme, in a gaunt D minor with prominent chilly tritone over a rumbling D pedal, reflected (according to Joachim) Brahms's state of mind after hearing that Schumann had thrown himself into the Rhine. Undoubtedly the *Sturm und Drang* passion of the concerto's first movement must draw much of its power from the traumatic events of early 1854. The movement is rich in thematic ideas; it is noticeable that the piano at first propounds only the emotionally soothing ones (in its meditative, Bach-like first entry, and solo statement of the grand, assuaging second subject), in contrast to the fevered passion of the orchestra. Not until the moment of recapitulation does Brahms allow the piano more than a glance at the opening theme: and then, in the movement's most dramatic stroke, the piano blazons it forth over the pedal D from the unexpected and choleric region of the dominant of A minor.

In his autograph full score of the slow movement, Brahms underlaid the words *'Benedictus qui venit in nomine Domini'* (Blessed is he that cometh in the name of the Lord) beneath the serene violin/viola theme in the opening bars, syllabically broken in the manner of a singing text. The music is closely akin to the sacred choral works he was writing in 1856, which included a project for a Mass. Taken together with the 'slow sarabande' that was later found appropriate in the *German Requiem*, this seems to constitute some evidence that the original symphony/sonata may have been conceived as a kind of instrumental 'Requiem for Schumann'. But *'Benedictus qui venit in nomine Domini'* is also the inscription over the door of the Benedictine abbey where Kreisler, the hero of E. T. A. Hoffmann's novel *Kater Murr*, finally gains some peace after his Romantic tribulations. *Kater Murr* was one of the young Brahms's favourite books, and he often used the pseudonym of 'Johannes Kreisler Junior', so the music here has a possible literary (and autobiographical) origin. Then again, in a letter Brahms also spoke of the Adagio as a portrait of Schumann's wife, Clara. Whatever the basis of its inspiration, this slow movement stands at the furthest possible remove from the first-movement Maestoso, as one of Brahms's profoundest evocations of a withdrawn, almost mystical, spirit.

The thrusting, energetic main theme of the Rondo returns us at once to the physical world. There is no attempt to escape the profundities of the first two movements: rather, the sense that they can only retain meaning through a continuing commitment to vigorous action. This strongly rhythmic and contrapuntal music engenders its own exhilaration; the broader, grander tunes of its episodes (which recall in outline the first movement's second subject) introduce the concept of hope; a brilliant fugue turns the energy to precise, constructive use; and the start of the coda, with bagpiping oboes and drone fifths in the cellos, affords us a brief glimpse of pastoral paradise regained, before Brahms brings the concerto to an end in a mood of fierce triumph.

© Malcolm MacDonald

∿ Piano Concerto No. 2 in B flat major, Op. 83 (1878–81)

1   Allegro non troppo
2   Allegro appassionato
3   Andante
4   Allegretto grazioso

Brahms completed his Second Piano Concerto at Pressbaum near Vienna in the summer of 1881, and dedicated it to Eduard Marxsen, his old piano teacher in Hamburg. The composer took the solo role in the premiere, given in Budapest on 9 November 1881, before playing the work on a triumphant tour of Austria, Germany and the Netherlands. Its reception was very unlike that accorded to his youthful D minor Concerto, completed in 1859, which had only slowly gained acceptance. Yet the B flat Concerto manifests many paradoxes of scale and utterance. The piano part is less overtly virtuosic than in the First Concerto, but presents the soloist with even greater technical challenges. Although the work's intimacy of discourse is often comparable to chamber music – witness the very opening, growing from a horn call of pure romance, answered by a piano solo of musing reverie – it is built on ample, quasi-symphonic lines, with four movements instead of three. And the first two, at least, are full of heroic bravura; hear the grand tutti the orchestra launches when it gets hold of the horn–piano theme. The whole work displays a leonine combination of gentleness and massive strength – but strength which is held in reserve or employed for athletic relaxation.

Thus Brahms seems to meld the principles of concerto and symphony – especially in the spacious first movement, which grows organically into a grand tonal network of interconnected ideas. The piano does not merely repeat the themes of the orchestral tutti but engages in a wide-ranging dialogue by continually varying them. Despite the generally optimistic tone, darkness and passion have their places – the former represented by sudden glimpses of distant tonal areas, the latter by the more choleric of the piano's monologues.

After this the D minor scherzo hints at real tragedy. Its first subject has an impetuous zeal, while the second is a haunting tune full of submissive pathos. An angry development then leads to the trio section's grand, Handelian D major theme before the scherzo music returns, urgent and volatile to the last.

The spirit of chamber music is most marked in the slow (third) movement, which is framed by an easeful, singing cello solo. The piano never has this tune, but muses upon its harmonic background in filigree passagework and decoration of the utmost plasticity. The overall impression is of self-communing improvisation, where motivic development dissolves into the stream of consciousness. In one episode, the clarinets introduce a quotation from Brahms's song 'Todessehnen' (Yearning for Death).

The last movement offers final relaxation, in a complex fusion of rondo and sonata form that wears its intricacy with insouciance. The piano summons up lilting, instantly memorable themes, in seemingly artless profusion – yet there is immense artfulness here. Not only in the many subtle rhythmic contrasts, but also in the 'gypsy' languor of the second-subject tune, in the Mozartian wit of the epigrams bandied about between soloist and orchestra, and in the easy confidence of scoring that allows Brahms to write grand, full-hearted tuttis without once requiring trumpets or drums.

It may not be provoking disbelief to hear this concerto as a kind of pianistic autobiography – by a composer for whom the piano, and piano music, lay at the centre of his creativity. The first movement's quality of carefully structured improvisation plausibly presents a portrait of the young virtuoso, responding to the voice of Nature (the horn theme) with a hugely confident display of pianistic technique. But the scherzo intervenes, in D minor – for Brahms a key of catastrophic associations (the First Piano Concerto, begun in the aftermath of Schumann's suicide attempt and incarceration in an asylum, makes this clear). However, the robust and enlivening 'Handelian' trio perhaps represents the saving grace of study, the power of the music of the past to strengthen and stabilise the composer – as Brahms's Baroque studies had strengthened him, issuing at length in his Op. 24 *Handel Variations*.

The Andante slow movement then indicates a period of withdrawal, of self-communing at the keyboard, almost of self-effacement. In Brahms's own solo output this mood is most clearly felt in the long series of late pieces which had begun during the 1870s with the Op. 76 Piano Pieces. The wonderful main theme, however, is entrusted to the solo cello: the piano muses round it, decorates it, dialogues with the cello as a subordinate partner. The extent to which this movement resembles a cello–piano duet suggests (quite apart from the tenderness of the main idea) some imaginative link with Clara Schumann. Perhaps Brahms was thinking of the 'Romanze' slow movement of her own Piano Concerto, which is even more of a cello–piano duo. The song quotation, too, is probably connected with his feelings for her.

The finale, with its Hungarian rhythms, its relaxed evocation of dance and song, evokes another side of Brahms's pianism: his sizeable output of music for enjoyment and relaxation, most notably in the *Hungarian Dances* and *Liebeslieder Waltzes*. This finale remains of the highest artistic quality (and is no relaxation for the pianist); but the popular elements blended in it are essential to any rounded portrait of its composer.

Malcolm MacDonald © BBC

✑ Violin Concerto in D major, Op. 77
(1878)

1 Allegro non troppo
2 Adagio
3 Allegro giocoso, ma non troppo vivace

During the later 1870s Brahms's life fell into a fairly regular pattern. He devoted three months or so of each winter to extended concert tours, as conductor and pianist; he spent most of the spring and autumn at home in Vienna; and he set aside the summer for long 'holidays', which in fact provided him with his best opportunities for sustained creative work. In 1876 he went to Sassnitz, on an island in the Baltic, and there put almost the final touches to his long-delayed First Symphony. In 1877 he discovered Pörtschach, a quiet village on the Wörthersee in Carinthia, where he composed most of the Second Symphony.

The following year, on his return from a genuine holiday – and a very enjoyable one – in Italy, he stopped off again at Pörtschach. 'I only wanted to stay there for a day,' he wrote to a friend, 'and then, as this day was so beautiful, for yet another. But each day was as fine as the last, and so I stayed on. If on your journey you have interrupted your reading to gaze out of the window, you must have seen how all the mountains round the blue lake are white with snow, while the trees are covered with delicate green.' And it was in these idyllic surroundings that the Violin Concerto came into being.

The concerto was intended for Brahms's friend Joseph Joachim, the greatest violin virtuoso of the age. As soon as the solo part was drafted, Brahms sent it to Joachim for his comments, and a detailed correspondence ensued; though, as the composer's biographer Karl Geiringer drily observed, 'it is characteristic of Brahms that he conscientiously asked his friend's advice on all technical questions – and then hardly ever followed it.' The work was given its first performance in Leipzig on New Year's Day 1879.

Brahms's correspondence with Joachim reveals that, at an early stage of drafting, the concerto was to have had four movements, including a scherzo – the plan which Brahms was to adopt a few years later for his Second Piano Concerto. But, in its completed form, the Violin Concerto has a classical three-movement shape – indeed, a strictly classical one, eschewing the formal innovation of the Mendelssohnian type of Romantic concerto and even of the later Beethoven concertos.

The three movements are separate, with no link between slow movement and finale; the first is a large-scale sonata-form movement, with a full orchestral exposition before the soloist's first entry; the slow movement is a straightforward A–B–A structure; and the finale is a rondo, with an acceleration in the coda at just the point at which many of Mozart's and Beethoven's concerto finales similarly turn for home. But the most self-consciously conservative feature of the work is that, in the first movement, Brahms provided the customary springboard of a chord for a cadenza, but did not write one himself. The one which Joachim composed for his own use has in general been adopted by succeeding generations of violinists.

As for the musical language of the work, it bears a distinct resemblance to the D major product of Brahms's previous Carinthian summer, the Second Symphony. The first movement in particular begins as if continuing the relaxed yet controlled triple-time progress of the first movement of the symphony. But it proceeds throughout by contrast between this lyrical vein and a more forceful manner, which is associated in particular with double- and triple-stopping in the solo part – a Joachim speciality.

The slow movement, in F major, is pure lyricism: it begins, unexpectedly, by giving the limelight to a solo oboe, accompanied only by the other wind instruments; and after the soloist's entry the wind continue to make telling contributions, dropping into the background only in the slightly slower, and richly ornamented, middle section.

The finale introduces a lighter note, one which Brahms would have hesitated to sound in a symphony: a flavour of Hungarian gypsy music. This is both an act of homage to Joachim, a Hungarian himself and composer of a concerto 'in the Hungarian style', and a reminiscence of Brahms's own youthful interest in gypsy music; and it proves an ideal way in which to end a work that so successfully combines a relaxed, holiday mood with Brahms's unique compositional mastery.

© Anthony Burton

℘ Concerto in A minor for Violin, Cello and Orchestra, Op. 102 (1887)

1 Allegro
2 Andante
3 Vivace non troppo

The Double Concerto of 1887 was Brahms's last orchestral work. In the remaining ten years, and twenty opus numbers, of his life, he concentrated on choral music, songs, chamber music (including the late group of clarinet works) and short keyboard pieces. The concerto's combination of solo instruments was at the time unique (given that Vivaldi's music was virtually unknown in the nineteenth century), and remains rare (though there are notable twentieth-century concertos for violin and cello by Delius and Sessions). Brahms had worked towards it in his three previous compositions: Op. 99 was the F major Sonata for cello and piano, Op. 100 the A major Sonata for violin and piano, and Op. 101 the C minor Trio for violin, cello and piano. The orchestral contribution to the Double Concerto, however, is no blown-up piano part, but is scored with all Brahms's usual, and still often under-rated, skill; in particular, it embraces a wide range of wood-wind textures which are full of character but do not obscure the acoustically vulnerable pair of soloists.

The concerto is, of course, an abstract piece; but it is not without what literary critics call a 'subtext', and one of considerable human interest. The work was written for, and first performed by, the great violinist Joseph Joachim and his quartet colleague Robert Hausmann. Brahms had enjoyed a long-standing association and friendship with Joachim, but it had been sundered in 1880 when Brahms had taken sides with Joachim's wife over the couple's divorce proceedings. The concerto was a gesture of reconciliation – and a successful one: when they came together to rehearse for the first performance, Brahms and Joachim spoke to each other for the first time in years. It has often been noted that the second subject of the first movement is very similar to the opening theme of the Violin Concerto No. 22, also in A minor, by Viotti – a once famous work which Joachim played frequently and which Brahms called his 'special delight'. But it is tempting to look further, and suggest that the cello part, while written for Hausmann to play, consciously or unconsciously embodies the gruff persona adopted by Brahms himself.

Viewed in this light, the introduction to the first movement, preceding the traditional long orchestral tutti, becomes an allegory of reconciliation. After four bars of stern orchestral prelude (foreshadowing the first subject), the cello launches into an expansive cadenza; then, after a short, eloquent passage for the wind (foreshadowing the second subject, with its echo of Viotti), the violin embarks on what promises to be a reply of equal length; but the cello intervenes in this after a few bars, and the two instruments go on together in perfectly balanced partnership – a partnership which is then maintained virtually throughout the work.

In the D major slow movement, the broad, expressive principal melody, played by the two soloists in octaves – but twice with subtle divergences of rhythm to reinforce the top of the melodic curve – is a perfect musical metaphor for a strong and enduring friendship. And the finale seems to review the course of that friendship: youthful high spirits in the main rondo theme; fine Romantic aspiration in the main subsidiary idea; later, perhaps, just a hint of strife. Then in the coda, in which a slowed-up major-key version of the rondo theme is wreathed in decorative arabesques and spun out in new flights of lyricism, there is a feeling that the friendship is being renewed and reaffirmed in later life, in a mood of autumnal tranquillity.

© Anthony Burton

Benjamin Britten (1913–76)

Born in Suffolk on 22 November 1913 (propitiously, the feast day of St Cecilia, patron saint of music) Britten began piano lessons aged five, composing songs for his mother by the age of ten. At thirteen he began composition studies with Frank Bridge before entering the Royal College of Music in 1930. His documentary scores for the GPO (General Post Office) Film Unit brought him into collaboration with W. H. Auden, a liberating force; in 1937 he not only attracted international attention with his *Variations on a Theme of Frank Bridge* at the Salzburg Festival, but also met the tenor Peter Pears, who would become his lifelong partner and an influential interpreter of his work. Britten revitalised English opera with his first stage triumph *Peter Grimes* (1945), launching the Aldeburgh Festival three years later. He performed often as a conductor and pianist, and though he wrote a significant number of chamber and choral works (among them three string quartets and the *War Requiem*, 1961) it is principally for his vocal and especially operatic output that he is remembered.

❧ Piano Concerto, Op. 13 (1938)

1 Toccata: Allegro molto e con brio
2 Waltz: Allegretto
3 Impromptu: Andante lento –
4 March: Allegro moderato, sempre alla marcia

Britten was twenty-four when he gave the first performance of this concerto at the 1938 Proms. In 1945 he replaced the original third-movement Recitative and Aria with the present Impromptu, based in part on incidental music to a BBC play, *King Arthur* (broadcast in 1937). The Piano Concerto was Britten's first large-scale, non-vocal work involving the full orchestra, and it has sometimes been held against the youth-ful composer that he did not take the opportunity to attempt a work of Brahmsian profundity. The concerto did much to establish that reputation for easy satisfaction with mere effects which dogged Britten even after his operatic successes of the 1940s.

It would do the composer no service to argue that, on the contrary, the concerto is after all a deeply serious symphonic structure of profound emotion. But its blend of exuberance and charm, by no means unadulterated by darker moods, indicates latent tension and uncertainty more than mere superficiality or glibness. The late 1930s was a period of great political and personal uncertainty, and the concerto can certainly be seen and heard as a product of the kind of ambivalence which had Britten producing vigorously paci-fist music, while at the same time the sophisticated self-consciousness of 'the Auden generation' pointed in rather different directions. Ten years after the concerto's premiere, one critic claimed to find 'something of the masochism of Isherwood's Mr Norris' in the finale, with 'the whip sounds of the slapstick orchestration'.

The opening Toccata, in sonata form, is the longest move-ment, and for all its echoes of Ravel and Prokofiev it is a resourceful and far from impersonal demonstration of the difficult art of sustaining a large-scale, steadily evolving musi-cal argument at a fast tempo. Contrasting lyrical material, initially subordinate, becomes increasingly important as the movement proceeds, notably after the cadenza. And that cadenza shows that Britten was well able to write imagina-tively for the instrument on which he was a master performer, but which he used reluctantly as a composer, save as accom-paniment to the voice.

Britten had shown his ability to write disturbingly evoca-tive waltz movements before, notably in the *Frank Bridge Variations*. In the concerto, the sad spirit of occupied Vienna haunts the music – never more so than in the initial viola solo – and although a lighter tone is also evident, there is less of the sardonic parody than in some other Britten waltzes. The mood deepens further in the Impromptu, whose form is not the rather casual structure suggested by the title, but a passacaglia whose variations are each linked by a solo flourish. The music – questing, yet never simply aimless – provides the concerto with its most reflective passages.

After it, the March rapidly accumulates a weighty energy in which exuberance and horror seem inextricably linked. With its swagger expressing both mockery and menace it provides a dazzling conclusion to an early work which fascinates all the more because it indicates so many of the composer's later concerns so clearly.

© Arnold Whittall

✺ Violin Concerto, Op. 15 (1939; rev. 1958)

1   Moderato con moto
2   Vivace – Cadenza –
3   Passacaglia: Andante lento

In the spring of 1939, with the outbreak of war inevitable, Britten followed his literary friends Auden and Isherwood and left England for North America. At the age of twenty-five he had already written the *Variations on a Theme of Frank Bridge* and the Piano Concerto, and had begun *Les illuminations*; now he turned to another orchestral work, the Violin Concerto, which he completed in Quebec Province on 20 September 1939. Although the concerto clearly owes much to Bartók, Stravinsky and Prokofiev, at the same time it reveals a consolidation of Britten's characteristically imaginative scoring, and of his highly original approach to structure in the use of a ground bass in the last movement, and in the application of a closely wrought inner logic to his motivic material – though ostensibly he still adheres to the classical three-movement concerto framework.

Despite the brilliance of orchestration and the virtuoso solo part – in both of which rhythmic vitality and touches of humour abound – the concerto is dark in overall character. A sense of foreboding and impending disaster is established at the outset by an ostinato figure assigned (as at the opening of Beethoven's Violin Concerto) to the timpani. Interpretations can all too easily be applied in retrospect, but the American composer Elliott Carter, reviewing the work at its premiere in New York on 28 March 1940, saw it as 'autobiographical', its appeal lying in 'its disarming frankness'. In some ways, at least, the Violin Concerto would seem to be an expression of the anxieties and tensions that impelled Britten to leave his homeland to its uncertain future.

The first movement, however, with its juxtaposition of lyrical and percussive elements, remains curiously detached, apart from the unsettling effect of its combination of intense melancholy and sense of implacability. Throughout the concerto the soloist explores the motivic material as if searching for an unforeseen resolution, most poignantly, perhaps, in the cadenza that leads from the central scherzo-like movement to the Passacaglia. Beginning with the main theme of the scherzo, the cadenza shifts back to the opening material and is still pensively reviewing the more lyrical vein when the trombones introduce the ground on which the last movement is based. This is the first of Britten's highly successful experiments with the ostinato principle; here the ground migrates throughout the orchestra, gradually extending its grip even as its rhythmic and melodic shape undergoes subtle transformations in a sequence of nine variations. The coda, marked 'Lento e solenne', strives towards a resolution, the orchestral texture clearing and moving in the manner of a slow procession as the tonality settles on D while the restless violin seems to offer up a prayer to some vaguely defined hope. Here is an early glimpse of the powerful emotional intensity of Britten's maturity.

© Tess Knighton

Max Bruch (1838–1920)

Even during his long lifetime, Max Bruch's output was over-shadowed by the success of his First Violin Concerto, stealing attention from his three operas, a number of sacred and secular cantatas, three symphonies, songs and chamber music. He was born in Cologne and studied with Reinecke and Ferdinand Hiller. Having completed his one-act opera *Scherz, List und Rache* (Op. 1) when he was twenty, Bruch embarked on a period of travel in Germany and Austria culminating in Mannheim, where his second opera *Die Loreley* was performed. He took posts in Koblenz and Sondershausen, concentrated on composition during the 1870s, then returned to conducting in the 1880s, with posts in Liverpool and in Breslau. His high standing as a composer was confirmed with a professorship at the Berlin Academy from 1891 until his retirement in 1911. Towards the end of his life, Bruch's choral works became less fashionable and his style appeared unadventurous. The *Scottish Fantasy* for violin and orchestra and *Kol nidrei* on Hebrew themes for cello and orchestra remain in the repertoire, displaying Bruch's wide-ranging interest in folk music.

◊ Violin Concerto No. 1 in G minor (1864–8)

1   Prelude: Allegro moderato –
2   Adagio
3   Finale: Allegro energico

Although he composed several choral and orchestral works (including three concertos for the violin and one for two pianos), Bruch's fame today rests largely on one piece – the Violin Concerto in G minor. He was at work on the concerto as early as 1864, and expressed in a letter that 'I do not feel sure of my feet on this terrain'. Sure or not, the work became enormously successful, although it was to undergo considerable revision before it reached its final state. Sadly, through his own misjudgement, Bruch made very little money out of his most famous work. He sold the concerto outright, thereby depriving himself of the considerable fortune he would have made from the work's lasting popularity with audiences.

The first movement is a rhapsodic prelude whose opening drum roll and sombre woodwind theme introduce an impassioned flourish for the solo violin. The orchestra soon settles down to a more regular rhythmic pattern, against which the soloist pits a new, dramatic theme. The contrasting second subject, introduced once again by the violin, is a long, cantabile melody that slowly climbs through the instrument's higher register via a series of ecstatic trills. The foregoing material is then treated to a clear-cut series of developments, culminating in a rich passage for full orchestra. The opening flourishes return, their rhapsodic gestures now heightened, to provide a transitional link to the next movement.

The central Adagio is the emotional core of the concerto. It unfolds as a string of lovely themes, the first three of which are introduced by the soloist. A fourth theme emerges from these, announced initially by horn and woodwind, while the solo violin overlays its own florid gloss. These themes reappear throughout the movement, sometimes transformed by the orchestra in glowing instrumental colours and often in decorated versions played by the soloist.

The final movement is a sparkling, dance-like Allegro energico with a strong Hungarian flavour, possibly in tribute to the Hungarian-born violinist Joseph Joachim, for whom Bruch wrote his concerto. After a few bars of 'wait for it' preparation, the soloist enters with the main theme, much of which calls for 'quadruple stopping' (playing all four strings at once). A transitional theme leads to the 'big tune' of the movement, a soaring, triumphant melody given first by the full orchestra and then sumptuously taken up by the soloist.

Having mustered his melodic forces, Bruch commences to reassemble them, often virtually unchanged, but moving effortlessly and effectively towards the concerto's exciting Presto finale.

Brendan Beales © BBC

Fryderyk Franciszek Chopin
(1810–49)

Perhaps more than any other major composer, Chopin has become associated with a single instrument, yet his achievements were no less far-reaching because of his concentration on the piano. He studied at the Warsaw Conservatory before moving to Paris, where he quickly found favour in aristocratic circles, played in salons and earned a living as a celebrity teacher. Challenging the prevailing appetite for showy virtuosity, he placed the greatest technical demands at the service of expression, particularly in his two sets of Études, Opp. 10 and 25. Alongside his cycles of generally smaller pieces – waltzes, preludes, mazurkas, nocturnes – lie milestones of the repertoire, particularly the four Scherzos and four Ballades, three sonatas (the second of which includes the best known of all funeral marches) and the late Barcarolle. By extending the range of the piano's emotional language, and developing the importance of texture and colour, Chopin became a direct influence on generations of composers including Liszt, Debussy, Rakhmaninov and Skryabin.

∾ Piano Concerto No. 1 in E minor, Op. 11
(1830)

1 Allegro maestoso
2 Romanze: Larghetto –
3 Rondo: Vivace

Chopin's two piano concertos are both early works, written before he reached the age of twenty-one. They were probably inspired by the virtuoso concertos of John Field and Johann Nepomuk Hummel, to which Chopin had been introduced by Josef Elsner, his teacher at the Warsaw Conservatoire; and in particular by a visit Hummel made to Warsaw in 1828, in the course of which the eminent pianist and the talented young student became firm friends. The following year Chopin composed his Concerto in F minor, later published as No. 2; then in the spring and summer of 1830 he followed it with the E minor. He gave the first performance of the latter at his farewell concert in Warsaw in October 1830, less than a month before he set out for Vienna and, eventually, Paris – never to return to his homeland.

After his departure from Poland, Chopin wrote only one other work including orchestra (the *Grand Polonaise* in E flat); apart from songs and a couple of cello pieces, he devoted himself exclusively to the solo piano. The orchestral contributions to his youthful concertos have been much criticised – the master orchestrator Berlioz, for example, called them 'cold and almost superfluous' – and there have been many attempts to improve them (the most recent and most drastic being 'chamber versions', suggested by Chopin's practice of rehearsing the concertos with the string principals alone). Certainly in the E minor Concerto the sound of the orchestral tutti, including four horns and a trombone, is thick and not especially effective; and there are rather too many passages that rely on the strings alone to accompany the soloist. But the effect of the muted strings in the slow movement is magical. And Chopin does give some characterful moments to several of the wind instruments, notably the first horn and the first bassoon.

Perhaps the mistake made by commentators has been to judge the concertos against the yardstick of the great 'symphonic' concertos of Mozart and Beethoven, when they really belong to a tradition of lighter virtuoso concertos in which the main interest lies in the solo piano part. And the same defence could be made against criticisms of unconventional features of their form. What is more important is that Chopin's formal schemes provide an effective platform both for some brilliant passagework, and for his unique gift for expressive melody and meaningful ornamentation.

The opening movement of the E minor Concerto finds room for two of the composer's finest melodies, in the midst of a great deal of bravura writing. The E major Romanze has all the intimate intensity of Chopin's nocturnes: it was probably inspired by the composer's undeclared love for the singer Konstancja Gladkowska, and was described by him (in an unusual excursion into poetic commentary) as 'giving the impression of someone looking fondly towards a spot which calls to mind a thousand happy memories'. The extrovert major-key finale strikes a nationalist note – as popular in Warsaw just before the anti-Russian uprising as it was to be later in Paris – by adopting the springing rhythms of a southern Polish dance, the *Krakowiak*.

© Anthony Burton

◌ Piano Concerto No. 2 in F minor, Op. 21 (1829–30)

1 Maestoso
2 Larghetto
3 Allegro vivace

Chopin's two piano concertos are both early works, composed during the period when he had completed his studies in Warsaw and was aiming to make a name for himself as a virtuoso pianist in the other major European capitals. After the success of his first journey to Vienna in August 1829 he returned to Warsaw and planned an extensive tour of Italy and Germany for the following year. He had already composed three works for piano and orchestra: the Variations on Mozart's 'Là ci darem la mano', the *Fantasy on Polish Airs* and *Krakowiak*; now he needed full-scale concertos for his repertory.

The Concerto in F minor was the first of the two to be written, and was performed by Chopin at the National Theatre in Warsaw on 17 March 1830, a few weeks after his twentieth birthday; the entire concert was such a success that it had to be repeated five days later. The E minor Concerto was composed later that year; but since it was the first to be published (in 1833, three years before its predecessor), it became known as No. 1. A similar reversal occurred with

Beethoven's first two piano concertos, one of the very few things Beethoven and Chopin have in common.

In contrast to the more symphonic type of concerto pioneered by Mozart and Beethoven, Chopin's models were the concertos of such early nineteenth-century composer–performers as John Field, Ignaz Moscheles, Frédéric Kalkbrenner (dedicatee of Chopin's E minor Concerto) and, perhaps most important, Johann Nepomuk Hummel, the pupil of Mozart whom Chopin had met in Warsaw in 1828, and who, before the emergence of Liszt and Chopin himself, was generally considered to be the finest pianist–composer of his day.

Chopin's concertos have been at the heart of the repertory for a century and a half. They bear the weight of an imposing tradition and variety of interpretation, which is surely some indication of greatness. But on account of both their formal layout and of the relationship between piano and orchestra, they have been subjected to the harshest criticism of any of his works. Much of this criticism misses the point. In this type of early nineteenth-century concerto, the orchestra and piano were rarely on equal terms, for the simple reason that the orchestra was there merely to provide a discreet accompaniment to the soloist's virtuosity. Indeed, when the composer–pianist travelled, he could by no means be certain of finding an adequate orchestra, and last-minute patching and arrangement was frequently the order of the day. Chopin often performed his concertos as solo works, or with the accompaniment of a small chamber ensemble of strings.

There have been various attempts to rewrite the orchestral parts of Chopin's concertos (by such distinguished musicians as Karl Klindworth, Carl Tausig, André Messager and Mily Balakirev). Some of these can be heard on older recordings, and are unconvincing. Chopin's own writing, whether for piano or orchestra, cannot be tampered with, as anyone knows who has heard the entertainment known as *Les sylphides*, a ballet score concocted from Chopin's piano music.

The opening orchestral passage of the F minor Concerto is in fact full of rhythmic and harmonic interest, but here, as throughout the concerto, the full orchestra is to be heard only at those points where the piano is silent: it is an alternation of forces, not a partnership. There is a certain amount of dialogue with the woodwind in the central development section, but apart from this the orchestral writing is largely limited to the strings, who colour and support the continuous discourse of the piano solo. In this relatively early work, the main characteristics of Chopin's mature piano style are already fully developed, most of them arising out of technical devices which turn the percussive piano into a singing instrument. The brilliance and poetry derive from such subtle features as use of the pedals, the spacing of chords and a wonderful freedom of rhythmic accent.

Ornamental melody is the prime feature of the Larghetto, whose outer sections are in the style of a nocturne, with a steady left-hand bass against ever more elaborately decorated right-hand traceries. The central section, where the piano delivers an almost vocal recitative over a background of tremolo strings, is a passage of pure Romantic rhetoric. According to Liszt, this was a movement that Chopin played frequently in private (as a solo); and while composing the concerto he admitted to a close friend that the movement had been inspired by his 'ideal', the young singer Konstancja Gladkowska.

Chopin's greatest public successes in his early years had been those works based on Polish dance measures, and so it was natural that he should feature them as finales in both of his piano concertos. In the F minor Concerto it is a mazurka, which sounds at first as though it will be the recurrent refrain of a rondo form, but the movement is in fact cast in an A–B–A form, with a brilliant final section introduced by a solo horn call and a turn to the major mode.

© Andrew Huth

Aaron Copland (1900–90)

Very much a child of the twentieth century, Copland left the musical conservativism of his native New York in 1921 to study with Nadia Boulanger in Paris. There, influenced by the rhythmic complexity of Stravinsky, he wrote his ambitious ballet *Grohg* and returned to the USA in 1924 with a commission from Boulanger for an organ symphony (later rescored as the First Symphony). Koussevitzky premiered Copland's jazzy *Music for the Theatre* and Piano Concerto in Boston. During the 1930s Copland adopted a simpler style that led to the wide appeal of his three ballet suites on American subjects, *Billy the Kid*, *Rodeo* and *Appalachian Spring*, as well as the patriotic *Lincoln Portrait* and *Fanfare for the Common Man*. He produced three film scores for Hollywood, and in 1950 wrote a Clarinet Concerto for jazz clarinettist Benny Goodman. In the 1950s and 1960s he returned to a more progressive style, but he gave up composing in the 1970s. He was a huge influence on the formation of a distinctive American music, not only through his compositions, but also as a writer, educator, administrator and supporter of younger composers.

✺ Clarinet Concerto (1948)

The jazz clarinettist and composer Benny Goodman became a dominant figure in post-war American music largely owing to his ability to ignore boundaries and to cross bridges. Equally at home in jazz and the classics, Goodman was not only the 'King of Swing' but the man who sought works for his instrument from, among others, Bartók, Hindemith, Bernstein and, in 1948, Aaron Copland. All of them, Copland especially, found Goodman's mixture of jazz techniques, improvisatory freedom, bitter-sweet lyricism and sharply etched rhythms well-nigh irresistible. Goodman paid

Copland the princely sum of $2,000 for exclusive rights to the concerto, quibbled only about a couple of high notes, got anxious about performing it for the first time, but eventually gave the premiere in November 1950.

The Clarinet Concerto is continuous, and unfolds as a natural sequence that moves from calm stasis to high excitement at the end. The opening is straight out of *Appalachian Spring*. Over a steady ostinato of pizzicato double basses, sighing violas and cellos, and the plangent accompaniment of the harp, the clarinet intones a slow expressive tune that instantly conjures up the wide open spaces and rolling plains of some imaginary, maybe Midwest American landscape – before the Fall (in both senses). Barely a hint of chromaticism troubles its unhurried progress; and when the high strings enter, with the parts now often in close imitation, the heat haze is almost palpable. With precise calculation, Copland tightens the screw, first nudging the tempo on imperceptibly, then inserting the odd bar in a different metre or increasing the dynamics, before this first undisturbed section of his concerto settles back into a quiet C major – and the first surprise.

For this is where Copland puts the cadenza, which is fully written out. The soloist has no room for his own manoeuvres, because this is the pivotal point in the concerto, structurally and thematically. The cadenza breaks the mood of serenity that has prevailed so far, and establishes the transition to the altogether different mood of the remainder of the work. Copland marks the cadenza 'freely'; but the score is crammed full of very precise indications about tempo, dynamics and articulation, and this long unaccompanied solo is one of the virtuoso peaks in the work, immensely difficult and exposed, and culminating in a ferocious fortissimo scale from one end of the instrument's range to the other.

The first entry of the piano signals the arrival of the new paragraph, a quick, rather Bartókian section, with lots of ostinato passages, stabbed staccatos, col legno effects and pizzicatos, and scurrying figures for the strings. Again the lack of orchestral wind and brass creates an open, uncluttered texture, leaving the way clear for the soloist, on his eventual entry, to rise above the fray with high staccato crotchets, at first still with little chromaticism in earshot, but gradually becoming more chromatic. Arpeggio figures abound, in both solo and accompaniment, which is ingeniously varied: now just violins, now with a solo viola playing harmonics, now with harp or piano prominent. Eventually the syncopations and offbeat emphases produce a fierce climax and set the scene for the final part of the work.

And here the jazz element that was such a preoccupation of Copland in the 1940s at last erupts to exhilarating effect. A racy theme that had briefly shown its head above the parapet back in the cadenza now surfaces again: 'with humor, relaxed', says the score, while the accompaniment begins on a solo bass: 'one stand, slap-bass style, forte, secco'.

From here on, to the wild Gershwin-like riff of the final bars, the excitement builds progressively, in a mixture of hoe-down and jam session. The key to Copland's magnetic energy here is rhythm – not only the increasingly frequent changes of pulse, and disruptive bars of 3/8 and 5/8 (Copland knew his Stravinsky), but also effervescent syncopations, all the more effective when the soloist is screaming at the top of his topmost register. The level of virtuosity increases still further over a pounding, descending four-note figure in lower strings and in the bass of the piano, until a series of clarinet flourishes and crashing chords from the orchestra brings this wonderfully assertive concerto to an appropriately brilliant end.

© Piers Burton-Page

Ernő Dohnányi (1877–1960)

Born in the Austro-Hungarian town of Poszony (now Bratislava), Dohnányi entered the Budapest Academy in 1894, where with Brahms's encouragement his Op. 1 Piano Quintet was given its premiere. On leaving the Academy Dohnányi began a successful career as a concert pianist, winning praise for his performances of the Viennese classical repertoire. He taught piano at the Berlin Musikhochschule from 1905 to 1915, but returned to Budapest in 1916 and began to exert a powerful influence on the country's musical life. From 1919 to 1944 he was music director of the Budapest Philharmonic; other posts included music director of the Hungarian Broadcasting Service and director of the Budapest Academy from 1934 to 1941 (when he resigned in protest at anti-Jewish laws). In 1949 he moved to Florida to teach at Tallahassee University. Dohnányi wrote in a more conservative and less nationalistic style than his compatriots Bartók and Kodály. Like his early idol Brahms, he worked largely in the Germanic classical forms. Among his output are two symphonies, four operas and a number of chamber works.

∾ *Variations on a Nursery Song*, Op. 25 (1914)

Introduction: Maestoso – Tema: Allegro
  1 Poco più mosso –
  2 Risoluto –
  3   –
  4 Molto meno mosso –
  5 Più mosso –
  6 Ancora più mosso –
  7 Waltz: Tempo giusto –
  8 Alla marcia: Allegro moderato –
  9 Presto –

10   Passacaglia: Adagio non troppo –
11   Chorale: Maestoso –
Finale fugato: Allegro vivace

Four years younger than Rakhmaninov, Ernő Dohnányi
was also an outstanding pianist. He was one of the first to
feature in his concerts neglected repertoire by the Viennese
classical masters – in 1920 he performed all Beethoven's
piano works, and in 1941 he gave a complete cycle of the
Mozart concertos – at a time when only a handful were in the
standard repertory.

Championed in his youth by Brahms, it was natural that
his own music should uphold the values of the great classical
tradition. From 1905 to 1915 Dohnányi taught at the Berlin
Musikhochschule, where he wrote some of his finest chamber music, including the Second String Quartet and the
Second Piano Quintet. Early in 1914 he returned to orchestral writing with the *Variations on a Nursery Song*, described
as 'for full orchestra with piano concertante', and dedicated
'to the enjoyment of lovers of humour and to the annoyance
of others'.

The meaning of the enigmatic dedication becomes clear
from the first chord. Having made his entrance and sat down
at the piano, the pianist might well think he has been booked
for the wrong night. For almost four minutes he has to sit
while the orchestra expounds a massive introduction, apparently heralding a work of epic proportions and tragic dénoue-
ment. All the hallmarks of doom are there – the minor key,
the brass chords full of foreboding, the anxious string figuration, the sinister 'fate' motif hammered out on the timpani
and reinforced by the full orchestra. This must surely belong
to some bloodstained drama by Verdi or Puccini, or at least to
a tragic symphony or overture by Brahms.

But then . . . every pianist has his day. After a fortissimo
chord on the dominant brings the sombre introduction to an
ear-shattering close, the 'theme' of these variations finally
makes its appearance, played in octaves, requiring at least

Grade 1 standard on the part of the pianist. And what is this theme? French children know it as the old nursery rhyme '*Ah, vous dirai-je, maman*', while in this country it is better known as 'Twinkle, twinkle, little star'. Mozart wrote a set of twelve variations on it for solo piano in 1778, in which he also stated the theme quite simply, in two parts.

Having kept the orchestra in check throughout the theme and Variation 1 (in which the piano dances off gleefully, at one point indulging in a little friendly competition with the harp, while the strings state the basic notes of the theme), Dohnányi allows the horns and woodwind to introduce Variation 2, another lightly scored, but this time heavily chromatic, variant in which the piano continues its rippling figuration. Variation 3 – a lush, Romantic dialogue between piano and strings – has definite hints of Brahms, or even Richard Strauss; while in Variation 4, the piano plays a subordinate role to a grotesque wind sextet consisting of piccolo, flutes, bassoons and contrabassoon.

In Variation 5 the mood changes completely. Accompanied almost imperceptibly by muted strings, harp and the faintest brass chords, and with the theme stated on the glockenspiel, the pianist is directed to put all possible pedals down, in order to sound like a musical box (or even a celesta – does one detect the saccharine influence of a certain Sugar-Plum Fairy?). Variation 6 continues in the same vein, but with oboes, clarinets and bassoons counterpointing the piano's sparkling figuration. In Variation 7, we are swept into the glittering world of the Waltz King; while Variation 8 – a military march for the woodwind, horns, timpani and double basses, with timid interjections for piano could easily come from a late nineteenth-century opera.

The marching timpani bass quickens its pace to lead in to Variation 9, in which the sinister, hollow sound of bassoons and horns, later joined by xylophone and col legno strings, evokes the graveyard frolics of Saint-Saëns's *Danse macabre* – or even Berlioz's Witches' Sabbath from his *Symphonie fantastique*. Towards the end, the piano finally summons up enough courage to interrupt these ghostly orchestral revels with its own forceful clarion call – the sort of double-octave flourish which opened many a nineteenth-century piano concerto. The bassoons skitter away into their graves, and the piano introduces a new note of dignity in a short passage marked 'Andante rubato'. This leads into the tenth variation, a majestic Passacaglia which pays homage to Brahms's *Variations on a Theme of Haydn* and brings the mellow tones of the strings – especially the violas – to the fore.

A coda for full orchestra leads into the last variation – a solemn chorale in which piano statements alternate with woodwind and brass. But after a quiet timpani roll, the piano resumes its former high spirits in a dazzlingly playful fugato finale. Just as before, a fortissimo dominant chord heralds a final statement of the theme in all its nursery simplicity – before cascades of piano arpeggios culminating in a six-octave glissando bring the variations to an end.

© Wendy Thompson

Henri Dutilleux (b. 1916)

A skilful painter of intense and refined orchestral colours, Dutilleux has won his reputation on the basis of a small number of works – he destroyed most of his music before the Piano Sonata of 1946–8. He was born in Angers, studied at the Paris Conservatoire and won a Prix de Rome in 1938 for his cantata *L'anneau du roi*. After returning to Paris following wartime duties he worked as an accompanist at the Paris Opéra, then headed a department at French Radio before leaving in 1963 to compose full-time. He wrote two symphonies during the 1950s and has produced a small number of fine works since the 1960s, among them the cello concerto *Tout un monde lointain . . .* (1967–70) for Mstislav Rostropovich, the string quartet *Ainsi la nuit* (1973–6), *Timbres, espace, mouvement* for orchestra (1976–9) and the violin concerto *L'arbre des songes* (1979–85) for Isaac Stern. *The Shadows of Time* (1995–7) was given its UK premiere at the BBC Proms in 1998, and in 2002 Anne-Sophie Mutter premiered the brief but sensuous nocturnal violin concerto *Sur le même accord*.

❧ Violin Concerto: *L'arbre des songes* (1979–85)

1 Librement [Freely] – Interlude –
2 Vif [Lively] – Interlude 2 –
3 Lent [Slow] – Interlude 3 –
4 Large et animé [Broad, with movement]

Since the death of Messiaen in 1992, Boulez and Dutilleux remain the foremost names in twentieth-century French music: Boulez representing the avant-garde, and Dutilleux the survival of the French traditions of clarity, economy, craftsmanship and *sensibilité* in direct descent from Debussy and Ravel.

As one would expect, Dutilleux has made many original contributions to his inheritance, particularly in the areas of continuous thematic growth and the imaginative subdivision of the orchestra, and the main areas in which he parts company with Boulez lie in his opposition to dogmatic systematisation and the concept of the 'work in progress'. He rarely resorts to any form of serialisation, carefully preserves the accessible concept of recurring pivot notes, hates 'prefabricated formal scaffolding', and seeks to make his imaginative compositions unfold in a free, seemingly improvisatory manner, with the sheer 'joy of sound' and the 'spirit of variation' uppermost in his mind. As with the secretive Debussy, his titles are of carefully chosen brevity and his message is spiritual rather than programmatic, although there is an equally broad cultural mind at work underneath and cross-references with the other arts permeate frequently.

We know, for instance, that Dutilleux's earlier cello concerto, *Tout un monde lointain* . . . (1967–70), was inspired by several poems by Baudelaire, whose aesthetic ideas he particularly admired. As Francis Bayer has suggested, it is thus perfectly possible that Dutilleux remembered Baudelaire's prose poem *Les projets* (1857) when he began work on *L'arbre des songes* in 1979, and especially its evocative line '*et la nuit, pour servir d'accompagnement à mes songes, le chant plaintif des arbres à musique*'. Dutilleux, however, remains characteristically non-committal on this point, simply explaining that 'the work grows rather like a tree, for the constant multiplication and renewal of its branches is the lyrical essence of the tree. This symbolic image, as well as the idea of a seasonal cycle, at the time inspired my choice of the true title, *The Tree of Dreams.*'

L'arbre des songes was commissioned by Radio France to commemorate the sixtieth birthday of the celebrated violinist Isaac Stern in 1980. But as Dutilleux the perfectionist again proved notoriously slow in completing his concerto, Stern did not perform it until 5 November 1985 at the Théâtre des Champs-Élysées in Paris, when the French National

Orchestra was conducted by Lorin Maazel. Dutilleux's aim was to integrate Stern with the orchestra, and to give him a challenging solo part that was devoid of any pure virtuosity. As most of Dutilleux's mature works interrelate, the structure in seven continuous parts (four movements, linked by three interludes) can be related to that of his string quartet *Ainsi la nuit* (1973–6), just as the *'thème des accords'* in *Tout un monde lointain . . .* has its counterpart in the *'thème du carillon'* which appears at (or near) the end of each interlude in the Violin Concerto on a separate group of 'tinkling', bell-like instruments. This becomes the predominant idea in the fourth movement, which functions both as a second scherzo and a summary finale/coda.

The three contrasting interludes each have a different character. The first, introduced by the bass clarinet, has a pointillist texture, while the second is a monodic response to the preceding scherzo. The third is at once static, humorous and functional. Dutilleux takes the pivot note A (around which the beautiful dialogue between solo violin and oboe d'amore gravitates during most of the preceding slow movement) and uses it as the logical basis for a brilliantly timed tuning-up exercise in which each group of the orchestra participates.

© Robert Orledge

Antonín Dvořák (1841–1904)

It was Brahms who recognised Dvořák's talent when, around 1875, he recommended the Czech composer to his own publisher, Simrock. Born in a village north of Prague in 1841, Dvořák worked as a viola player at the Provisional Theatre, then as an organist. The success of tours in the 1880s led to wider recognition as a composer, and his appointment in 1891 as director of the newly founded National Conservatory of Music in New York. During his three years in America he was influenced by Negro and indigenous Indian music, composing the 'New World' Symphony and the 'American' Quartet, Op. 96. But the pull of his homeland, whose folk music and pastoral beauty was reflected strongly in his music, was great. He returned to a post at the Prague National Conservatory, later becoming director. He never achieved the success of his older compatriot Smetana in the field of opera, but wrote three concertos (for violin, cello and piano), some fine string quartets, and established the Czech oratorio with his *Stabat mater* in 1883. He is best known for his symphonies and his sets of *Slavonic Dances*, originally written for piano duet, then arranged for orchestra.

∾ Cello Concerto in B minor, Op. 104 (1894–5)

1 Allegro
2 Adagio ma non troppo
3 Finale: Allegro moderato

With his Cello Concerto, Dvořák said goodbye to America. It was the only composition to come out of his third and final season as director of Mrs Thurber's National Conservatory in New York. He began work on the first movement on 8 November 1894, and by 30 December that year had completed the first two movements in full score. The sketch of the final movement is headed 'New Year 1895', and it was completed in full score by 9 February 1895. On his return to Bohemia, however (he couldn't wait to get there, judging by the many hints at Czech music in the Finale), Dvořák took the piece up again. During composition, he had learnt of the illness of his sister-in-law and former beloved, Josefína Kounicová, and had worked into the slow movement a reference to a favourite song of hers. Josefína died on 27 May 1895, and on his return Dvořák extended the coda of the third movement as a reflection of his feelings. He completed this revision on 6 June 1895.

After writing the Cello Concerto, Dvořák made a surprising shift in the final decade of his career. He continued to write operas – including his masterpiece *Rusalka* (1901) – but for the orchestra he composed no more symphonies or concertos, but rather a series of symphonic poems. These were not based on the sonata, ternary or rondo structures that lie behind so much of his earlier orchestral music. Instead their construction mirrors – often quite slavishly – the folk ballads by K. J. Erben which gave them their titles. So it was with the Cello Concerto that Dvořák said goodbye not only to America, but also to the symphonic principles on which many of his previous works had been written.

A concerto, especially one for cello, seems an odd choice to have ended with, in view of Dvořák's somewhat dismissive comments on the instrument's tone (the middle range sounds fine, he said, but it 'makes a nasal whine at the top and grumbles at the bottom'). Moreover, Dvořák's two earlier concertos, for piano and violin respectively, hardly rank among his most successful or popular pieces. Maybe he felt that it would be difficult to write another symphony after the 'New World', given so triumphantly in New York in December 1893. As it happens, when this symphony was played again in New York in March 1894, it was coupled with the Second Cello Concerto of Victor Herbert – a former cellist at the Metropolitan Opera and a colleague of Dvořák's at the National Conservatory (now best remembered as the composer of over forty operettas, including *Naughty Marietta* and *Babes in Toyland*). Dvořák was impressed at the way Herbert used trombones to support the solo instrument in the slow movement, and his enthusiasm for Herbert's piece and the promptings of his friend Hanuš Wihan (cellist of the Czech Quartet) seem to have been the chief reasons behind his own decision to write a cello concerto, a decision which, as he wrote to his friend Alois Göbl, surprised even himself.

Dvořák could not have gone out on a more magnificent work. The first movement has all the structural tautness of the great Seventh Symphony, combined with the melodic richness and orchestral inventiveness of the Eighth. The chief problem of a cello concerto – the balance between the solo instrument and the orchestra – seems only to have stimulated his imagination. There are daring combinations of cello and solo wind instruments that make the standard orchestra he uses sound anything but conventional. It was a work that set a benchmark for all later cello concertos, and several of its ideas fertilised works as different as those of Elgar and Shostakovich.

The concerto is cast in three movements: sonata form, a slow movement with a contrasting middle section and a varied reprise, and a rondo that begins briskly with an infectious march but ends gently and elegiacally with the tribute to Josefína.

The sonata-form first movement is conventional in its double exposition (one for orchestra alone, one with cello), and its clearly differentiated themes – the first in the minor, the second in the major. It begins with an arresting declamatory theme emphasising the key-note B and providing a hint of modality by its reference to the flattened leading note, A natural. The noble second theme on the horn is, as Donald Tovey once wrote, one of the most beautiful themes ever given to that instrument. We know Dvořák was pleased with it too, not only because he said so in his letter to Göbl, but because of the stunning climactic use he made of it to initiate the recapitulation. The development is brief, though not at all perfunctory. It contains a particularly haunting version of the declamatory theme, here 'molto espressivo e sostenuto' for cello against a hushed background of tremolo strings and a countertheme for flute. Towards the end of the development there is a taxing passage for cello in double stops which, to the terror of all potential soloists, suddenly flies up the scale (in octaves) to land triumphantly on the key-note B for a fortissimo version of the horn theme; thus the original order of themes from the exposition is reversed. This is not an uncommon procedure in a minor-key work, though usually it is to allow the minor-key first theme, and thus its allied mood, to colour the end of the movement. Here, however, Dvořák continues in the major and ends optimistically with a grandiose major-key transformation of the opening declamatory theme.

The Adagio begins with a simple, heartfelt tune for solo clarinet against a wind ensemble whose restraint recalls Brahms. The tune is repeated by the cello and then extended by two clarinets and punctuated by cello flourishes. A middle section takes the key to the minor with a dramatic fortissimo for full orchestra. This forms a brief introduction to Josefína's tune on the cello, a variant of the middle section of Dvořák's song 'Leave me alone' (from his Op. 82). It is heard twice in varied forms, sectioned off by the dramatic introduction. In the return to the first section, the heartfelt tune is played on three horns, now a solemn chorale whose drum-beat accompaniment on the lower strings ominously suggests a funeral march. Its continuation on the cello provides a 'quasi cadenza' (the solo instrument is imaginatively joined by the flute and then bassoons) before a final statement of the tune.

The last movement is a rondo whose chief theme is splendidly led up to with an anticipatory march rhythm. The episodes in between get longer and more indulgent. Most indulgent of all, however, is the sixty-bar coda extension which Dvořák added in memory of Josefína. Surprisingly, it does not dwell entirely on her theme, but instead mostly recalls the declamatory theme of the first movement.

Dvořák understandably repudiated the virtuoso cadenza that the concerto's dedicatee, Wihan, proposed in its place, and wrote a stern warning to his publisher Simrock not to print this or any other alteration without his express permission. And it was not Wihan who had the honour of the first performance under Dvořák in the Queen's Hall, London, on 19 March 1896, but a young and inexperienced English cellist, Leo Stern.

© John Tyrrell

✑ Violin Concerto in A minor, Op. 53 (1879–82)

1   Allegro ma non troppo
2   Adagio, ma non troppo
3   Finale: Allegro giocoso, ma non troppo

A story related by one of Dvořák's pupils suggests that he preferred his Violin Concerto to his great Cello Concerto. While the Violin Concerto is certainly a much-loved part of the repertoire, the judgement of history has favoured the Cello Concerto. His preference for the Violin Concerto may have had much to do with his notorious mistrust of the timbre of the cello; it may also reflect Dvořák's own instrumental expertise, since he was a good viola player and, when occasion demanded, an able violinist.

Dvořák wrote the Violin Concerto during the summer of 1879 when his reputation was fast acquiring an international dimension with the success of his *Moravian Duets* and the first set of *Slavonic Dances*. Moreover, the friendly intervention of Brahms had found him a publisher. Another important figure who had begun to notice the Czech composer was Brahms's friend, the violinist Joseph Joachim. Dvořák visited Joachim in Berlin at the end of July 1879 and presumably discussed his new concerto; whatever the subject of their conversation, the concerto was eventually dedicated to Joachim.

This, however, was far from being the end of the story. Joachim recommended numerous revisions which Dvořák, an almost compulsive reviser of his own works, undertook meticulously. While it is not possible to assess the extent of these revisions since Dvořák destroyed the original material, it is clear from a letter that the changes were very far-reaching indeed, touching every aspect of the concerto's musical fabric and organisation. Even these alterations were not enough for Robert Keller, an adviser of Dvořák's publisher Simrock, who wanted the composer to write an ending for the first movement rather than letting it lead straight into the slow movement. For Dvořák, the time for accommodation was past, and he refused. Simrock accepted his judgement and in 1883, four years after its completion, the concerto was published. It is interesting to reflect that Joachim may have been in agreement with Keller since he never performed the work; the premiere was given in 1883 by Dvořák's friend the violinist František Ondříček.

Even by Dvořák's standards, the concerto is a richly lyrical work. The first movement begins boldly with a forceful unison statement from the orchestra answered with a bittersweet melody by the violin. Another exchange between solo and orchestra and a cadential flourish leads into the main part of the movement in which the violin is rarely silent. A miniature cadenza initiates an exquisitely crafted link into the slow movement whose rapt melodic lines are interrupted by a stormy minor-key central episode anticipating the slow movement of the Cello Concerto composed sixteen years later. The finale is close to the world of the *Slavonic Dances* written the year before; it opens with a main theme with the cross-rhythms of the Czech *furiant*. This ear-catching melody is frame for a number of memorable episodes, including a reflective D minor interlude, before the exhilarating end.

Jan Smaczny © BBC

Edward Elgar (1857–1934)

Elgar rose from humble beginnings (his father was a piano tuner and organist) to become Britain's leading composer: he was knighted in 1904, awarded the Order of Merit in 1911 and became Master of the King's Musick in 1924. Born in Worcester, he failed in his early attempt to establish himself in London, though his reputation grew steadily during the 1890s. The *Enigma Variations* of 1899 first brought him to national attention, followed closely by his darkly imaginative *Dream of Gerontius* (1900). He was over fifty when he produced his First Symphony, the first of his large-scale orchestral works, which was followed by the Violin Concerto, the Second Symphony and the Cello Concerto. After the death of his wife in 1920 he lost the will to compose, though in 1932 the BBC commissioned his Third Symphony. Elgar left 130 pages of sketches for the symphony at his death, which were elaborated by the British composer Anthony Payne. Fittingly, the completed work was finally premiered by the BBC Symphony Orchestra in 1998.

∾ Cello Concerto in E minor, Op. 85 (1919)

1 Adagio – Moderato
2 Lento – Allegro molto
3 Adagio
4 Allegro – Moderato – Allegro, ma non troppo

The Cello Concerto was the last important work that Elgar wrote. Its first performance, in October 1919, with the composer himself conducting, opened the first post-war season of the London Symphony Orchestra at the Queen's Hall. Most of the time available for rehearsal was taken by the other works in the programme, which were conducted by Albert Coates, and as a result the concerto suffered. Ernest Newman wrote in the *Observer*: 'The orchestra was often virtually inaudible, and when just audible was merely a muddle. No one seemed to have any idea of what it was the composer wanted.'

How the light tread of the music became a shamble can be imagined. Yet Newman himself did have an idea of what Elgar wanted: 'Some of the colour is meant to be no more than a vague wash against which the solo cello defines itself.' He went on to speak of 'that poignant simplicity that has come upon Elgar's music in the last couple of years', by which he was referring not to patriotic and topical pieces such as *The Spirit of England*, but to three chamber works – a string quartet, a violin sonata and a piano quintet – which had been given their first performances at the Wigmore Hall the previous May.

Yet the Cello Concerto also harked back to Elgar's last symphonic work, *Falstaff* (written in 1913), even though that was on a much more expansive scale. *Falstaff* contrasts bluff rhetoric and wistful reverie in a similar way, and the *Times* music critic H. C. Colles's perception in it of 'a mind that can think on a big scale, but loves to play with children far more' could apply equally to the concerto. Elgar's portrait of Falstaff was one of contradictions, but throughout, he wrote, 'runs the undercurrent of our failings and sorrows'. Falstaff was a man left behind by events, and by the end of the 1914–18 war Elgar felt the same had happened to him.

In *Falstaff* Elgar had perfected the manipulation of episodes, the ability to change the subject without losing sight of it, and in the Cello Concerto he applied that mastery to a four-movement symphonic plan and gave it a sense of fluidity and caprice.

In the concerto, the solo cellist doubles as narrator and protagonist, introducing and interrupting the course of events by way of linking them. His opening recitative is sketchily recalled at the end of the first movement, then cast aside as he scribbles ideas for the scherzo; after the first orchestral flourish of the finale he extends, in a sort of cadenza, a line connecting the shape of the original recitative to the finale's main subject.

The slow third movement, in its distant key of B flat major, remains apart, like a brief dream that reaches no conclusion. But Elgar does not leave it at that: towards the end of the finale the music broadens in a tide of lyrical passion which brings the Adagio back. It does not have the final say, for however strong the elegiac strain may be in the concerto, it is, in the classic sense of the word, a comedy.

© Adrian Jack

❧ Violin Concerto in B minor, Op. 61
(1907–10)

1 Allegro
2 Andante
3 Allegro molto

Elgar began his Violin Concerto in 1907 but then laid it aside until 1909. The triumphant first performance was given in the Queen's Hall, London, on 10 November 1910 by Fritz Kreisler, to whom the concerto is dedicated. Opposite the first page of the score Elgar wrote a quotation in Spanish: '*Aquí está encerrada el alma de . . . . .*' ('Herein is enshrined the soul of . . . . .'). Beyond saying that it was feminine, Elgar never revealed whose soul was concealed by those five dots. His own name has five letters; so had his wife's Christian name, Alice; so had the nickname 'Pippa' by which a close friend, Julia (also five letters) Worthington, was known to the Elgars. There is documentary evidence of the special connection between the concerto and Alice Stuart-Wortley, daughter of the painter Millais. 'Our own concerto', he called it in letters to her over the years; and he referred to some of its most tender themes as 'Windflower themes', 'Windflower' being his private name for Mrs Stuart-Wortley. Or do those dots hide Helen (five letters again) Weaver, to whom Elgar was briefly engaged in 1883 and who sailed out of his life to

New Zealand, leaving him heartbroken? We shall never know, and the matter would be of merely peripheral interest were it not that the music, for all its grand design and opulence, is of a peculiarly expressive intimacy which seems to betray a deep personal experience. There is no mistaking or ignoring the note of passionate regret for what might have been, or even what had been.

Elgar was himself a fine violinist and his concerto certainly enshrines the soul of the instrument itself. The soloist is called upon to be orator, singer, poet, conjurer and wizard, such is the expressive and technical range of the writing. The first movement begins with a long orchestral tutti in which several themes are heard. The first of these is a motto theme for the whole concerto and is stated at once by the full orchestra. It is this, transfigured to 'nobilmente', with which the soloist enters and proceeds to expand, decorate and ennoble all the themes so far heard. In particular the second subject, announced almost casually in the opening tutti, becomes a most tender and evocative melody, and is also strong enough to survive its later violent treatment from the orchestra in a development section that has something of a fantasia about it.

The slow movement, in the key of B flat, is in perfect contrast to the tempestuous first movement. The writing for the orchestral strings is of exquisite beauty and throws into even stronger relief the soloist's eloquent rhapsodising. From its opening peacefulness the movement passes through several impassioned climaxes and an episode in D flat to an even deeper tranquillity. Two points should be noted: that the soloist never plays the main theme in its original form, always a variant of it, and that at one point Elgar daringly scores for the violin and trombones, to memorable effect.

The long finale begins quietly with rapid and brilliant ascending passages for the soloist as an introduction to the quick and vivacious march-like main theme of the movement, announced by the orchestra and taken up forcefully by the soloist. The movement then becomes an elaborate vehicle for the soloist's virtuosity, with themes from the first and second movements recalled in altered form. Just as the music seems to be moving towards a conventional ending, it goes into the tonic minor, the scoring is thinned away to almost nothing except a muted horn, and the long accompanied cadenza begins. This is much more than a further opportunity for the soloist to show skill; it is an epitome of the whole concerto, reviewing the themes, musing on them, elaborating them, revealing their close relationship to each other. At first the accompaniment is merely a magical 'thrumming' by the strings – pizzicato tremolando – but other instruments join in as the cadenza progresses. It ends with the violin recalling the opening theme of the concerto and playing it slowly and expressively, but with a finality that buries the past. Without a pause the violin re-establishes the brisk tempo of the opening of the finale and the concerto ends brilliantly and expansively. Elgar's own reaction to the work was 'It's good! awfully emotional! too emotional, but I love it.' Perhaps, in spite of all he said, those five dots merely conceal the name Elgar.

© Michael Kennedy

Manuel de Falla (1876–1946)

With Albéniz and Granados, Falla cultivated the heritage of Spanish music to create a new nationalist idiom which produced, in his case, a small number of gem-like works of the highest quality and individuality. Falla was born in Cádiz and studied in Madrid with Felipe Pedrell from 1902. He composed a number of *zarzuelas* (traditional Spanish operettas) without great success, and left for Paris with the score of his opera *La vida breve* (A Brief Life). In Paris he met Dukas, Debussy, Ravel and Stravinsky, and *La vida breve* was staged at the Opéra-Comique. He returned to Madrid in 1914 completing his *Noches en los jardines de España* (Nights in the Gardens of Spain, 1914) and his two popular ballets: *El amor brujo* (Love, the Magician, 1914–15), and *El sombrero de tres picos* (The Three-Cornered Hat, 1916–19 for Diaghilev's Ballets Russes). In 1920 he settled in Granada, where he wrote his puppet opera *El retablo de maese Pedro* (Master Peter's Puppet Show, 1919–22) and Harpsichord Concerto for Wanda Landowska (1923–6). Falla spent his last years in Argentina, leaving his 'scenic cantata' *Atlántida* unfinished (it was later completed by a pupil and first staged in 1962).

∾ *Nights in the Gardens of Spain*: symphonic impressions for piano and orchestra (1911–15)

1 En el Generalife: Allegretto tranquillo e misterioso
2 Danza lejana: Allegretto giusto –
3 En los jardines de la Sierra de Córdoba: Vivo

By a strange paradox, that most typically Iberian evocation, Manuel de Falla's *Nights in the Gardens of Spain*, was conceived in Paris, by a composer who, though born in Andalusia, had never yet seen the gardens of Granada and

Córdoba that his music so graphically evokes. Originally it was intended for solo piano. The Catalan pianist Ricardo Viñes, another Parisian resident and a close friend of Debussy and Ravel as well as of Falla, persuaded the composer that the work would be better cast in orchestral form.

Despite the subtitle 'symphonic impressions', there is nothing particularly symphonic about the writing. Nor is this a concerto. Instead, it is one of the most overtly impressionistic, even extrovert, of Falla's scores. In later years, in such works as the Harpsichord Concerto or the unfinished 'scenic cantata' *Atlántida*, he was to delve deeper into the Spanish soul; here the shimmer of an Andalusian night is an almost tangible backdrop to each of the three movements.

The ghost of Debussy (especially the Debussy of *Ibéria*) is never far away, particularly in the gossamer scoring: the first movement, depicting the Generalife Gardens beside the Alhambra in Granada, frequently makes magical use of sul ponticello strings and distant horns.

The central 'Dance in the Distance' leads straight into the final movement, 'In the Gardens of the Sierra de Córdoba', in which vigorous sections suggestive of some gypsy fiesta alternate with a slow Andalusian tune played in high octaves, whose final appearance is over a static, thrumming accompaniment in the strings: the effect is timeless and remote, an echo of that *andalucismo universalizado* to which Falla always aspired.

© Piers Burton-Page

César Franck (1822–90)

Franck showed early signs of a promising pianistic career, studying at the conservatoire in his home town of Liège and undertaking a concert tour of Belgium at the age of twelve. In 1835 his family moved to Paris where Franck entered the Conservatoire. He wrote a number of piano pieces, including a concerto, and an oratorio, *Ruth*, was premiered in 1846. He married in 1848, and took a number of teaching and organist posts before becoming organist at Ste Clotilde in 1858. Here, according to his pupil d'Indy, he would 'stir up the fires of his genius in admirable improvisations'. Franck was appointed organ professor at the Paris Conservatoire in 1872, which finally brought him recognition after a series of disappointingly received works. Most of the works for which Franck is now remembered were composed after this appointment, and the majority of these – the *Prelude, Chorale and Fugue* for piano, the *Symphonic Variations* for piano and orchestra, the Violin Sonata and the Symphony in D minor – were written in his last six years.

∾ *Symphonic Variations*: for piano and orchestra (1885)

At the heart of Franck's late-life decade of creative fulfilment, which ran from the Piano Quintet of 1879 to the *Chorales* for organ in 1890, are three works involving piano whose modest lengths contain powerfully intense musical arguments. The *Prelude, Chorale and Fugue* and the *Prelude, Aria and Finale* are, or ought to be, high points of the nineteenth-century French solo repertoire. Only their reliance on a large hand-span, which for most pianists makes many passages awkward to play, has kept them from becoming as familiar as the sonatas of Chopin or Liszt. The *Symphonic Variations*, in contrast, have always been one of Franck's best-known achievements.

Yet they are about as unshowy as a solo-and-orchestra work can be. To be sure, they have their tricky moments too, but fewer of them, and the piano is not left out on its own at the times they occur. Rather, the exposed passages, and particularly the main themes, have a rich sonority and an expressive warmth that between them are as gratifying to the performer as to the listener.

As befits a spiritual descendant of Beethoven, Franck achieved a variation technique that goes much further than the simple theme-with-variations format. There is such an episode at the centre of this piece, in which the variations are few and straightforward. But the theme is itself made by a variation process, evolving out of the stark announcement for strings in octaves that opens the work. And another theme is up for variation too, the one with which the piano makes its first entry. This supplies the main business of the free-flowing introductory section, and it returns after the theme-with-variations episode to generate a mysterious, transitional-feeling slow interlude and eventually a boisterous finale. Sharp ears will notice that both themes emerge in new guises as this finale proceeds.

First performed in 1885, the work had an immediate influence on contemporary French music; the *Symphony on a French Mountain Song* by Vincent d'Indy, Franck's most faithful follower, appeared the next year with piano leading orchestra through an exhaustive exploitation of just one theme. But since then the *Symphonic Variations* have taken their place in a longer line, which not only begins with Beethoven and his ceaselessly varying late quartets and continues through the concertos of Schumann and Liszt with their ingenious transformations of themes, but echoes on as far as the concertante instruments of Messiaen's *Turangalîla Symphony* – not so far removed from the French symphonic tradition as it may at first sound.

© Robert Maycock

George Gershwin (1898–1937)

Having left school at fifteen to accompany a Tin Pan Alley song-plugger, Gershwin was set for a career in musicals; and his first Broadway show, *La La Lucille*, opened in 1919 when he was still aged twenty. The influence that the jazz idiom could have on the classical world became clear with the success of his *Rhapsody in Blue* in 1924, after which Gershwin turned more and more to so-called classical forms. His Piano Concerto in F followed a year later and in 1928 came his brilliantly colourful tone poem *An American in Paris*. Meanwhile he had struck up a partnership with his gifted lyricist brother Ira resulting in a sequence of songs and shows. Not wanting to stifle Gershwin's highly developed talents, both Ravel and Nadia Boulanger declined to give him lessons (Ravel famously commented that given the amount the young American was earning, it was he who should be giving the lessons). Musicals and songs for films continued to flow, but Gershwin's most ambitious and influential project was the 'folk opera' *Porgy and Bess* (1935). He died suddenly, before he was forty, of a brain tumour.

❧ Piano Concerto in F (1925)

1 Allegro
2 Adagio – Andante con moto
3 Allegro agitato

'Many persons thought the *Rhapsody in Blue* was only a happy accident,' Gershwin once said. 'Well, I went out, for one thing, to show them that there was plenty more where that had come from. I made up my mind to do a piece of absolute music.'

The impetus for his new work, which Gershwin started out by thinking of as a 'New York' concerto, had come from an unexpected source. Familiar with the *Rhapsody in Blue*, Walter

Damrosch, the conductor of the New York Symphony Society, boldly suggested the work to Gershwin, who was more than happy to accept the commission and to agree to appear as the soloist. A contract was signed in April 1925, with a performance date in view for December the same year – a schedule which by today's standards would be considered by no means comfortable.

Damrosch was sixty-four at the time of the commission, and a long-established figure on the New York musical scene. Via his German father, a violinist and conductor, he had received a thorough musical grounding, and his roots were firmly in the great European tradition of the nineteenth century. But if his request to Gershwin at first sight looked unexpected, then Damrosch was also, as a conductor, interested in new musical developments, and in a fortunate position to further the tastes of his regular audience.

Gershwin was due to visit London in the spring of 1925, and was not able to start work until his return. But it seems that once he settled to it, inspiration flowed freely. We even know the precise dates between which Gershwin composed the concerto: 22 July and 10 November 1925. He seems to have kept composition and orchestration in separate compartments, a division of labour which has sometimes loaned fuel to his critics. The last month of work was devoted solely to orchestrating his draft score.

He had, by this stage in his career, plenty of people around him who were only too willing to help and advise – and in some cases to claim the credit. His friend William Daly, who regularly conducted Gershwin shows from the pit, played the embryonic accompaniment on a second piano. Oscar Levant, who was later to make a celebrated recording of the concerto, was already by 1925 becoming a noted Gershwin disciple. A third close friend of this period was the composer and pianist Kay Swift. All three probably offered their reactions.

Not surprisingly, then, argument has sometimes raged about the full extent of Gershwin's originality, here and elsewhere. In his other world of musical comedy, paying arrangers to orchestrate a piano score was the norm; in the classical world, even Gershwin's admirers became defensive about their hero's known technical inexperience in matters of form and instrumentation. Matters were not helped, either, by a probably ironic statement on the part of the composer himself, a week before the premiere, that when starting work on the concerto he had gone out and bought 'four or five small books on musical structure to find out what concerto form actually was'!

Nor was Gershwin's mind, throughout the long summer, concentrated exclusively on the concerto. He was also at work on a new Broadway piece, *Tip-Toes*, with his brother Ira, and writing songs for Hammerstein's *Songs of the Flame*. Even so, Gershwin was not one to miss an important deadline; and he didn't. Indeed, whether out of eagerness or insecurity, Gershwin decided that he did not want to wait until the first rehearsal before hearing the results of his summer's work. At his own expense, he hired the Globe Theater in New York for an afternoon, as well as an orchestra of about fifty musicians, and the concerto was tried out for the first time before a small audience of friends and admirers. The run-through was conducted by Daly, who suggested cuts, not all of which Gershwin was prepared to accept. And Gershwin himself apparently was still inserting or trying out revisions of his own.

The existence of a full score in Gershwin's hand is not conclusive proof of anything other than that Gershwin himself found the writing of a fair copy the proper end of the compositional process. His habit of trying out work in progress semi-publicly – in the concerto's case also among the students attending his friend Ernest Hutcheson's summer piano masterclasses in upstate New York – meant that many and various voices had all had their say long before the first performance. It hardly matters. What is clear is that Gershwin took final responsibility, and is entitled to the full and final credit for a work of bold and blazing individuality.

The concerto's premiere took place on the afternoon of 3 December 1925, when it was preceded by Glazunov's Fifth

Symphony and Henri Rabaud's *Suite anglaise* – and by a thunderstorm. Gershwin himself supplied a brief commentary, which is by far the best summary of its shape and sound and provides all that is necessary by way of a listening guide:

> The first movement employs the Charleston rhythm. It is quick and pulsating, representing the young enthusiastic spirit of American life. It begins with a rhythmic motif given out by the kettle drums, supported by other percussion instruments, and with a Charleston motif introduced by bassoon, horns, clarinet and violas. The principal theme is announced by the bassoon. Later, a second theme is introduced by the piano.
>
> The second movement has a poetic nocturnal atmosphere which has come to be referred to as the American blues, but in a purer form than that in which they are usually treated.
>
> The final movement reverts to the style of the first. It is an orgy of rhythms, starting violently and keeping to the same pace throughout.

Much of the reaction to Gershwin's concerto, not surprisingly, continued to concentrate on the questions that had often preoccupied American commentators earlier. Was a synthesis between jazz and the concert hall possible? And which way had Gershwin turned? Where should he go now?

The neatest summary, perhaps, came when a columnist in the *World* reported in mock-Pepys fashion on going to a party: 'Then G. Gershwin the composer came in, and we did talk about musique and about going ahead regardless of advice, this one saying Do not study and that one saying, Study; and another saying, Write only jazz melodies, and another saying, Write only symphonies and concertos.'

Gershwin himself, fortunately, remained untroubled by such demonstrations of intellectual confusion. Maybe the concerto does show the occasional flaw – moments when the music momentarily loses its way before reviving with a new theme, or moments when a particular section is stretched out beyond its natural length. But even Homer nodded; and Gershwin's concerto is also stunningly rich in melody and harmony, rhythm and texture. This is, somehow, music of both passion and melancholy which transcends the idiom of its own era, even while carrying generous echoes of its time and place.

For if Gershwin himself deleted the title reference to New York at a fairly early stage, it is hard to resist the images that the work itself sets up. We have the analogy with Gershwin's own later *American in Paris* to act as a precedent for hearing, in the upward sweep of the piano's phrases, or the brassy orchestration, a cityscape that is very obviously Manhattan: not just skyscrapers and traffic, but the chatter of Broadway and even, in the slow movement, a vision of the city in the quieter hours of the night. The poetic raptures of this fine movement in turn dissolve into the brassier, breezier rhythms of the finale, where the stridency and rush of New York in full flood reassert themselves in vibrant, extrovert fashion.

© Piers Burton-Page

∽ *Rhapsody in Blue* (1924)

By 1924, the American band leader Paul Whiteman had achieved fame as 'The King of Jazz' and felt it was time the US public was taught to take jazz more seriously. Though he himself specialised in slickly rehearsed big-band arrangements that held enormous appeal for dance-hall crowds but were frowned upon by dedicated jazz connoisseurs for their lack of any real openings for improvised spontaneity, Whiteman nevertheless craved recognition for jazz as 'a new movement in the world's art of music'. So he organised a matinée concert at New York's Aeolian Hall, that sanctum of serious classical music, and gave Gershwin – already famous as the composer of Al Jolson's hit-song 'Swanee', and well established on Broadway – just a month to come up with a new 'jazz concerto' to headline the event. Boldly billed as 'An Experiment in Modern Music', the concert was scheduled significantly for

12 February – Abraham Lincoln's birthday – an ideal date for the publicity-conscious Whiteman to proclaim the emancipation of jazz.

On the day, an increasingly sceptical audience sat through twenty-four separate movements before solo clarinettist Ross Gorman sounded the rising glissando that launches the *Rhapsody*. Gorman had sprung this effect on Gershwin to enliven rehearsals; in the manuscript it had been written out as a seventeen-note scale. With its following chuckling phrase, it would become the most famous opening bar in American music. Gershwin's own pianism bedazzled an audience dotted with such musical celebrities as Rakhmaninov, Kreisler and Stravinsky. Despite its technical shortcomings, the verve and originality of the piece saved the day. An elated Whiteman signed off with (of all things) Elgar's *Pomp and Circumstance* March No. 1.

Neither Gershwin nor Whiteman were close to the folk roots of jazz. They were operating within the terms of white, commercialised big-band jazz. Nonetheless, the Aeolian Hall concert was a genuine attempt to explore the potential of 'symphonic jazz'. Gershwin explained:

> Jazz I regard as an American folk music. I believe it can be made the basis of serious symphonic works of lasting value. There had been so much chatter about the limitations of jazz. Jazz, they said, had to be in strict time. It had to cling to dance rhythms. I resolved, if possible, to kill that misconception with one sturdy blow. I wanted to show that jazz is an idiom not to be limited to a mere song and chorus that consumed three minutes in presentation.

The nearest classical models are the flamboyant concertos of Liszt, with their similar looseness of form and continuous transformation of tiny motifs. Gershwin's virtuosic solo part revels in syncopated ragtime rhythms, Rakhmaninov-style chordal melody over sonorous left-hand arpeggios, Lisztian fireworks, bullet-like repeated notes with crossed hands, saloon-bar broodings in the left hand, and oriental motifs evoking New York's Chinatown. That we can today enjoy the heart-tugging, central slow theme is thanks entirely to Whiteman's expert arranger, Ferde Grofé, who had speedily orchestrated the young composer's original two-piano sketch, and persuaded him to keep the theme in when Gershwin himself wanted to reject it as being 'tripe, sentimental . . . just too cheap'.

Gershwin said of the *Rhapsody*: 'If I had taken the same themes and put them into songs they would have been gone years ago.' For him, concert music had a future, compared with the fragility of Broadway. For us, this quintessential picture of metropolitan America in the Jazz Age remains as fresh as when, on that February afternoon in 1924, Whiteman – poised to bring in the band at the end of Gershwin's partially improvised cadenza – followed the advice Grofé had scrawled in the score: 'Wait for nod.'

© Rodney Greenberg

Edvard Grieg (1843–1907)

Of Scottish descent on his father's side, Grieg was born in Bergen and studied for four years at the Leipzig Conservatory, where he was influenced by German Romanticism. But it was during later studies in Copenhagen that the importance of Norwegian folk music became apparent to him, and this realisation found early expression during the 1860s in the *Humoresques* and the first book of *Lyric Pieces* for piano. Grieg settled in Oslo in 1866 and after his Piano Concerto (1868) returned less frequently to the larger Germanic forms, although his output includes a sonata for piano, three for violin and one for cello, as well as a string quartet which Debussy admired. His marriage in 1867 to his cousin Nina Hagerup inspired many of his 180 or so songs; he continued his series of *Lyric Pieces* (numbering around sixty) and he wrote incidental music for theatre (for Ibsen's *Peer Gynt* and Bjørnson's *Sigurd Jorsalfar*). His most characterised music matches the idiom of Norwegian folk music with an almost impressionistic gift for sound-painting.

✤ Piano Concerto in A minor, Op. 16
(1868; rev. 1907)

1 Allegro molto moderato
2 Adagio –
3 Allegro moderato molto e marcato

The popularity of Grieg's Piano Concerto has led to some distorted judgements over the years, but there is no questioning the impact of the work on the life of its composer. Grieg wrote it in the summer of 1868, when he was staying with his wife and baby daughter in the Danish town of Søllerød – a happy time for him which resulted in a rare burst of creative activity. Enormous success has attended the Concerto ever since Grieg himself gave its first performance in Copenhagen in April 1869: Liszt praised it when the composer visited him in Rome later that year, and for the rest of his life Grieg was in great demand throughout Europe as soloist or conductor in performances of it.

In fact, he was never really able to escape from the shadow of the piece that first made his name, and there were times when he even felt that constant involvement in performances of it was obstructing his maturer creativity. Nor was he ever truly satisfied with the details of its orchestration, which he continued to tinker with for years. The most startling example of his lack of confidence in his own initial inspiration was the reassignment – at Liszt's suggestion – of the first movement's tender second theme to a solo trumpet; although Grieg later thought better of this bizarre piece of scoring and returned the theme to the cellos, it was incorporated, along with various other Liszt suggestions, into the first published score, issued in Leipzig in 1872. The version we know today actually dates from as late as 1907, when Grieg and Percy Grainger together produced a new, revised edition.

If the Piano Concerto was Grieg's first notable success, however, it also marked the end of a chapter in his creative development. Hitherto he had still followed the central European tradition of large-scale sonata-form composition (having produced in the previous eight years a piano sonata, two violin sonatas and a symphony), but his success with these forms had been limited, and it seems that it was at the time of the Piano Concerto that he decided that such music was not for him; thereafter he favoured more intimate forms, and completed only three more sonata-type works. This is ironic, because the Piano Concerto is arguably his most satisfying attempt at large-scale composition, combining a sound, no-nonsense approach to the formal problems of the Romantic concerto with keen melodic invention and a fitting sense of the heroic. His own attractive musical personality is also well in evidence, and the folk elements which were later to become such an important part of his style are unmistakable.

It has often been observed that the work owes much in formal outline to Schumann's concerto in the same key, written during the 1840s. This is particularly clear when the two opening movements are compared: both start with a dramatic descent from the top register of the piano to the middle; both present their first theme in the woodwind, to be copied by the soloist; both have central development sections with a similar outline (wind interplay accompanied by arpeggios from the piano, which then emerges to hold centre stage); and both movements end with a passage in a faster tempo. But to say that Grieg consciously modelled his concerto on Schumann's seems fanciful, however inexperienced he might have been in writing music of this kind: nobody has suggested that he needed a model for his symphony or three early sonatas, and it seems more likely that Grieg, who had come to admire Schumann's work during his student days in Leipzig, absorbed the older composer's example as an unwitting consequence of close familiarity.

If the first movement owes an unconscious debt to Schumann, the other two are more clearly products of Grieg's own invention. The second is a haunting Adagio in D flat major whose song-like opening theme is at first stubbornly ignored by the piano, which prefers to follow its own dreamy course. The orchestra continues to nudge it gently in the direction of the first theme, however, until in the end the piano relents and takes it up in a sonorous and assertive restatement. The mood subsides as the movement draws to its close, but a brief woodwind fanfare and a flourish from the piano plunge us straight into the finale.

This opens with a perky theme based on the characteristic dance-rhythm of the Norwegian *halling*, but after a brief, chordal second theme has come and gone the mood changes dramatically for an extended interlude featuring a wistful new theme. This is then lovingly developed by the soloist, and although the return of the opening material eventually sweeps it aside, it is this theme that has the last word as it triumphantly brings the movement – and Grieg's large-scale orchestral ambitions – to an end.

© Lindsay Kemp

Sofia Gubaidulina (b. 1931)

In the years since the death of Shostakovich, one of the leading voices of the Russian avant-garde, along with Alfred Schnittke, has been Sofia Gubaidulina. She has drawn inspiration from a variety of religious and philosophical principles, linguistic theory and mathematical series. Born in Christopol in the Tartar Republic, she studied at the Kazan Conservatory then at the Moscow Conservatory, and founded the improvisation group Astreia, which actively worked with non-Western and folk instruments – a number of which, such as the *bayan*, *koto* and *dombra*, appear in her work. She first came to international attention in the 1980s when Gidon Kremer toured with her *Offertorium* for violin and orchestra. The concepts of opposition and religious symbolism feature in her titles, though she speaks of the importance of intuition in composing and believes strongly in the mystical qualities of music, partly apparent in her careful placement of silence as well as sound. In addition to Kremer, her champions include the viola player Yuri Bashmet, the cellist Mstislav Rostropovich and the conductor Valery Gergiev, who conducted the first performances of her *St John Passion and Resurrection*.

❧ Viola Concerto (1996)

As far back as she can remember, Gubaidulina has been fascinated by the quality of sounds. Her ear has always been as interested in colour, texture and timbre, as in pitch and rhythm. As a small child in Kazan in the years before the Second World War, she amused herself by coaxing unusual noises out of the grand piano, because, she says, she was bored by the beginners' piano pieces she was supposed to be playing. Later, as a student in Moscow in the early 1960s, she made friends with the young percussionist Mark Pekarsky and was impressed by his maverick approach to instruments. She particularly noticed his almost ritualistic reverence for the most perfunctory of everyday noises, the intensity of his concentration on the very moment a human hand or beater touches the surface of a drum or gong.

In the mid–1970s she formed an improvisation group, Astreia, with two friends, Viktor Suslin and Vyacheslav Artyomov. All three composers had become frustrated with the more usual, formal and academic ways of making music in the old Soviet capital. The idea of Astreia was to play and invent unexpected musical ideas in an atmosphere of almost childish fantasy and freedom. There were experiments with different instruments, exotic folk instruments and children's toys, and later more conventional instruments played in unconventional ways.

So it's hardly surprising that in her composed music, especially from the 1970s onwards, Gubaidulina took the greatest care with the smallest details of tiny sounds. She especially loved to draw our attention to the sounds behind the sounds, to the sometimes barely audible noises that inevitably go along with the production of simple 'musical' notes that are all we are usually supposed to be listening to. Often in her music of that period we find ourselves intensely aware of the thud of a hammer hitting a piano string . . . or the sandpapery rustle (present at the same time as the musical note) of a rosined bow drawn across a violin string . . . or the whisper of human breath just before the emergence of a note on a wind instrument. Especially memorable are the delicate breathing sounds from cello and free-bass accordion in the chamber concerto *Seven Words* (1982).

But there is another side to this composer's character. However interested in detail she is, she is just as much concerned with form. Without form, detail, for Gubaidulina, cannot mean anything. No matter how pretty or alluring or sinister a sound might be, it only makes sense when heard against the background of a clear, large-scale, architectural and dramatic design.

Form, for Gubaidulina, is a matter of proportion. But there are different kinds of proportion and different ways in which it can be used. Sometimes, as in the chamber cantata *Perception* (1983) and the symphony '*Stimmen . . . verstummen . . .*' (1986), Gubaidulina exploits the famous and ancient Fibonacci number series (1, 2, 3, 5, 8, 13, etc.), so widely observed in painting, architecture, nature and even in the music of many other composers. Once, in her homage to J. S. Bach, *Meditation* (1993), she took the elaborate proportional structure of Bach's last chorale, 'Vor deinen Thron tret' ich hiermit', and made that her supporting structure. In her choral and orchestral *Alleluia* (1990) she played with numerical proportions derived from the different wavebands of the colour spectrum.

Over the last two decades three large-scale concertos for stringed instruments stand out in Gubaidulina's list of works. And in these the subtle balance between her concern for detail and her concern for form is particularly well observed. The first was *Offertorium*, a violin concerto for Gidon Kremer, which she worked on between 1980 and 1986. This was the piece that first brought Gubaidulina's name to most Western listeners. It was followed in 1993 by a cello concerto for David Geringas, with a title taken from a poem by the Chuvash writer Gennadi Aigi, *And: the festivity at its height . . .*

The Viola Concerto is the third of this cycle, written in 1996 for Yuri Bashmet, and first played by him with the Chicago Symphony Orchestra conducted by Kent Nagano in 1997. Like the earlier two concertos, this is in a single movement in several sections. Unlike the previous two, however, there is no special poetic or religious title. This apparently trivial fact reflects the greater asceticism and understatedness of Gubaidulina's recent manner. This concerto is one of the barest and most laconic scores she has written.

In a note the composer comments that the Viola Concerto is 'dedicated to the great violist of our times, Yuri Bashmet . . . to a performer who possesses astonishing opulence of colours and an enormous range of emotional states, from extreme expression to the most profound mysticism of sound'. She adds that the piece is also dedicated 'not only to the performer, but to his instrument. The peculiar mysteriousness and veiled quality of the viola's timbre has always been something of an acoustic enigma to me, and an object of rapture.'

Two features of the orchestration deserve special mention. One is the quiet but dramatic appearance at two points in the score of the honeyed sound of three Wagner tubas (played by the horn players). The other is the continuous presence of a concertante group of four solo strings (violin, viola, cello and double bass). Eerily tuned a quarter-tone lower than everyone else, these four make a kind of semi-chorus, mediating between the soloist and the rest of the orchestra.

There are seven sections. The first three form an introduction and double exposition. After the very opening, where the soloist gropes his way up and down the whole range of his instrument on the octaves of the single note D, the strings enter with what Gubaidulina calls 'a specific rhythmic figure' (one might also call it a melody), which 'emerges . . . repeats itself several times and delineates . . . the form'. The development, like the exposition, falls into three parts. First comes a long unfolding cantilena for the soloist, accompanied to start with only by a few low instruments – including, for the first time, the Wagner tubas – but bit by bit drawing in the rest of the orchestra. After a shimmering eruption into the highest register, a mysterious, dream-like passage recalls fragments of the work's opening. The development ends with an extended paragraph of fast music, a *perpetuum mobile* leading to a sonorous peroration. The Wagner tubas make their second and last appearance in the concerto's coda, at once a recollection of the opening and a suggestion of the beginning of something new.

© Gerard McBurney

Joseph Haydn (1732–1809)

Haydn trained in the choir of St Stephen's Cathedral in Vienna, and in 1757 became Kapellmeister to the Morzin family. In 1761 he landed a position at the court of the wealthy Esterházy family. During his many years in the family's employment, Haydn claimed he was exposed to little external musical influence, but the position allowed him scope to write anything from dances to full-scale operas, and 'forced me to become original'. One of the first composers to develop the string quartet (of which he produced sixty-eight), he also extended the form and expressive range of the symphony – writing no fewer than 106. He composed a number of dramatic works and was released from the Esterházy court – in 1790, in his late fifties – in order to visit London. He enjoyed two highly successful visits, composing his twelve 'London' symphonies, and produced two great oratorios – *The Creation* (1798) and *The Seasons* (1801) – as well as his six late masses for the Esterházy family.

∿ Cello Concerto No. 1 in C major
(*c.* 1765)

1   Moderato
2   Adagio
3   Allegro molto

Haydn entered the service of the Esterházy family in 1761 at the age of twenty-nine. His appointment was as Vice-Kapellmeister to the ageing Gregor Werner, with the promise that he would succeed to the full position. Musical duties at the court were divided into two: Werner was entrusted with running the church music, Haydn with the instrumental music. In the months following Haydn's appointment a virtually new orchestra was established at the court, consisting of players of Haydn's age, many of whom he had known from his days as a freelance composer in Vienna. The new Vice-Kapellmeister had, therefore, enviable working conditions: a rich and supportive patron, and players who were eager and capable.

Clause 5 of Haydn's contract required him to 'appear daily (whether here in Vienna or on the estates) in the antechamber before and after midday, and enquire whether a high princely order for a musical performance has been given'. These 'musical performances', in front of a small, select audience of the Prince and his guests, included vocal music (arias from contemporary operas) as well as instrumental music. Over the years Haydn's main contribution to these concerts was to be over fifty symphonies, but in the early 1760s he also composed several concertos for members of the orchestra, which no doubt gratified the players as much as they pleased the Prince. There were concertos for the violin, cello, double bass, flute and horn. In around 1765 Haydn began entering his compositions in a draft catalogue and all these works were duly noted. Some of the works themselves have, however, disappeared; the double bass concerto is still missing, as is the flute concerto. It is possible that they still survive in some uncatalogued archive in Europe. Certainly, scholars and players can take heart from the fact that one of the violin concertos was rediscovered only in 1950, and the C major Cello Concerto eleven years later, in 1961, when a set of contemporary parts, formerly from Radenín Castle in Bohemia, turned up in the National Library in Prague. Since that time the concerto has established itself as a regular part of the cello repertoire.

Haydn's cellist was Joseph Weigl, who stayed for eight years at the Esterházy court before returning to work in Vienna. Haydn was godfather to his son, also called Joseph, who later became a popular composer of German opera. As well as being a skilful player, Weigl must have been a sympathetic musician, for this concerto is undoubtedly the finest of the Esterházy concertos from the 1760s, and in Haydn's entire output of concertos it is surpassed only by the Trumpet Concerto, composed much later, in 1796.

Unlike Haydn's contemporary symphonies, which usually open with a brisk Allegro, the first movements of many of his Esterházy concertos are moderately paced. In the Cello Concerto the tempo encourages a sturdy poise, complemented by the dotted figuration of the opening theme and the occasional multiple stopping. Throughout the movement virtuosity is skilfully woven into the fabric of the music.

The traditional stylistic source for slow movements in eighteenth-century concertos was the operatic aria. Haydn had first learnt the contemporary Italian style from the celebrated composer and teacher Porpora in the mid-1750s, and in the early years at the Esterházy court he had his first opportunity to compose Italian vocal music on a regular basis. Slow movements in his instrumental music, too, soon reveal this influence and, like this Adagio, they are virtually arias without words; the cellist (or should we say the tenor?) even enters with a traditional *messa di voce* – that is, a long held note designed to show off a singer's breath control. Like the first movement, the Adagio culminates in a cadenza.

The concluding movement is an energetic Allegro molto with a great deal of nervous tension, produced by the repeated notes of the accompaniment, the bold contrast between forte and piano and the wide compass of the melodic material (particularly that of the soloist). The occasional deflection into the minor key adds momentary passion to the good humour.

© David Wyn Jones

Paul Hindemith (1895–1963)

A gifted violinist from an early age, Hindemith studied violin and composition at Frankfurt's Hoch Conservatory. After serving in the German army and while leader of the Frankfurt Opera Orchestra (1915–23) he produced three controversial one-act operas. Throughout the 1920s he was a prominent member of Europe's modern-music scene, playing viola in the Amar Quartet, which he founded in 1921 to promote new music. Alongside his often expressionistic, parodying scores of the 1920s he wrote much instrumental music for amateurs and children (*Gebrauchsmusik*), believing in the importance of music's role in everyday life. His opera *Mathis der Maler* (1934–5), based on the life of the painter Matthias Grünewald, was banned by the Nazi regime, and in 1935 Hindemith left Germany. He counselled on Turkey's music education programme and in 1940 he moved to the USA, becoming professor at Yale where he taught and founded the Yale Collegium Musicum as a workshop for the revival of early music. Though he took US citizenship in 1946 he returned to Europe in 1953 to a post at Zurich University. Despite his early experimentalism, Hindemith's polyphonic skill represented a distinctly German trait that could be traced back to Bach.

∾ *Trauermusik* (1936)

> Langsam – Ruhig bewegt – Lebhaft – Chorale: 'Vor deinen Thron tret' ich hiermit'

In January 1936 Hindemith was in London, where he was scheduled to play the solo part in the British premiere of his new viola concerto, *Der Schwanendreher*, which he had first performed in November in Amsterdam. His new compositions were already banned in Nazi Germany, and his peripatetic life as a composer–performer was now, of necessity, largely carried on abroad. But on 21 January – the day before the scheduled concert – King George V died. BBC protocol ruled that, at this time of national mourning, the scheduled Queen's Hall concert should be replaced by a studio concert; and that instead of Hindemith's concerto some appropriate funeral music should be played.

However, Sir Adrian Boult and Edward Clark, the Schoenberg pupil who was head of the BBC Music Department, were avid that Hindemith should – 'at all costs', as he later wrote to his publishers – still take part. It was decided that the funeral music should be specially written by Hindemith himself. So from 11 a.m. to 5 p.m. that day he engaged in what he described as 'some fairly hefty mourning', with a team of copyists engaged to transcribe the results. The end product was *Trauermusik* ('Music of Mourning') for viola and string orchestra (or piano), which Hindemith premiered in the national broadcast with the BBC Symphony Orchestra under Boult the very next day. 'How doleful we all were,' the composer later recalled, 'many of the musicians weeping.'

This would be remarkable enough as a story of Hindemith's fabled professionalism and versatility; but the work he produced in those six hours has far outlived the occasion for which it was written. Indeed it remains a shining example of an 'occasional' composition which is a distinct contribution to the general repertoire, and is one of Hindemith's most justly celebrated pieces. The 'fairly hefty mourning' to which he ironically referred must have been fuelled, not so much by the death of the King, as by a strong vein of personal sorrow, no doubt occasioned by his current uncertain position as a German artist, and his growing fears for the direction in which his country was being taken by its new Nazi masters. For the *Trauermusik* is a grave, shapely, and unexpectedly eloquent lament. The music, in Hindemith's most exalted vein but with a quality of intimacy that comes out most clearly in the version with piano, is closely allied to the reflective portions of the Grünewald-inspired opera *Mathis der Maler*, which he had completed the year before, and also points forward to the ballet *Nobilissima visione*, inspired by the life of St Francis of Assisi, which would occupy him in 1937.

The single movement is divided into four sections. The rhythm and melodic contours of the first are closely modelled (though without quotation) on the opening of the slow movement, 'Grablegung' (Entombment), of the symphony Hindemith had extracted from his as-yet-unperformed *Mathis* opera. The second section, in a serene 12/8 pulse, is more songful – even, one may fancy, with a flavour of English folk song, though it is more likely the idiom of the *Schwanendreher* concerto, based upon medieval German folk songs, that is recalled here. A livelier, more determined section follows, but the energy quickly dissipates into renewed expressions of lamentation on the viola. The concluding part of the work is a free elegiac invention on Bach's chorale 'Vor deinen Thron tret' ich hiermit' (Before thy throne, O God, I stand): 'very suitable for kings,' commented Hindemith, who went on to observe that the melody is well known in England as the psalm tune 'The Old Hundredth'. In these final bars, among the most moving he ever wrote, personal expression and the requirements of time and place become a seamless garment.

© Malcolm MacDonald

John Ireland (1879–1962)

Ireland was born in Cheshire to literary parents who both died during the boy's early teens. At fourteen he entered the Royal College of Music, studying piano and theory before learning composition with Stanford as a contemporary of Vaughan Williams, Holst and Frank Bridge. He earned a living as organist at St Luke's, Chelsea, from 1904 to 1926, and from 1923 to 1939 he taught at the College, where his students included E. J. Moeran and Britten. Inspired by the writing of Arthur Machen, he wrote a number of works associated with ancient British rituals and mysteries, beginning with *The Forgotten Rite* (1913) and including *Mai-Dun* (1921), inspired by a prehistoric fortification in Dorset. His Piano Concerto (1930) remains his most popular large-scale work, though he produced many piano pieces, chamber music and an important contribution to the English song repertoire.

❧ Piano Concerto in E flat major (1930)

1 Moderato
2 Lento espressivo –
3 Allegro – Allegretto giocoso

John Ireland's Piano Concerto – one of his finest and most representative works – enjoyed considerable popularity at the Proms for nearly thirty years. Between 1930 and 1958 it was included in twenty out of the twenty-nine seasons, often on the Last Night. Then it was dropped, together with a good many other regularly appearing works, in order to make way for new kinds of musical experiences at these concerts. In the 1979 season, however, it was included again, to mark the centenary of Ireland's birth on 13 August; it was received with enthusiasm by the Prom audience, for many of whom it would have been a new work.

The circumstances in which the concerto came to be written are set out in John Longmire's book, *John Ireland: Portrait of a Friend*. When Ireland was in his middle forties, his brief and unfortunate marriage was annulled, leaving him bitter, detached, often lonely. At the Royal College of Music, where Ireland was a professor, a girl of eighteen, Helen Perkin, was sent to him as a composition pupil. She was a gifted pianist, and already knew and admired some of Ireland's piano music. In brief, a close friendship quickly developed between them. In John Longmire's words, 'She was his muse, his inspiration, and his constant companion; spring and summer met in an ideal friendship, and teacher and pupil were inseparable.' Together they explored all that meant most to Ireland, including his favourite authors (George Moore, Hardy, Aldous Huxley, D. H. Lawrence), various art galleries, and the English countryside, the spirit of which was so often beautifully conveyed in his compositions – sometimes, like Sibelius, extending to legendary aspects.

Ireland stated that the idea of composing the Piano Concerto first occurred to him when he heard Helen Perkin playing Prokofiev's Third Concerto; and the influence of some of Prokofiev's bravura writing can be detected in the first and third movements of Ireland's work. There is a personal touch: the solo violin passage at the end of the slow movement is a quotation from a string quartet by Helen Perkin (with which she won a Cobbett Prize). Throughout the spring and summer of 1930, in fact, Ireland was writing this concerto with Helen Perkin very much in mind. Because of the smallness of her hands, there are no wide stretches, no massive chords such as we normally find in Ireland's piano writing. The slow movement is full of a deeply felt nostalgia, a suggestion of the fleeting, insubstantial nature of present happiness.

The theme announced by the strings at the very beginning is a kind of motto for the whole work, reappearing in various guises. Other themes overlap from movement to movement, giving further unity to an overall structure which is basically traditional, but moulded by the composer in a highly personal manner. Never is there display for its own sake; neither is there undue reticence. The pianist has technical problems to solve, and often virtuosity is required – but everything is musically valid, and a wide range of feeling is explored.

As was natural, the work was dedicated to Helen Perkin, who gave the premiere at the Proms in 1930 with Henry Wood conducting the BBC Symphony Orchestra.

© David Cox

Oliver Knussen (b. 1952)

Knussen's father was principal double bass of the London Symphony Orchestra, and his early exposure to music led to the premiere of his First Symphony with the LSO when he was only fifteen. In 1970 Knussen made the first of many visits to the Tanglewood Summer School, studying with Gunther Schuller. He honed his technique during the 1970s in works such as *Trumpets* for soprano and three clarinets (1975), *Ophelia Dances* (1975) and the chamber orchestra piece *Coursing* (1979), often using serial principles. Following the premiere of his successful Third Symphony (1973–9) at the BBC Proms in 1979, much of the 1980s was spent on his fantasy-opera double bill on children's stories by Maurice Sendak, *Where the Wild Things Are* (1979–83) and *Higglety Pigglety Pop!* (1984–5; rev. 1999). He developed an international conducting career, championing the works of many living composers, and also promoted their work at the Aldeburgh Festival and Tanglewood Music Center. He was principal guest conductor of the Residentie Orchestra, The Hague (1992–8), and for four years from 1998 was Music Director of the London Sinfonietta. He writes slowly and meticulously; in 2002 he completed a Violin Concerto for Pinchas Zukerman, co-commissioned by the Pittsburgh and Philadelphia orchestras.

∾ Horn Concerto (1994; rev. 1995)

Intrada – Fantastico – Cadenza – Envoi

Oliver Knussen has described the horn as 'perhaps my favourite instrument of all'. His love for it goes back to early memories of hearing Barry Tuckwell as principal horn in the London Symphony Orchestra throughout the 1960s. 'The wish to compose something for Barry Tuckwell had been somewhere in the back of my mind for almost as long as I can remember,' he explains, but it was not until the composer's early forties that this concerto was conceived and completed (in just two months) for performance in Suntory Hall, Tokyo, on 7 October 1994, with Tuckwell himself as soloist under Knussen's direction.

The concerto is in a single continuous movement divided into four parts and lasts about thirteen minutes. The opening 'Intrada' immediately establishes D minor as the home key, although this is a highly personal interpretation of that key, with much emphasis upon keys a semitone above or below (E flat and C sharp). The horn enters shortly after the opening and introduces the work's main thematic idea, gently oscillating around the pitches A and D.

In the main part, headed 'Fantastico', the music takes on a progressively darker, more nocturnal hue (at one point Knussen had considered calling the piece *Night Air*). This turbulent central section includes numerous fleeting allusions to several loosely nocturnal works from earlier this century by a variety of composers including Mahler, Shostakovich and Britten. These are punctuated by increasingly violent chords from the whole orchestra, leading to a climax, at which point the horn has an extended and dramatic cadenza. This leads directly into the concluding 'Envoi', in which distant fanfares pass between the horn and the orchestra. The horn concludes the work with a brief reminiscence of the main theme.

© Julian Anderson

György Ligeti (b. 1923)

A Jew born in Transylvania, Ligeti's studies at the Budapest Academy were interrupted by the war. His father and brother were killed at Auschwitz; Ligeti survived and began teaching at the Academy from 1950. His dissonant, chromatic style was banned under the Communist regime and in 1956, following the failed uprising in Budapest, Ligeti illegally crossed into Austria. Now able to explore Europe's musical experimentalism, he worked at West German Radio's electronic music studio in Cologne (1957–8). The shifting sound clusters of his orchestral work *Atmosphères* aroused attention in 1961, and seven years later Stanley Kubrick featured his *Atmosphères*, *Aventures*, *Requiem* and *Lux aeterna* in the film *2001: A Space Odyssey*. After the seminal, concise Chamber Concerto (1969–70) and the anarchic opera *Le grand macabre* (1974–7), he developed an intricate polyrhythmic style as heard in the Piano Concerto (1985–8). A heart condition slowed down his output from 1979, by which time he had held teaching posts in Stockholm, Stanford and Hamburg. In 1985 he began his still-ongoing series of Études for piano; these wonderfully innovative pieces are establishing themselves as modern classics of the genre.

∾ Piano Concerto (1985–8)

1 Vivace molto ritmico e preciso –
2 Lento e deserto
3 Vivace cantabile
4 Allegro risoluto, molto ritmico –
5 Presto luminoso: fluido, costante, sempre molto ritmico

Ligeti's Piano Concerto belongs to that late period of the composer's work which began, after a long creative silence, with the Horn Trio in 1982. It was a startling departure for audiences familiar with the old Ligeti of slowly changing washes of colour and gently unwinding skeins of murmuring 'micropolyphony', shattered now and then by a sinister–comic gesture. Now all the elements of music that had had to be stifled in that search for a 'textural' music – melodic profile, pulse, clearly definable harmonies – were suddenly readmitted. Even the mistunings of the horn's natural harmonics (an ear-catching effect which reappears in the Piano Concerto) were part of a distinct melody line rather than one element in a wash of colour.

This was in no way the mellowing of advancing age, or a sign of those neo-Romantic times (in fact Ligeti declared 'I hate neo-Expressionism and I can't stand the neo-Mahlerite and neo-Bergian affectations'). It was more a sign of the musical discoveries he made during those silent years, above all the exuberantly complicated polymetrical canons for player piano of Conlon Nancarrow, and the dense choral polyphony of the Banda Linda people of central Africa. But just as Ligeti hates neo-Expressionism, so too he would hate any overt quotation of exotic musical cultures, and you'll catch no hint of anything African in the Piano Concerto. What you will hear are clear echoes of Bartók, the one unchanging deity in Ligeti's musical pantheon.

The very opening of the Piano Concerto has a Bartókian feel, with its restless shifting of the pulse, and a harmonic tang of the right hand on the white keys and left hand on the black. There are other echoes too, including – ironically, given Ligeti's diatribe against 'neo-Bergians' – a reminiscence of Berg in the parallel sixths of the third movement. But these echoes are hugely distanced from their model by the alienating games Ligeti plays with the material. The reference to Berg is the accidental result of a momentary obsession with parallel sixths.

More common are the vastly complicated metrical games Ligeti plays, which have the effect of alienating straightforwardly cheerful or (in the second movement) droopingly expressive melodies. More often than not, piano and orchestra will have different time signatures, and within the orchestra different families will group the orchestral pulse in different ways. The effect is of an exuberant machine whose many spinning cogs start to skitter out of control. This is an old Ligeti conceit, and sometimes we'll hear a familiar gesture from the composer's past – for example, a hectic pattern which skitters right to the very top of the piano, and then reappears, in comic–surreal fashion, at the very bottom (the difference is that the effect is no longer the main event, in fact it's buried in so much eventfulness that you could easily miss it).

There are five movements in all, the helter-skelter odd-numbered ones where the piano leads, and two slower ones where the piano plays a modest role. The first of these, marked 'Lento e deserto', begins with a typical Ligeti witticism: piccolo and bassoon unfold a closely intertwined duet whose peculiar desolate quality comes from its range, which is uncomfortably low for the piccolo, and uncomfortably high for the bassoon. Oddest of all is the fourth movement, described by Ligeti as a 'geometric vortex', in which 'the ever-decreasing values produce the sensation of a kind of acceleration'.

Ivan Hewett © BBC

Franz Liszt (1811–86)

While Chopin's musical language grew out of the idiom of the piano, Liszt – inspired by Paganini's sensational Paris appearances in 1831 – succeeded in exploding the notions of what was considered possible on the instrument. Hungarian by birth, he toured Europe as a teenage pianist and settled in Paris, where he established himself as the leading virtuoso of the day. Also unlike Chopin, Liszt ventured into orchestral and choral music, and drew direct inspiration from literary and pictorial sources. He invented the orchestral tone poem, which became both a vehicle for his literary imagination and a suitable medium for his technique of progressively transforming themes. After an affair (1833–44) with Countess Marie d'Agoult, he was appointed to the court in Weimar, where he lived with Princess Carolyne Sayn-Wittgenstein. A devout Catholic, he took minor orders in 1865 while living in Rome. The *Études d'exécution transcendante* (1851), three books of *Années de pèlerinage* and the dramatic B minor Sonata figure among his most significant piano music, and his greatest orchestral achievement is *A Faust Symphony* (1854–7).

∾ Piano Concerto No. 1 in E flat major (1849; rev. 1853, 1856)

1 Allegro maestoso –
2 Quasi adagio – Allegretto vivace – Allegro maestoso –
3 Allegro marziale animato

It is a little surprising that Liszt, the great composer–pianist, wrote only seven works for piano and orchestra, of which the most important by far are the two concertos and the *Totentanz*. The main reason for this is that the circumstances of his life made his appearances as a pianist with orchestra relatively infrequent. Until around the age of thirty-five almost all the music he wrote was for piano solo. Such collections as the *Études d'exécution transcendante*, the *Harmonies poétiques et religieuses* and the *Années de pèlerinage*, usually revised in later years, represented a peak of piano technique and of Romantic sensibility and are still regarded as a formidable challenge to the solo player.

Liszt pioneered the idea of the solo recital (the term was coined for him in London in 1840), and in the years up to 1848 his travels as a virtuoso pianist stagger the imagination. The physical and mental strain of these tours, which took him all over Europe, from small market towns in Ireland to the Sultan's palace in Constantinople, was enormous, and in 1848 he decided on a complete change of life: he settled in Weimar, where he had been offered the post of Court Music Director, and never again played in public for money. His main preoccupation during the Weimar years was orchestral composition, and from the late 1840s and 1850s come the symphonic poems and the *Faust* and *Dante* symphonies. His usual tendency was to compose at great speed, and then revise meticulously, often repeatedly. Several of his large-scale works grew from ideas which had occurred to him many years earlier.

The earliest traces of the First Piano Concerto date back as far as 1830. It was the year in which he first met Berlioz, and a year before his formative encounters with Chopin and Paganini. Not yet twenty, he was emerging as a formidable piano virtuoso, but as a composer he had not yet achieved anything significant. The concerto passed through at least five different stages: substantially completed in 1849, soon after he settled in Weimar, it was then thoroughly revised in 1853, and again in 1856 before publication. Liszt gave the first performance of the concerto on 17 February 1855. The Weimar orchestra was conducted by Hector Berlioz, and the concert formed part of a week-long festival of Berlioz's music which included a revival of *Benvenuto Cellini* and the first German performance of *The Childhood of Christ*. In future years the concerto was far more associated with Liszt's pupils

– such remarkable players as Hans von Bülow and Carl Tausig – than with the composer himself.

Liszt's division of the score into three separate movements is a little misleading. The work is in fact played without a break between movements, and the second movement is a two-in-one structure containing slow movement and scherzo. This overall plan results in a work of great concentration, almost unique among nineteenth-century virtuoso concertos for lasting under twenty minutes in performance.

From its first performance the concerto has been criticised for its basic material. There is some justice in this, for most of its themes are not particularly distinguished in themselves. Far more important, though, and the reason why the concerto has always been prized by players and listeners, is that these plain themes are subjected to the process of variation and transformation that was Liszt's greatest contribution to the development of musical form in the nineteenth century. An important model was Schubert's 'Wanderer' Fantasy for solo piano (1822; arranged by Liszt for piano and orchestra some time before 1852); among Liszt's own works the technique reaches a peak in the B minor Piano Sonata and the *Faust Symphony*; its implications were vital for Wagner's music dramas, and had important consequences far into the twentieth century.

The concerto opens in bravura style, with full orchestra and thundering piano set in opposition; but much of the movement later develops in a more intimate manner, with the piano subtly blended into the orchestral texture, or delicately accompanying solo instruments.

After a brief modulating introduction by the orchestral strings, the slow movement features the piano in an extended solo whose sustained melody derives from Chopin's nocturne style and the long-spun, Italianate vocal lines of Bellini. This gives way to the mocking, Mephistophelean side of Liszt, as the scherzo section is introduced by triangle with pizzicato strings. The use of the triangle caused huge offence to some of Liszt's contemporaries. He vigorously defended it, though he was not always happy about the way it was played and removed the offending instrument from many places in the finale because, as he said, 'ordinary triangle virtuosi . . . usually come in wrong and strike it too hard'.

The concerto's finale is both recapitulation and conclusion. The opening march is a transformation of the slow movement's nocturne, and indeed all the material in this movement is a transformation of earlier themes, appearing in a single brisk march tempo until the pace is tightened for the exciting final Presto.

© Andrew Huth

❧ Piano Concerto No. 2 in A major (1839; revs 1849–1861)

In one of the most heartfelt tributes ever paid by one composer to another, Hugo Wolf declared of Liszt that 'with the utmost security he has created a new form in the sense that he willingly gave priority to the poetic idea, then, in order to develop the idea artistically, he had to depart, inevitably, from the traditional symphonic form . . . He had to let the musical form be determined by the substance of the poetic outline.' Cynics have been known to suggest that Liszt's 'creation' was as much by accident as by design. Yet even if one is sceptical about the effectiveness of those 'inevitable' departures from the traditional symphonic form, there is still great fascination in observing the ways in which the two aspects of Liszt's personality – the improvising virtuoso and the conscientious constructor of substantial musical structures – contrive to live and work together.

First sketched as early as 1830, before the concerto eventually designated No. 1, the A major piano concerto reached its definitive form only in 1849, and there were further, minor revisions over the next twelve years. Whatever the reasons for this long period of gestation – reprehensible indecisiveness, praiseworthy open-mindedness – the result is a characteristic Lisztian blend of the flexible and the clear-cut, a pianistic showpiece in which the orchestral contribution is crucial, and a strongly unified single-movement structure within which there is ample variety of tempo, texture and tonality. It is perfectly possible to regard the whole work as cast in an elastic but unambiguous sonata form. Yet the traditional, cumulative progress through exposition, development and recapitulation is here pushed rather into the background by a scheme in which side-roads are as significant as the main highway.

The concerto begins with one of those languid lyrical melodies that might seem ideal for a nocturne but unpromising as the starting-point for a symphonic composition. Liszt shows his awareness of the danger in the soloist's more decisive answer to the initial elaboration of the first theme: for the moment, however, this decisiveness is only a gesture for future reference. The first theme returns, even more seductively orchestrated, and the melody proliferates through horn, oboe and cello solos. Only gradually do the piano's decorative flourishes grow into a fully-fledged cadenza demanding a complete change of mood and a clear assertion that this is indeed a piano concerto. With the onset of a martial second section the main argument of the work, between lyric and dramatic characteristics, is fully joined. The martial music (not yet in march time) ends with another brief solo cadenza, and the fastest music so far (Allegro agitato assai) follows, to complete the exposition. This episode includes a passage for orchestra alone, developing the main motives, but with the return of the soloist the mood grows less hectic. There is a codetta in which the 'agitato' theme is strikingly transformed into a shapely lyric phrase for the strings. Then, after another cadenza, the central section of the concerto begins.

As befits a developmental episode, the work's first subject reappears, now in 4/4, with the piano accompanying a solo cello. This refined, poetic atmosphere is maintained through various changes of harmonic perspective, and passages in which the soloist dominates alternate with passages in which the piano adopts a supporting role. Then, after the most extended cadenza so far, the martial music returns, now in proper march time and bringing with it references to the earlier 'agitato' motive. The result is music which is much less episodic than what has gone before, forming an extended, dramatic development to complement the lyrical rumination which has preceded it.

As the development unfolds, the texture gradually thins out, but the mood does not relax. Rather, there is an increase of tension leading to the recapitulation, which begins with the concerto's first idea transformed from dreamy meditation into hyperactive march. The 'agitato' material is also brought back, and a huge, expectant climax is built up. This might be the moment for a final bravura cadenza but, having included so much cadenza-style writing earlier in the work, Liszt now gives the soloist a second, varied recapitulation of the first theme, hinting at the possibility of a more relaxed mood, and therefore of ending the work with a return to the tranquillity of its opening. As the piano retreats into its role of accompanist to orchestral soloists this outcome seems a real possibility, and even after the cadenza that ends this section a quiet ending would be conceivable. In the event, however, Liszt the showman conquers Liszt the dreamer, and the music returns to drama and display. The coda begins with scherzo-like lightness, but as the solo part becomes increasingly assertive, including some spectacular double glissandos, so the martial mood and material re-establish themselves, and carry the concerto to a forceful, triumphant end.

© Arnold Whittall

✌ *Totentanz*: paraphrase on the *Dies irae* for piano and orchestra (1849; rev. 1853, 1859)

It is surprising how little we know about the origin and composition of much of Liszt's music. In the case of the *Totentanz*, however, we can pinpoint the very moment of its inception: the afternoon of 5 December 1830, when Liszt attended the first performance of the *Symphonie fantastique* by Berlioz, whom he had met for the first time the previous day. The intonation of the *Dies irae* plainchant in the symphony's finale, with growling ophicleide and tolling bells, obviously made a deep impression on the nineteen-year-old Liszt, who later made a transcription of the score for solo piano.

An episode from 1832 indicates how the *Dies irae* continued to prey on his mind. That spring Paris was in the grip of a cholera epidemic. The roads to the cemeteries were blocked with hearses, and scenes worthy of the most morbid Romantic fantasy were occurring daily in the streets. Against this macabre background, we hear of the tenants of a building in the Rue de Provence banding together to clamour for Liszt's eviction after he had kept them awake all night playing the *Dies irae* 'from dusk to dawn in countless variations'. (He soon left the building of his own accord, and one hopes he found more understanding neighbours.)

Many accounts suggest that the *Totentanz* took shape while Liszt was travelling in Italy with Marie d'Agoult in 1838–9, and refer to the frescos of *The Triumph of Death* in the Campo Santo at Pisa as a possible inspiration for the piece. The figure of Death, part woman, part bat, hovers over the corpses of kings and peasants strewn on the ground. Liszt was certainly much impressed by these frescos (long thought to be by Orcagna, but now attributed to Francesco Traini), and they may well have provided a further stimulus to a composition based on the *Dies irae*. In actual fact, the character of what he eventually composed has more in common with a later artistic convention: it was only in the century following the Pisan frescos that the Dance of Death, showing dancing skeletons leading all sorts and conditions of men to the grave, appeared in European iconography. Liszt's title suggests something far more like the Germanic Expressionism of Holbein's famous series of engravings *Der Totentanz* (1538).

The exact pictorial source is less important than the verbal and musical associations of the *Dies irae* itself. This thirteenth-century Latin poem vividly describing the terrors of the Last Judgement soon became a central part of the Requiem Mass.

Berlioz was the first to quote the plainchant to which it was sung, and these simple but memorable musical phrases subsequently acquired a heavy and powerful symbolical charge of death, decay, terror, judgement, the sinister, the grotesque and the supernatural.

As far as we can tell, the *Totentanz* was first written down in 1849, soon after Liszt had abandoned the life of a touring virtuoso and settled in Weimar. It was revised in 1853, and again in 1859. The first performance was given by Liszt's son-in-law Hans von Bülow in The Hague on 15 April 1865, and the work was published later that year. Liszt was not present; by then he had settled in Rome. He himself never played the piece with an orchestra, and the first time he heard it in this form was on 6 May 1881, when it was played by his pupil Eduard Reuss in Baden-Baden.

Soon after this performance, Liszt was visited by Alexander Borodin, who recounted the scene in a letter to César Cui:

> When I told him that I should like to hear his *Totentanz*, which I considered the most powerful of all works for piano and orchestra for its originality of idea and form, for the beauty, depth and power of its theme, the novelty of its instrumentation, its profoundly religious and mystical sentiment, its Gothic and liturgic character, Liszt became more and more excited. 'Yes,' he exclaimed, 'look at that now! It pleases you Russians, but here it is not liked. It has been given five or six times in Germany, and despite excellent performances it turned out a complete fiasco.'

Perhaps German audiences in the 1860s found such blatantly Gothic Romanticism distasteful; they would certainly have been shocked by the music, which is at times quite brutally, aggressively modern. Significantly, the piece later became a great favourite of Béla Bartók, who played it frequently. The enthusiasm of Borodin and his Russian colleagues is reflected in much of their music: the *Totentanz* clearly made a very deep impression on Musorgsky, particularly in his *Songs and Dances of Death*, completed in 1877. As for a Russian of a later generation, Rakhmaninov's music is almost unthinkable without the constant spectre of the *Dies irae*.

Liszt's own fondness for his *Totentanz* hardly needs explanation. The theme which had haunted him for so long dominates the piece – Death has no rivals – and is subjected to a brilliant series of variations: harmonic, rhythmic, orchestral, and above all, pianistic. The opening is stark and threatening, as piano and drums underscore the first appearance of the *Dies irae* on brass, low wind and strings.

The transformations begin almost at once: they include swooping up-and-down glissandos, an insinuating dance, a repeated-note fugato, a reflective canon, a triumphant march, hunting-horn whoops, and a wild tarantella. Liszt here displays the Mephistophelean side of his character with bravura devilry, revelling in charnel-house virtuosity.

© Andrew Huth

Witold Lutosławski (1913–94)

Lutosławski hoped to continue his studies in Paris after graduating in piano and composition from the Warsaw Conservatory in 1937. But military service intervened, during which he was captured by the Germans before escaping to Warsaw (his brother was not so fortunate, and died in Siberia). His *Variations on a Theme of Paganini* (1941) for two pianos, was written for himself and his composer contemporary Andrzej Panufnik, with whom he played in Warsaw's cafés. In 1949 Lutosławski's First Symphony (1947) was banned, and in the following years his output included much folk music, including children's songs, until the extrovert *Concerto for Orchestra* (1950–4) established his national reputation. His fondness of aleatoric, or chance, principles, was first explored in *Jeux vénitiens* (1961) and in many works of the 1960s. After the Symphony No. 2 (1965–7) and the Cello Concerto (1969–70) he developed a more melodic style in the Double Concerto for oboe and harp (1980) and Symphony No. 3 (1981–3). He died a year after the premiere in Los Angeles of his Symphony No. 4.

∾ Cello Concerto (1969–70)

On a concert tour to Poland some time around 1968, Mstislav Rostropovich asked Lutosławski to write a cello concerto for him. 'I can't guarantee I will play it well,' Lutosławski reported the cellist as saying, 'but I will certainly play it very often.' In order to give the composer an insight into his playing Rostropovich gave him a private performance of Britten's First Cello Suite; Lutosławski responded with a tape of his most recently completed work, the song cycle *Paroles tissées*, written for Peter Pears. Encouraged by a commission from the Royal Philharmonic Society in London, Lutosławski composed the concerto in 1969 and the early months of 1970, sending the score page by page to Rostropovich, who gave the first performance at the Royal Festival Hall in October 1970.

Together with the manuscript Lutosławski also supplied an extra-musical explanation of the work, mapping out a dramatic scenario in which the solo cello and the orchestra were cast as adversaries, and in which the cello appears to be vanquished, only to rise again in the final pages. Doubtless Rostropovich identified strongly with such a heroic protagonist, especially at a time when he himself was in direct conflict with the Soviet authorities because of his public support for the Soviet dissident writer Alexander Solzhenitsyn. Shortly after the premiere he was to find himself removed from his position at the Moscow Conservatoire and banned from foreign travel. But Lutosławski always denied that the concerto had any detailed programme, or that it could in any way be construed as a late twentieth-century counterpart to Strauss's *Don Quixote*: the scenario he sketched for Rostropovich registers only the barest outline of what is essentially an intricate and vivid abstract musical argument.

The concerto is cast in a single movement, playing for just over twenty minutes, but it falls into four sharply differentiated sections, corresponding approximately to a traditional fast–slow–fast concerto plan, prefaced by an introduction for the cello alone. That beginning, strikingly characterised by the sequence of repeated Ds with which it opens, provides the nearest approach to a conventional cadenza in the work; the cello introduces itself with a protean collection of ideas of vastly divergent character and mood. Yet this wealth of thematic material proves to be unrelated to the confrontational journey on which the cello and orchestra then embark; the trumpets interrupt the soloist's musings with an aggressive outburst that will serve as punctuation throughout the concerto.

In its second section the concerto moves from monologue to dialogue: it is made up of four linked episodes, in each of which the cello sets out upon an attempt to come to terms with groups of orchestral instruments, predominantly woodwind, only to have each encounter cut short by the brass before it can reach any kind of conclusion. Their final intrusion is extended to announce the beginning of the third section, in which the strings join with the cello in developing a long, increasingly expressive cantilena. Such music provides both the concerto's moment of repose and its expressive core: it is essentially a three-part song with soloist and strings singing out their melody in the outer sections, finally building it to an impassioned climax, and a central episode in which the cello lines strike increasingly iridescent colours from the orchestra.

The return of the strident brass material cuts across all such niceties, but on this final occasion the remainder of the orchestra is swept into the attack. The cello then takes up the challenge and the music proceeds in a succession of battering exchanges, until inevitably the greater force prevails; after climaxing in a series of eleven savage hammer-blows, the cello is reduced to scraps of material, with all energy spent. Then, however, the music regroups, and the solo instrument is given its own glorious climax in the coda, rising through its entire range to end the concerto triumphantly, as it began, with repeated notes – this time, though, settling on high A rather than D.

© Andrew Clements

ஐ Piano Concerto (1988)

1   = c. 110
2   Presto
3   = c. 85 –
4   = c. 84

One of the last works Lutosławski completed as a 'traditional composer' was a *Concerto for Orchestra* (1954), which in retrospect seems a fond farewell to the folk music that had funded so much of his early output. He subsequently wrote three fully fledged solo concertos, each of which explored and redefined aspects of the concerto tradition in terms of his own constantly renewed technical resources. The single-movement Cello Concerto, completed in 1970, examined the classical relationship between the solo instrument and the orchestra, resolved into dialogues between the cello and selected orchestral soloists rather than in confrontations in dense tuttis. Ten years later, the Double Concerto for oboe and harp with strings and percussion harked back to eighteenth-century models; its lucid elegance and ritornello backgrounds conjure up an ironic detachment, while the folk-song tinges to the thematic material seem to hint at Lutosławski's own stylistic past.

The Piano Concerto (written for Krystian Zimerman and premiered by him at the 1988 Salzburg Festival) also combines wishful backward glances with a reassessment of tradition. In this case it is the development of the piano concerto since Brahms that is the focus of interest; elements of the 'symphonic concerto' are filtered and sorted, while references to many of the most significant piano concertos of this century – oblique and often textural rather than direct – are scattered through all four movements. The formal scheme – four movements played without a break but made utterly distinct, the second a scherzo and the last constructed over a chaconne-like bass – itself suggests Brahmsian links. While Lutosławski's development during the 1980s was characterised by ever greater technical assurance, it also saw his music move closer to traditional formal outlines, though characteristically moulding them very precisely to its own needs.

What he produced here, however, appears to be a concerto written both as a commentary upon the progress of the form since Brahms and an exercise in nostalgia as sophisticated and potent as that of the Double Concerto. The ghosts of Rakhmaninov, Bartók and Ravel, who lurk behind not only the solo piano writing but also many orchestral touches, too – the eruption of high clarinet and muted trumpet in the final movement, for instance, inescapably conjures up Ravel's G major Concerto – are those of composers who were vital ingredients in Lutosławski's early style. And this was also his first mature solo work for the instrument that provided his living and lifeline during the Second World War, when he played piano duets in Warsaw cafés with his student contemporary Andrzej Panufnik.

A high proportion of the Piano Concerto is fully notated. There is, Lutosławski acknowledged, less use of the controlled chance procedures in this work than in any other major score since *Jeux vénitiens* of 1961, though a later technical device, 'chain form', dominates the finale. There the piano's episodes are superimposed upon the repetitions of the chaconne theme in such a way that their beginnings and ends do not coincide until the final pages of the work, where they provide a natural point of climax. But the glinting textures with which the concerto opens are obtained by superimposing *ad libitum* lines. These passages provide the frame for a sequence of fugitive, almost casual motifs for the piano, and the first movement is constructed from two statements of this material intercut with two paragraphs in which a more extended lyrical melody is elaborated by the soloist, its profile given sharper definition by the persistent octaves in the keyboard part.

The central pair of movements is dominated by the piano, and both contain substantial solo passages. In the second a bravura cadenza provides the climax for what Lutosławski described as 'a kind of *moto perpetuo*, a quick "chase" by the piano against the background of the orchestra', while the third is framed by a piano recitative that leads directly into the presentation of a cantabile Largo theme that the soloist immediately decorates and embellishes. The function of the orchestra here is to heighten the tension; with its entry the central section of the movement begins and the music takes on a far more rhetorical character until the return, via a delicious sequence of decorative swirls, to a shortened statement of the Largo melody.

The chaconne theme emerges in the double basses from the final chord of this reprise. The theme itself, cryptic and punctuated with rests, departs from Baroque practice by being fundamentally melodic rather than harmonic, and its statements are confined to the orchestra. The piano's excursions, widely various, pursue a seemingly independent course. The forces combine to close the concerto: the orchestra restates the chaconne theme elided, without the rests; the piano launches a last recitative, this time with the orchestra, and plunges into a Presto coda that is unambiguously conclusive.

© Andrew Clements

James MacMillan (b. 1959)

James MacMillan is a composer of committed religious and political beliefs, whose convictions lie behind all his varied musical output. He was born in Ayrshire, and studied at Edinburgh and Durham Universities, before lecturing briefly at Manchester University. His move back to Scotland in 1988 coincided with a concentration on the dual influences of Scottish folk music and his Catholic faith, often with political resonances. *Búsqueda* ('Search', 1988) intersperses the Latin Mass with poems by Argentinian mothers of the disappeared; *The Confession of Isobel Gowdie* for orchestra, premiered at the BBC Proms in 1990, centres on the trial of a Scottish Reformation Catholic 'witch'. Another persecuted woman became the subject of his first full-length opera, *Inès de Castro* (1991–5). He has written a number of concerto and concertante works including *Veni, veni, Emmanuel* (1991–2) for the percussionist Evelyn Glennie, which received over 280 performances in its first decade, a Cello Concerto (1996) for Mstislav Rostropovich, and two clarinet concertos. He is now Composer/Conductor of the BBC Philharmonic.

❧ *Veni, Veni, Emmanuel* (1991–2)

Veni, Veni, Emmanuel, a concerto for percussion and orchestra, is in one continuous movement and lasts about twenty-five minutes. Dedicated to my parents, it is based on the Advent plainsong of the same name, and was started on the first Sunday of Advent 1991 and completed last Easter Sunday (these two liturgical dates are important, as will be explained later).

The piece can be discussed in two ways: on one level it is a purely abstract work, in which all the musical material is drawn from the fifteenth-century French Advent plainchant; on another, it is a musical exploration of the theology behind the Advent message.

Soloist and orchestra converse throughout as equal partners, and a wide range of percussion is used, including tuned, untuned, skin, metal and wood sounds. Much of the music is fast and, although the piece is seamless, it can be divided into a five-sectioned arch, beginning with a bold, fanfare-like 'overture', in which all the instrument types to be employed are presented. When the soloist moves to gongs, unpitched metal and wood, the music melts into the main meat of the first section – music of a more brittle and knotty quality, propelled by various pulse-rates evoking an ever-changing heartbeat.

Advancing to drums and carried through a metrical modulation, the music is thrown forward into the second section, characterised by fast, chugging quavers, irregular rhythmic shifts and the 'hocketing' of chords from one side of the orchestra to the other. Eventually the music winds down to a slow central section which puts cadenza-like expressivity on the marimba against a floating tranquillity in the orchestra, hardly ever rising above *ppp*. The orchestra repeats the four chords which accompany the words '*Gaude, Gaude*' in the plainsong's refrain over and over, layered in different instrumental combinations and in different speeds, and evoking a distant congregation murmuring a calm prayer in many voices.

A huge pedal crescendo on E flat provides a transition to section four, which reintroduces material from the 'hocket' section under a virtuoso vibraphone solo. Gradually one becomes aware of the original tune floating slowly behind the surface activity. The climax presents the plainsong as a chorale, followed by the opening fanfares, which provide a backdrop for an energetic drum cadenza. In the coda the all-pervasive heartbeats are emphatically pounded out on timpani and other drums as the music reaches an unexpected conclusion.

The heartbeats which permeate the piece, representing the human presence of Christ, offer a clue to its wider spiritual priorities. Advent texts proclaim the promised day of liberation from fear, anguish and oppression, and my work attempts to mirror this in music. I found its inspiration in the following text from Chapter 21 of the Gospel according to St Luke:

> There will be signs in the sun and moon and stars; on earth nations in agony, bewildered by the clamour of the ocean and its waves; men dying of fear as they await what menaces the world, for the powers of heaven will be shaken. And they will see the Son of Man coming in a cloud with power and great glory. When these things begin to take place, stand erect, hold your heads high, because your liberation is near at hand.

At the very end the music takes a liturgical detour from Advent to Easter – right into the Gloria of the Easter Vigil, in fact – as if the proclamation of liberation has found embodiment in the Risen Christ.

James MacMillan © BBC

Felix Mendelssohn (1809–47)

The grandson of a philosopher, Mendelssohn combined musical precociousness of a Mozartian order with a lifetime of learning and travelling. He gave his first performance as a pianist aged nine, and composed thirteen early string symphonies between 1821 and 1823. By the time of his first visit to London, aged twenty, he had already spent time in Paris. After returning to Berlin, where he had studied philosophy with Hegel, he undertook a major tour of Europe, which inspired the 'Scottish' and 'Italian' Symphonies as well as the *Hebrides* overture. He became conductor of the Lower Rhine Music Festival, Music Director of the Leipzig Gewandhaus Orchestra (1835), and founded the Leipzig Conservatory (1843). He showed vivid scene-painting ability in his overtures (especially *A Midsummer Night's Dream* and *Calm Sea and Prosperous Voyage*), but he produced some of his best work in the standard classical forms: an enduringly popular Violin Concerto, seven string quartets and two piano concertos. Of his three oratorios, *Elijah* was especially favoured by the English choral societies of the Victorian era.

∾ Piano Concerto No. 1 in G minor, Op. 25 (1832)

1 Molto Allegro con fuoco –
2 Andante –
3 Presto – Molto allegro e vivace

Mendelssohn's First Piano Concerto has always suffered from an undeserved reputation for frivolity. Perhaps this is why it featured as the test piece in the story (maliciously related by Berlioz) of the piano competition in which the participants were so numerous that the nervous pianists began to notice a progressive loosening of the keys: by the time the last competitor was ready to walk on to the platform, the piano began the piece by itself. The concerto's 'lightweight' status is partly Mendelssohn's own fault; he described it himself as a 'hastily sketched matter', and it has customarily been dismissed in a few brief sentences in most literature on the composer ever since.

In a letter written from Rome in the autumn of 1830 the twenty-one-year-old Mendelssohn mentioned 'a Piano Concerto that I would like to write for Paris [which] is beginning to whirl about in my head'. The piece was finally finished and performed in Munich the following year, on Mendelssohn's return journey from Italy. On 17 October 1831 he gave the premiere of the concerto at a charity concert in the presence of the King and Queen of Bavaria. The programme, all of his own works, also included the overture to *A Midsummer Night's Dream* and the First Symphony in C minor, both written a few years earlier. Mendelssohn reported that the concerto in particular was very well received. He played it again in Paris, in London and at the Leipzig Gewandhaus. The London audience was especially appreciative, demanding a second hearing; a review praised the composer's performance as 'an astonishing exhibition of piano-playing'. Nearly forty years later, the work was performed at a Mendelssohn memorial concert in Leipzig by the original dedicatee, a pianist named Delphine von Schauroth whom Mendelssohn had met in Munich. She is not known to have played it in public during his lifetime.

The perceptive London critic of the *Athenaeum* described the G minor Concerto as a 'Dramatic Scene for the Piano', and both in style and structure it resembles a fantasia rather than a traditional three-movement concerto. It belongs to a group of works, including the Second Piano Concerto, the Violin Concerto and the 'Scottish' Symphony, in which Mendelssohn experimented with form by linking the movements together and by introducing elementary cyclic principles. In this he was undoubtedly influenced by Weber's *Konzertstück* for piano and orchestra (1821), and his own concerto may have provided a model for Schumann's, written over a decade later. Thus the fanfare-like motif that supplies the transitional passage between the first movement and the Andante returns at the opening of the finale, as do the grandiloquent, recitative-like gestures of the soloist that open the piece after the briefest of orchestral introductions – a mere seven bars. (This non-thematic orchestral 'scene-setting' was to be abbreviated still further in Mendelssohn's masterpiece in the form, the Violin Concerto.) Thematic connections between the outer movements are further strengthened when the opening Allegro's second subject reappears fleetingly in the tonic key just before the coda of the finale.

© Wendy Thompson

∾ Violin Concerto in E minor, Op. 64 (1844)

1 Allegro molto appassionato –
2 Andante –
3 Allegretto non troppo – Allegro molto vivace

This elegant, impassioned work, composed three years before Mendelssohn's death, rebuts two ancient but persistent notions: that his attitude to musical form was conservative and unadventurous, and that inspiration deserted him in the final period of his life. The work is full of unconventional strokes that are no less so for their apparently effortless ease.

The first occurs at the outset, in the dream-like, troubled opening, where the soloist, not waiting for a formal orchestral exposition of themes, enters in the second bar with a noble, long-breathed melody above a sustained clarinet and bassoon chord, rustling violins and violas, and a soft pulsation of drums – an idea of genius which seizes the listener as powerfully as the opening of Beethoven's Violin Concerto. No less striking is the colouring of the G major second theme, as it is introduced when the long, throbbing minor-key section finally comes to rest: the solo violin simply sustaining a long, low G while woodwind play the tune – a sound as original as it is beautiful.

Yet another innovation is the placing of the violin cadenza: not, as normally, at the end of the recapitulation but much earlier, at the end of the development. Typical, too, is the magical way the cadenza's virtuoso flourishes are integrated – by means of a diminuendo combined with a gradual resumption of tempo – into the reprise of the main theme, whose return is made to seem both mysterious and inevitable. Unexpected, skilfully managed transitions are a feature of the score, like the sudden gleam of trumpets which, after the reprise of the second theme, recalls the music to the agitations of E minor and, from there, leads to the stormy conclusion.

Like several of Mendelssohn's large-scale works, the concerto flows without a break. The solo bassoon emerges from the final chord of the first movement still playing its (dominant) B, which functions as a leading note and ushers in the C major Andante. This is music as tuneful and raptly lyrical as the Allegro's second theme, borne forward on a gentle pulse and filled with that serene yet yearning mood that Mendelssohn made his own. The more agitated middle section, in A minor, raises the temperature, with an ominous motif in repeated notes on trumpets and drums, and restless string figurations that are carried over into the reprise of the opening.

In its turn, the Andante leads straight into the interlude, a wistful, rhapsodic Allegretto, first in A minor, then in the home key of E minor, and then turning with a smile to E major – whereupon the finale bursts in, with commanding fanfares, rapid flourishes for the soloist, and the first movement's menacing trills now turned to delight. From here until the triumphant end, the pace never falters, embracing glittering passagework, march rhythms and a broad cantabile theme, all worked together in a tour de force of unstoppable momentum. Indeed, the whole work refutes any idea of decline, so abundant is it – whether we think of the Andante's unending melodic span, the finale's delicate, brilliant textures, the softer, darker glow of the first movement, or the unfailingly imaginative treatment of the solo violin.

© David Cairns

Wolfgang Amadeus Mozart (1756–91)

More than two hundred years after his death, Mozart stands as a focal figure of Western classical music, not only for his astonishing precocity and inventiveness, but for the staggering range and quality of his music. His father Leopold, a violinist, paraded his son's talents around the European capital cities when he was as young as six. By sixteen, Mozart had absorbed a variety of musical fashions, having travelled to England, Germany, France, Holland and Italy. He worked for the Prince-Archbishop in Salzburg during his teens, producing symphonies, concertos and masses as well as operas. In 1780 he went to Munich to compose *Idomeneo*, his first great opera, and the following year he moved to Vienna, where in the four years beginning in 1782 he wrote fifteen of his twenty-seven piano concertos, which he played himself in concerts. *The Marriage of Figaro*, the first of his three operatic collaborations with the court poet da Ponte, appeared in 1786, followed by *Don Giovanni*. In his last three years he set his last da Ponte text, *Così fan tutte*, and wrote two highly contrasted operas, *Die Zauberflöte* and *La Clemenza di Tito* (1791), as well as the three final symphonies (Nos 39–41) and the gem-like Clarinet Concerto. He left his Requiem incomplete at his death.

∾ Clarinet Concerto in A major, K622 (1791)

1 Allegro
2 Adagio
3 Rondo: Allegro

Mozart's last great instrumental composition owes its existence to the clarinettist Anton Stadler, for whom it was written in the autumn of 1791. In part, it owes its greatness to him as well. Stadler was not only one of the foremost clarinettists of his day, a man whose playing was noted for its softness and voice-like quality, he was also a good friend of the composer, having already inspired him to create the superb Clarinet Quintet in 1789. The clarinet was a relatively new instrument at that time, and Stadler, always fond of the unearthly sound of its lower register, had developed a model which gave extra notes at the bottom end. In the event, this particular variant (now known as the basset clarinet) did not catch on, but it was at least around long enough for Mozart to compose both the Quintet and the Concerto for it and thereby insure it against total obsolescence.

What really distinguishes the Clarinet Concerto, however, is that it is a culmination of Mozart's unsurpassed achievements as a master of the concerto form, an effortless coming together of all the elements – structural coherence, appealing tunefulness, virtuosity and a talent for melodic characterisation carried over from his work in the opera house – with which he himself had moulded the concerto into a sophisticated means of expression. This had been accomplished above all in the great series of piano concertos which he composed for himself to play during the 1780s, but his orchestral use of wind instruments had always shown a strong affinity for their distinctive colours and expressive abilities, and if his concertos for flute, oboe, bassoon and horn did not match the inspiration of his piano concertos, it was perhaps only through frustration at their various technical limitations. In the clarinet – an instrument which combined vocal eloquence with the piano's ability to be brilliantly virtuosic over an unusually wide compass – Mozart found an instrument that suited him perfectly.

The original score of the Clarinet Concerto has long been lost (it seems the impecunious Stadler may even have pawned it), but in 1801 a version was published for 'ordinary' clarinet, with the solo part adapted to avoid the special low notes of the original. This is the form in which the work was known and played for a century and a half, but in the past fifty years it has become increasingly common to perform it on a reconstruction of Stadler's basset clarinet, and to restore the 'missing' low notes.

Perhaps the most impressive thing about the Clarinet Concerto is its apparent simplicity. This is a work with no great surprises or alarms, only music of perfectly pleasing melodic charm and structural 'rightness'. The first movement is unusually long and expansive, and has that relaxed but generous lyricism which characterises the two piano concertos Mozart had already composed in the same key. The finale is a suave and witty rondo with a memorable recurring theme. But it is the central slow movement that brings some of the loveliest music not only of this concerto but also of Mozart's entire output. The exquisite tune with which it begins and ends – presented delicately by the soloist at first, then warmly echoed by the orchestra – is essential Mozart, deeply moving yet at the same time noble and restrained. Commentators in the nineteenth century were apt to dismiss this concerto as old-fashioned, even 'grandfatherly'; in our age, more understanding of Mozart's talents, it has become one of the best-loved compositions in the classical repertoire.

© Lindsay Kemp

❧ Horn Concerto No. 3 in E flat major, K447 (1787)

1 Allegro
2 Romance: Larghetto
3 Allegro

One of the more unusual distinctions of Mozart's output is the number of works that feature a solo horn. While horn concertos are by no means rare in the classical period, they are not as common as those for flute or oboe. Mozart composed four, plus several single movements (some incomplete) and a quintet for horn and strings. Most of this music, if not all, was written for a close friend, Joseph Leutgeb.

Leutgeb was born in Vienna in 1732 and grew up in the same musical circles as his exact contemporary Joseph Haydn. For a short while in 1763 Leutgeb was a member of Haydn's orchestra at the Esterházy court, before moving on to Salzburg. There he became a firm friend of the Mozart family. He was a rather larger-than-life character, who encouraged the laddish aspect of Mozart's personality. Several symphonies and orchestral serenades from the time have daringly high horn parts designed to challenge, if not taunt the player. Leutgeb had married Barbara Plasseriani, the daughter of a sausage and cheese merchant from Vienna, and in 1777 the couple returned to Vienna in order to run the business – a good investment against the time when Leutgeb's abilities went into decline. He disappeared from Viennese musical life in the 1790s, but continued to live in the city as a successful trader until his death in 1811.

All Mozart's solo music for Leutgeb dates from the period 1783 to 1791 when both were living in Vienna and Leutgeb was at the peak of his abilities. He may have been a dolt – on the manuscript of one work Mozart called him an 'ass, ox and clown' – but he must also have been a player of superb ability. He had mastered the contemporary technique of hand-stopping – altering the pitch of the note by careful manipulation of the hand inside the bell of the instrument – so that Mozart was not restricted to the notes of the harmonic series. (The invention of valves in the nineteenth century made this skill redundant, but Mozart's writing still sets formidable challenges for the modern player.) In addition, Leutgeb was clearly a performer of great sensitivity. Mozart certainly called him an ass, but the music he wrote for him is a better indication of his esteem and affection.

Mozart's Third Horn Concerto was probably written in 1787; nothing is known of any public performances by Leutgeb. Unlike the other horn concertos, this one has the distinctive sound of clarinets and bassoons in the orchestra, rather than oboes and bassoons. As well as virtuosity, the first movement explores the warm, lyrical properties of the horn, aspects of the instrument that are more fully exploited in the following Romance. The finale, a rondo, is a 'hunting' movement, full of swagger and bravado.

© David Wyn Jones

∾ Horn Concerto No. 4 in E flat major, K495 (1786)

1 Allegro moderato
2 Romanza: Andante
3 Rondo: Allegro vivace

One of Mozart's lifelong friends was Joseph Leutgeb. Twenty-four years older than Mozart, he was born in Salzburg in 1732. From 1763 he played the horn in the court orchestra; Mozart was later a Konzertmeister at the court, and his father, Leopold, was Deputy Kapellmeister. Leutgeb married the daughter of a Salzburg cheese and sausage merchant and helped to run the business. He was more talented than the run-of the-mill court musician and undertook several journeys throughout Europe as a soloist, including a trip to Paris in 1770, where he played concertos in the celebrated Concert Spirituel. He moved to Vienna in 1777 where he continued to play the horn and run a cheese and sausage business. In Vienna, Mozart wrote at least three of his four horn concertos for him, as well as a horn quintet.

The present concerto dates from the summer of 1786 and was composed in the weeks following the premiere of *The Marriage of Figaro*. Although numbered in the nineteenth century as the fourth horn concerto it was, in fact, the second to be completed; No. 3 was probably finished in 1787 and No. 2 was completed after Mozart's death by Süssmayr. Mozart clearly admired Leutgeb as a horn player, and his affection for the man is suggested by the many jocular remarks written onto the autographs of the music he composed for him. On the six pages of the autograph manuscript of K495 that have survived Mozart makes childishly comic use of four different inks: his normal black, plus blue, red and green.

Leutgeb was a resourceful master of hand-stopping – altering the pitch of the note by adjusting the position of the right hand in the bell of the instrument. In the decades before the invention of valves this enabled horn players to sound notes between those of the harmonic series. Accomplished players like Leutgeb achieved great dexterity, as is shown time and time again in this concerto.

Mozart also responded readily to the natural warmth of the sound of the horn. In the first movement all the material shows a natural inclination towards the lyrical, and in the central development section, where one might expect some bravura passagework, there is an entirely new melody, in C minor. The slow movement is headed 'Romanza', a leisurely movement featuring a cantabile theme alternating with contrasting sections. Towards the end of the movement the orchestration acquires a telling depth of sonority when short phrases from the solo horn and first violins are supported by an accompaniment underpinned by repeated notes on the orchestral horns. Mozart, like all composers of the day, made willing use of the horn's association with the hunt, actual or symbolic. The eager 6/8 rhythms of the finale are immediately suggestive of the hunt but, for those listeners who know the composer's operas, there is irony too. The multicoloured score had teased Leutgeb; now it is we who are the willing victims of the music's mocking bravado.

© David Wyn Jones

∾ Piano Concerto No. 17 in G major, K453 (1784)

1 Allegro
2 Andante
3 Allegretto – Finale: Presto

One of the most remarkable aspects of Mozart's early years in Vienna was how quickly he established himself in the social circles of the aristocracy and bourgeoisie. For a series of subscription concerts in 1784 Mozart acquired the sponsorship of over 170 individuals; he may not have known each one of them personally, but it is clear that it was the fashionable thing to support the talent of this pianist–composer.

One of his most committed supporters was Gottfried Ignaz von Ployer, a member of the new nobility who represented the interests of Salzburg in government circles in Vienna and also held office in the chancellery. His niece Barbara (affectionately known as 'Babette') was nineteen years old in 1784 and an accomplished pianist. She became a favourite pupil of Mozart. That year he wrote two concertos for her to play in private concerts (*Hauskonzerte*) at the family homes in the centre of town and in the suburb of Döbling. The Piano Concerto in E flat (K449) was performed in March and the one in G major (K453) in June. The day before the first performance of the G major Concerto, Mozart wrote an enthusiastic letter to his father about the event, a letter that also conveniently name-drops Paisiello and Sarti, two of the most respected opera composers of the time.

> Tomorrow there is to be an academy concert at the country place in Döbling of the Agent Ployer, where Miss Babette will play her new concerto in G – and I will play the quintet for piano and wind instruments [K452] – and then both of us the grand sonata for two pianos [K448]. I shall fetch Paisiello with the carriage, to give him a chance to hear my compositions and my pupils playing – if Maestro Sarti had not been obliged to leave today, I would have taken him there too.

The history of the virtuoso piano concerto in the nineteenth and twentieth centuries has too often blinded modern listeners to the fact that many of Mozart's piano concertos, such as the G major, were written for performance in private surroundings with small forces, rather than in public; in that sense, they are chamber music rather than grand public confrontations in the manner of piano concertos by Beethoven, Schumann, Brahms, Grieg and others. Mozart's G major

Concerto is one of his most enchantingly subtle works, prolific in its melodic charm and, as in all great chamber music, the listener is a privileged eavesdropper, not someone who is addressed directly.

The work begins almost casually, with the first violins only (in Döbling in 1784 it could well have been only one player), before the rest of the ensemble join in. The opening theme is the first in a wonderful procession of ten contrasting ideas, by turn whimsical, theatrical, pensive and comic. The piano enters, discusses some of the existing ideas, before announcing one of its own. As a respite from this luxurious display of melody, the middle portion of the movement is a fantasia-like section, largely devoid of any references to the main themes. In the recapitulation, soloist and orchestra review the thematic material of the movement in an entirely new order and with the insertion of a cadenza for the soloist.

The slow movement is even more lavish, characterised by melodic decoration in flute, oboe and bassoon as well as piano, and by several highly charged changes of harmonic direction initiated by the piano. In mood the movement is a perfect realisation of the 'sentimental', the display of spontaneous feeling that was so fashionable in art, literature, opera and drama in the second half of the eighteenth century.

Feeling is set aside in the last movement in favour of a no-nonsense set of variations on the simplest of tunes. After five contrasting variations, Mozart adds what he termed a 'finale' – that is, a much faster section, as at the end of an opera, in which soloist and orchestra vie with each other to spit out the words, as it were, before the main theme is played at breakneck speed to conclude the movement. Babette von Ployer was clearly a pianist capable of bravura as well as feeling.

© David Wyn Jones

∿ Piano Concerto No. 19 in F major, K459 (1784)

1 Allegro
2 Allegretto
3 Allegro assai

The peak of Mozart's success with the Viennese public came in the mid–1780s. In the spring of 1785 Leopold visited Vienna and found his son at the centre of a whirlwind of activity. 'Every day there are concerts,' he reported back to his daughter, 'and the whole time is given up to teaching, music, composing and so forth . . . It is impossible for me to describe the rush and bustle. Since my arrival your brother's fortepiano has been taken at least a dozen times to the theatre or to some other house.'

On a practical level, piano concertos were the best way for Mozart to combine his talents for composition and performance in a way that was satisfying both to him and to his listeners, and it is not surprising that they should have been an important feature of many of his Viennese concerts. After his move to Vienna he composed only six symphonies, at least three of which were intended expressly for audiences in other cities; the tally of piano concertos for the same period is seventeen. But these concertos were also Mozart's most important instrumental legacy, a giant advance in the development of a still-youthful genre and an example for other composers to follow, comparable to Haydn's achievements with the symphony and the string quartet; for many listeners they continue to encapsulate Mozart's compositional genius no less than do his mature operas.

The F major Concerto, K459, is the last of six Mozart composed in 1784, and it amply reflects the self-assured frame of mind in which the composer must have found himself. There is an outgoing ease of manner to the work, epitomised as much by the utter cordiality of the opening as by the relaxed warmth of the middle movement, with its gently lolling dialogues between piano, flute, oboe and bassoon. But it is the finale which most readily conjures in the mind the scene described by Leopold; a vigorous rondo infused with fugal textures of uncommon vitality, it makes a fitting conclusion to a work in which we can witness a young, supremely talented composer revelling in his own skill with unreserved confidence and joy.

© Lindsay Kemp

❦ Piano Concerto No. 20 in D minor, K466 (1785)

1 Allegro
2 Romance
3 Rondo: Allegro assai

The decade that Mozart spent in Vienna from 1781 until his death was when he truly found his own voice as a composer, and nowhere is this new maturity and individuality better shown than in his piano concertos of the period. Altogether he wrote seventeen of them while in the Imperial capital, mostly for himself to play at the public and private concerts that helped provide him with financial support, and they were thus the works with which he was most closely associated by his audiences. More importantly, it was with them that he established the piano concerto for the first time as a sophisticated means of personal expression, rather than a vehicle for polite public display.

The high point in the series came with the five concertos composed in the period of just over a year from the beginning of 1785. K466 – completed and first performed in February 1785 – is chronologically at the head of this group but, musically speaking, too, it stands out in many ways. The composer's father Leopold, visiting Vienna at the time, heard the premiere, and a little over a year later was organising a performance by a local pianist back in Salzburg. He later described the occasion in a letter to his daughter:

Marchand played it from the score, and [Michael, brother of Joseph] Haydn turned over the pages for him, and at the same time had the pleasure of seeing with what art it is composed, how delightfully the parts are interwoven and what a difficult concerto it is. We rehearsed it in the morning and had to practise the rondo three times before the orchestra could manage it.

One can well imagine the impression the piece made in the composer's home town; there can be few clearer demonstrations of how far Mozart had left Salzburg behind him.

D minor is a relatively unusual key for Mozart, and therefore a significant one. Later he would use it both for Don Giovanni's damnation scene and for the Requiem, and there is something of the same grim familiarity with the dark side – a glimpse of the grave, it seems – in the first movement of this concerto. The opening orchestral section contrasts brooding menace with outbursts of passion, presenting along the way most of the melodic material that will serve the rest of the movement. Even so, it is with a new theme, lyrical but searching and restless, that the piano enters; this is quickly brushed aside by the orchestra, but the soloist does not give it up easily, later using it to lead the orchestra through several different keys in the central development section. The movement ends sombrely, pianissimo.

The slow second movement, in B flat major, is entitled 'Romance', a vague term used in Mozart's day to suggest something of a song-like quality. In fact this is a rondo, in which three appearances of the soloist's artless opening theme are separated by differing episodes, the first a drawn-out melody for the piano floating aristocratically over gently throbbing support from the strings, and the second a stormy minor-key eruption of piano triplets, shadowed all the way by sustained woodwind chords.

Storminess returns in the finale, though this time one senses that it is of a more theatrical kind than in the first movement. This is another rondo and, although the main theme is fiery and angular, much happens in the course of the movement to lighten the mood, culminating after the cadenza in a turn to D major for the concerto's final pages. An unthinkingly conventional 'happy ending' to send the audience away smiling? Perhaps so, but the gentle debunking indulged in by the horns and trumpets just before the end suggests that Mozart knew precisely what he was doing.

© Lindsay Kemp

◈ Piano Concerto No. 21 in C major, K467 (1785)

1 Allegro maestoso
2 Andante
3 Allegro vivace assai

To have a favourite among Mozart's piano concertos is not to proclaim it the best. We can well understand why Beethoven liked the impassioned K466 in D minor and K491 in C minor, and seems to have been specially impressed by the second of them. Forced to decide between them, our judgement might swing from movement to movement; and if marks for each movement were totalled they would have incurred a foolish assessment of incomparables, e.g. the rondo finale of the D minor and the variation finale of the C minor. Asked to judge only middle movements and say which, in all the concertos, did and still does bring most wonder, we should be likely to name the Andante of this K467. We can understand why it has been poached by purveyors of background music and by television advertisers, for it became known as the *Andante-rêve* – the dream andante. For one writer this music recalls a stage setting of the Elysian Fields in Gluck's *Orfeo*, with the Blessed Spirits moving between pillars of light that filtered to spectators through gauze curtains.

The score alarmed Mozart's father. He stayed with Wolfgang's family in Vienna for several months of 1785 and heard two of the piano concertos given that year – K466 in D minor and this C major. Surprised at the contrast in public taste between Salzburg and Vienna, Leopold was overjoyed at the enthusiastic reception of the D minor work; but surely some people would be offended at unconventional harmonies in the slow movement of the C major Concerto, and was not his son too bold with the piano triplets pacing duplets in the melody given to muted strings? Surprise this movement must have caused, yet Leopold's letter home reports rapturous applause during which 'many were in tears'.

The splendid first movement gives no premonition of Mozart's 'Romantic' vein except in an idea that comes late in the initial orchestral statement. It is heard again when the orchestra finishes the first concerted section – hence the term 'ritornello' – and its chromatic harmony imparts a tender Schumannesque yearning in strong contrast with the martial strut of the first theme and its company. That theme is all-pervading in the orchestral ritornellos, but the word 'company' rather than 'derivatives' is deliberately chosen.

Dittersdorf, a contemporary admirer of Mozart, and him-self no mean composer, wished he had time to relish one beautiful idea before it was outshone by another, for surely Mozart was too prodigal with his melodic invention. Beethoven's economy, his expansion of fewer ideas, would bring him greater admiration than Mozart if Mozart's unri-valled integration of many ideas were not as impressive. That martial first theme of K467 might have been immediately developed by Beethoven; Mozart immediately follows it by others but frequently refers to it throughout the movement.

In a Mozartian rondo the prolific sequence of ideas is made more obvious by a design which presents and re-presents the main one as a whole 'tune' ending with a full close. Between its recurrences (if it is to be worthy of previous movements) subsidiary ideas and figurations, perhaps with 'bridges' formed by derivations from the main one, call for symphonic expansion, none the less admirable for a certain hilarity. (Tovey considered the hilarious finales to Haydn's sym-phonies and quartets to reveal his most brilliant command of form.) Mozart's finale can be likened to a visit to the fairground after leaving haunts of the dignified, then of the soulful. Liszt was not malicious when he rejoiced in Mozart's 'piano concertos for wind instruments and orchestra'. Among the wind instruments do we imagine a fairground organ?

© Arthur Hutchings

✎ Piano Concerto No. 22 in E flat major, K482 (1785–6)

1 Allegro
2 Andante
3 Allegro – Andante cantabile – Allegro

When Mozart began this aristocratic concerto in December 1785, he was entitled to be in a confident mood. Since his arrival in Vienna four years earlier, he had found the musical sophistication of the Imperial capital conducive both to his creativity and to his fortunes: he had married; his opera *Die Entführung aus dem Serail* had been a great success; and he had achieved fame and popularity with a series of piano concertos he had written for himself to play. Earlier that year, his father had visited him and reported home on his hectic lifestyle.

As 1785 neared its end, and with the composition of *The Marriage of Figaro* in progress, it seems unlikely that it could have occurred to Mozart that his fortunes would soon decline, for all that he had recently had to write the first of a series of letters to friends asking for money. Yet although the nine piano concertos he had already composed in Vienna represent part of one of the most important contributions made by a single composer to any musical genre, there is evidence to suggest that Viennese audiences were beginning to find his music to be 'over-composed', in the sense of being needlessly rich in melodic invention, chromatic and contrapuntal detail, and perhaps expressive weight as well. Whereas in the Lenten concert season of 1785 Mozart had given concerts virtually every night, the same period in 1786 would see him give only one.

K482 is certainly a rich work, both in melody and in orchestral colouring. The first movement contains a wealth of themes, some of which (including the one with which the piano makes its first entry) are heard only once; and although the opening rightly suggests that this will be a movement of great expansiveness, the ceremonial grandeur which it promises is often undermined, not least by the use for the first time in a Mozart concerto of mellow clarinets instead of bright oboes. A deepening understanding of wind scoring in general – and of the clarinet's liquid tones in particular – was another benefit of Mozart's move to Vienna; this work is just one of many to show how much he had begun to relish using the orchestra's wind section as an entity in itself – an intention signalled here from the very first bars.

Winds also feature prominently in the second movement, in which the intense C minor theme announced by the strings (with violins muted) is varied three times in combination with the piano. After each of the middle two variations, however, there is a contrasting episode, the first a serenade-like section for woodwind and horns, and the second a perky duet for flute and bassoon with string accompaniment. Whatever Mozart's audiences were beginning to find hard to take in the mid-1780s, it was clearly not pathos of this kind, for at the first performance of this concerto the slow movement was encored.

The finale is a rondo of the jaunty 'hunting' type whose seemingly uncontroversial and suave course is unexpectedly interrupted by an extended section in the style of a slow minuet. It is a trick that Mozart had played eight years earlier in another E flat Concerto, K271, and it is no less effective here in adding a soft extra layer to this most comfortably appointed of concertos.

© Lindsay Kemp

❧ Piano Concerto No. 23 in A major, K488
(1786)

1 Allegro
2 Adagio
3 Allegro assai

By the spring of 1786, Mozart's popularity with the Viennese public was about to begin its decline. The previous year he had performed in concerts virtually every night during the Lenten season, but now the same period saw him appearing only once. The feeling among listeners (some connoisseurs included) that Mozart's music was over-elaborate, even over-filled, was perhaps starting to kick in. For the fact is that even those works of Mozart's which seem most straightforward on the surface can hold surprising depths, or can leave us taken aback by sudden turns into new and totally different emotional worlds. Such changeability no doubt left some listeners feeling uncomfortable, although, of course, it is just this ability to encompass in one work so many facets of the human condition – and to do it with an unobtrusive ease amounting almost to subterfuge – that makes Mozart's concertos the ones we listen to today rather than those of Kozeluch, Hummel or even Haydn.

K488 was composed in March 1786, at the same time as Mozart was working on one of the most generous and humanly perceptive of all operatic masterpieces, *The Marriage of Figaro*, and whatever audiences thought of the concerto then, today it is one of his most frequently performed. It is not unreasonable to suppose that its popularity owes as much to the contrasting and complex emotions it invokes as to its undoubted and enduring attractiveness.

The first movement is amiable and gentle, a mood reinforced by a scoring which omits trumpets and drums and includes clarinets but not oboes. Pianistic brilliance, too, is rejected in favour of a lyrical landscape on which the sun frequently shines, but in which the occasional threat of clouds prevents things from spilling into exuberance; even the end of the movement is cheerful in a subdued sort of way.

It is the darker side, however, that emerges in the slow movement, although so magnified as to take us into the realms of heart-rending pathos. 'Adagio' is a relatively rare choice of tempo marking for Mozart; the selection of key, F sharp minor, is a unique one. Cast in the lilting dance rhythm of a *siciliana*, and with the anguished complaints of the piano seemingly incapable of consolation from the tender contributions of the orchestra, it is the kind of movement which only Mozart could have written.

It is the piano, however, which in an instant transforms the atmosphere in the opening notes of the finale, a bustling rondo which brings the work to an exhilarating close as if nothing had ever been wrong in the world. There is a story of how once, when Mozart was improvising in front of an audience he considered insufficiently attentive, he suddenly broke off, executed a few cartwheels, dived under the table and abruptly left. Such mercurial behaviour is never easier to imagine than when listening to this perfect, priceless concerto.

© Lindsay Kemp

✎ Piano Concerto No. 24 in C minor, K491 (1786)

1 Allegro
2 Larghetto
3 [Allegretto]

In the first part of 1786 Mozart's fortunes in Vienna appeared to change. As the year began, he was at the height of his popularity. Substantial quantities of his music were being advertised in the daily press, he had received a commission to compose the German opera *Der Schauspieldirektor* (The Impresario) and, an even more rewarding breakthrough, he was working on his first Italian opera for the court theatre, *The Marriage of Figaro*. As a pianist he was particularly well known, appearing regularly in public and private concerts: between February 1784 and March 1786 no fewer than eleven piano concertos were completed by the composer in readiness for these concerts. This unendingly resourceful series of works concluded with the Piano Concerto in C minor, which Mozart entered in his catalogue of compositions on 24 March 1786. Two weeks later, on 7 April, he gave a concert in the Burgtheater when, it is assumed, this new concerto was played for the first time.

Apart from the date and venue, nothing is known about this concert; there are no contemporary accounts and it is not mentioned in any extant letter by the composer. What is known is that this was the last concert that Mozart gave in Vienna's leading venue. Commentators on Mozart's life have always blamed the 'fickle Viennese' for the composer's change of fortune around this time, but this seems too easy, if not uncharitable. Was there something in the music that worried the public? The C minor Concerto provides some clues.

The idea of writing a concerto in the minor key was extremely unusual, going against the tradition (which Mozart had earlier fully exploited) that works in the genre should be outgoing and assertive, displaying the soloist to maximum advantage. Music in the minor key, as heard in opera and symphonies, was usually either poignant or flamboyantly aggressive. Both types are found in this concerto, but for the most part the minor key defies categorisation; there is an undermining uncertainty throughout.

The very opening is highly individual: *piano* dynamic, not forte, mannered phrasing, and an octave unison melody that within eleven bars contains all twelve notes of the chromatic scale; it is only the entry of the oboes that channels the music towards something approaching convention.

Thirteen months earlier Mozart had completed another concerto in the minor mode, K466 in D minor, in which the finale had moved towards D major. In K491, however, Mozart maintains the sound of the minor right through to the end of the concerto. The slow movement, a rondo, is in a contrasting E flat major, but the first episode (announced by oboes, bassoons and, later, flute) takes the listener back to C minor. In the finale, a set of variations, the sound of C major is allowed only one appearance – in the fifth variation, led by solo oboe – before the music returns remorselessly to the minor.

Minor-key music in the classical period had always featured a richer harmonic language than music in the major key, often using well-worn turns of phrase. Mozart, too, used such clichés in order to provide coherence, but – crucially – he also used the same harmonies in unconventional ways and in highly concentrated dosages. To adopt a rather crass analogy with cooking, the ingredients are the same but the quantities and the recipe are highly individual. The tutti that follows the opening theme contains enough chromatic writing to last Gluck an entire opera, and the theme of the finale owes much of its effect to the unstable harmony that initiates the penultimate phrase of each section (second inversion, rather than the usual first inversion).

Mozart's operas were often criticised for the over-richness of their instrumental writing. The same might well have been said of this concerto. It has the largest orchestra ever used by Mozart in a concerto: one flute, two oboes, two clarinets, two bassoons, two horns, two trumpets, timpani and strings. The power of these instruments is to be felt in the tutti section, their eloquence in the many passages of dialogue between the piano and solo wind, and their depth of colour in the slow movement, which is almost a concerto for piano and wind band, an indoor serenade.

The use of the minor key and the wealth of the harmonic language and instrumentation are, as always in a mature piano concerto by Mozart, supported by unending lyrical inspiration and resourceful keyboard writing. Were the Viennese fickle, or was it genuine stupefaction?

© David Wyn Jones

❧ Piano Concerto No. 25 in C major, K503 (1786)

1   Allegro maestoso
2   Andante
3   Allegretto

In the last decade of his life Mozart composed seventeen concertos for the piano, Nos 11–27 in the familiar numbering. Of these, twelve (Nos 14–25) were written in a particularly concentrated period of two years from 1784 to 1786. It was during this period that Mozart's popularity in Vienna as a pianist and composer was at its height; the C major concerto, the last in this marvellous creative burst, was completed in December 1786. The date of its first performance is not known, but it is thought to have been played at one of the four subscription concerts that Mozart is believed to have held during Advent that year.

For the next twenty years or so it was one of the most frequently performed of all Mozart's concertos, played by Mozart himself, his son Franz Xaver, his pupil Johann Nepomuk Hummel and possibly by the young Beethoven. Part of its appeal, no doubt, lay in its assertive stance, as in the opening gesture, derived from the long Austrian tradition of bright C major orchestral music distinctively coloured by trumpets and timpani. But into this most public of keys and sonorities Mozart injects an individuality of harmonic colour and thematic argument that ensures that the concerto is one of the most sophisticated that the composer ever wrote.

The work's sophistication surfaces within a few seconds, as the grand opening subsides to a *piano* dynamic and bassoons and oboes utter a quiet call; the full orchestra reasserts itself, but this time the woodwind call deflects the music to the minor and to a passage of intricate thematic writing. The grandeur, pathos, argument and brilliance of these opening bars are later joined by lyricism and, as soon as the pianist enters, virtuosity and a constantly varying relationship between soloist and orchestra. The sheer range of expression is unmatched in any concerto first movement by Mozart; the ease with which it is guided and controlled is astonishing.

1786, the year of this concerto, was also the year in which *The Marriage of Figaro* received its premiere in Vienna. The close stylistic link between the opera and this concerto is apparent in the slow movement. The orchestra, with prominent woodwind writing, sets the scene for the disconsolate prima donna, who gradually draws the audience into her confidence; but no prima donna could match the range and agility of the decoration found in Mozart's piano writing.

If in the slow movement one begins to imagine the presence of the opera's Countess, then in the last movement it is Figaro who comes on stage, buoyant, confident, and with any momentary doubts soon forgotten. Like most of the finales of Mozart's mature piano concertos, this movement is a sonata-rondo, a main theme alternating with contrasting sections, the first of which is later repeated. Most of the thematic writing is allocated to the orchestra, with the piano providing a bravura display of boundless vitality. Having already demonstrated a matchless mastery of composition, Mozart now dazzlingly vanquishes all rival performers.

© David Wyn Jones

ꙮ Piano Concerto No. 27 in B flat major, K595 (1788–91)

1 Allegro
2 Larghetto
3 Allegro

The special position this concerto holds in the affections of Mozart-lovers has owed much to the notion that, written in the composer's last year (Mozart entered it in his thematic catalogue of works on 5 January 1791), it expresses the resignation and weariness of spirit which had overtaken him after two years of dwindling success and reduced productivity. And it cannot be denied that such an interpretation suits this gentle work, in which the ebullient virtuosity and extrovert gestures that had characterised the great piano concertos of the mid-1780s are rejected in favour of an altogether more personal species of utterance, as if Mozart had tired of the rat race of public display.

Modern research into the composer's manuscript paper – and in particular its watermarks – has forced us to modify this view of the work, for it now appears that it was drafted in incomplete score as early as 1788. No doubt Mozart shelved it when the prospect of a performance vanished (it could have been intended for the same projected subscription series that possibly prompted his previous concerto – the 'Coronation' – and the three last symphonies). His return to it at the start of 1791 may well have been in response to the need for a work to play at a benefit concert for the clarinettist Joseph Bähr on 4 March.

This is not to diminish K595, however. If its wistful lyricism can no longer be slotted quite so conveniently into the chronological details of Mozart's life – if it is no longer the 'work of farewell' that Alfred Einstein dubbed it – then its purely musical value as a composition of noble and restrained beauty remains for all to hear.

Like the G minor symphony (No. 40), this concerto opens with a bar of accompaniment before the first theme appears, a wistful violin melody which sets the mood for the rest of the movement. This is a world away from the outgoing style of the concertos of the mid-1780s, and it is surely significant that the military woodwind figure which punctuates this theme with a rhythm so characteristic of Mozart's concertos is now a tired shadow of its proud former self. As the opening orchestral section continues, a feeling of longing persists, helped by the music's frequent turns to the minor, and the atmosphere is hardly changed at the entry of the soloist, where, instead of an operatic opposition of themes, we find the piano coming in with an uncontroversial restatement of the first theme; thereafter it is content to take over the material of the orchestral exposition and contribute only one significant theme of its own, an agonised passage inserted between the first and second themes. The central development section, for all its restless modulations, perpetuates such fatalism with its surface smoothness and ease of arrival at the moment of reprise, and the movement closes in the same quiet vein in which it had started.

The resigned and unargumentative mood of this first movement carries over into the second, an E flat Larghetto in ABA form. As in the Allegro, soloist and orchestra are here very much in thematic and spiritual accord, with the other instruments providing unquestioning support for the piano's quiet complaints, offering sympathy and the occasional outburst of consolatory warmth. At the coda, it is hard to disagree with Cuthbert Girdlestone's suggestion that 'the flute and first violins seem, gracefully but firmly, to be leading the piano off the stage'. This is music whose elegant simplicity of expression easily matches that of the more celebrated slow movement of the C major Concerto, K467.

The final rondo brings something, at least, of the brilliance of Mozart's earlier concertos, but if its playful demeanour suggests that the composer has turned his back on the sadnesses of the preceding movements, a continued flirtation with the minor mode and an insistent preoccupation with the least stable part of the principal theme are enough to remind us of less complacent emotions. The resulting, faintly nostalgic feel makes this movement a fitting close to a work in which, perhaps, we can after all hear Mozart recalling happier days.

© Lindsay Kemp

∾ Violin Concerto No. 4 in D major, K218
(1775)

1 Allegro
2 Andante cantabile
3 Rondeau: Andante grazioso – Allegro non troppo

Mozart's output of violin concertos is disappointingly small. Five works seems like pretty short measure from a composer whose twenty-seven concertos for piano constitute one of the most important contributions ever made to a single genre, while the frustration of violinists is increased by the fact that all five are relatively early works dating from the mid–1770s.

The shortage is surprising when one considers Mozart's musical background and upbringing. His father Leopold was the author of one of the eighteenth century's most influential and trenchant treatises on violin playing (published in 1756, the year of Wolfgang Amadeus's birth) and accounts of the boy composer's triumphs as a performer throughout Europe suggest that, at that stage at least, he was equally proficient on the violin as at the keyboard. 1769 saw his appointment – while still only thirteen – to the post of Konzertmeister of the Archbishop of Salzburg's court orchestra, and in the years that followed Wolfgang's letters to his father contained a number of reports of his successes as a violinist. 'I performed a symphony and played Vanhal's Violin Concerto in B flat, which was unanimously applauded,' he wrote from Augsburg in October 1777. Leopold's own rating of his son's ability was also high, and in the opinion of Antonio Brunetti, Mozart's successor at the head of the Salzburg orchestra, Mozart 'could play anything'.

Even so, it is not known for what precise purpose, or for whom, Mozart composed the five concertos, still less why four of them should all date from the same year, 1775. (The first concerto, K207 in B flat, previously thought to be contemporary with the others, is now known to have been written in 1773.) There is no apparent objection to the view that Mozart composed these works with the intention of performing them himself, though there seems to have been no particular occasion for them and there is no actual evidence, any more than there is for the promising theory that they were written for Brunetti, an accomplished violinist for whom Mozart is known to have later composed some isolated concerto movements (including substitutes for some of the movements in these concertos).

Whatever the truth of the matter, it is interesting that the style of solo writing in the violin concertos is significantly different from that of the highly virtuosic concertante movements which Mozart included in a number of orchestral serenades composed at about the same time, works which we know he also performed. In the concertos – and especially in the last three – the accent is not on technical brilliance but on lyricism, on an eloquent, personal expressiveness which we now recognise as truly Mozartian, but which in 1775 signalled a new stage in the composer's maturity. At the same time these works demonstrate for the first time some of the expertise in the manipulation of concerto form, in the balancing of solo and orchestral passages and in the imaginative and flexible ordering of thematic material, which were later to contribute to the greatness of the piano concertos.

The D major Concerto, K218, ably demonstrates the nineteen-year-old Mozart's new-found strengths. Its themes are lean and muscular, and the organisation of their presentation and return is handled with great skill. The first movement's opening fanfare, for example, returns to inaugurate the first solo, transformed by its reappearance in a high register (a feature of this work) into a lyrical statement; but it is then omitted from later sections of the movement and the recapitulation, which starts instead with one of the new themes that the violin had introduced earlier.

The radiant Andante cantabile second movement is a relatively simple structure, but even here there is subtle attention to formal detail, with the orchestra keeping one tiny thematic element to itself for the two tutti passages that frame the movement.

The finale is more diffuse, but in spite of its rondo theme's juxtaposition of 2/4 Andante and 6/8 Allegro – as well as its introduction of an eccentric bagpipe-like episode – it still manages to maintain coherence through deft manipulation of the listener's expectations.

© Lindsay Kemp

∾ Violin Concerto No. 5 in A major, K219 (1775)

1   Allegro aperto
2   Adagio
3   Rondeau: Tempo di Menuetto

As a child prodigy and as an adult, Mozart's solo performances were primarily as a pianist, and most of his twenty-seven concertos for the instrument were written to display his own talents. But Mozart was also a very proficient violinist, who, during the 1770s, practised and played that instrument as frequently as he did the piano.

This concentration of interest at this period was encouraged by several factors. Wolfgang's father, Leopold, was one of the most respected violin teachers of the time, who, in the year of Mozart's birth, had published the influential *Treatise on the Fundamental Principles of Violin Playing*; he naturally encouraged his son's aptitude. Three journeys to Italy had exposed Wolfgang to some of the leading violinists of the day, so that Leopold's solid training was complemented by experience of Italian flair, while in Salzburg orchestral works such as serenades and cassations, played at weddings and other social occasions, often included several concerto-like movements for the violin. Mozart's interest in violin playing reached its peak in 1775, when he composed four of his five concertos for the instrument. The A major is the last, the autograph carrying the following inscription: 'Concerto di

Violino. Di Wolfgango Amadeo Mozart Salisburgo li 20 di decembre 1775'.

The tempo heading of the first movement, 'Allegro aperto' (an 'open' allegro) is one favoured by Mozart at the time, implying frankness and vigour in equal part. Following the tuneful orchestral ritornello, the soloist enters not with a statement of the principal theme, as would have been the normal practice, but with a complete change of tempo and mood, before embarking on the main business of the movement. The return to the 'aperto' music demonstrates Mozart's authority as a player, lyrical writing in a high register contrasting with rhythmic writing that descends to the lowest register of the instrument.

The lyricism of the Adagio movement is less theatrical, probing a single mood with beautifully controlled decorative writing for the soloists. Contemporaries seem to have regarded this movement as rather difficult listening, to judge from the response of Antonio Brunetti, a violinist at the Salzburg court; he persuaded Mozart to provide a substitute movement (K261) on the grounds that the original was 'too studied'.

The last movement is a Rondeau: a sectional structure alternating a main theme (a formal minuet, but with a delightful spry ending, almost an afterthought) with contrasting episodes. Of the four episodes the most vivid is the third, a 'Turkish' interlude evoking the janissary bands of the Sultan's army, but diminishing their menace with exaggerated comedy.

© David Wyn Jones

↬ Sinfonia concertante in E flat major, K364 (1779)

1   Allegro maestoso
2   Andante
3   Presto

The title 'Sinfonia concertante' was commonly applied in the late eighteenth century to a hybrid type of composition, usually a sort of lightweight symphony or divertimento with important solo parts for two or more instruments; but whatever Mozart's contemporaries might have understood by the term, there is nothing lightweight or hybrid about the present work. It is a full-scale concerto for violin and viola – indeed the only significant concerto ever written for this combination – and an outstanding landmark in Mozart's development.

The work was composed some time in the late summer or early autumn of 1779. In January Mozart had returned to Salzburg from a sixteen-month tour which, far from being the triumph anticipated by himself and his family, had been soured by professional failure and the death of his mother in Paris, and by the rejection of his love by Aloysia Weber in Munich. Mozart was now nursing the wounds to his self-esteem, and fretting at the limitations of a provincial environment which gave him too few opportunities to show what he was capable of.

We do not know of any particular occasion for which the Sinfonia concertante might have been composed, nor for whom it was written (although Mozart, an excellent player of both violin and viola, would presumably have played one of the solo parts). Neither is there documentary evidence of any performance, in Salzburg or elsewhere. The piece was only published eleven years after Mozart's death, and the manuscript has disappeared.

Even if the precise date of composition is unknown, we do know that this was a period during which Mozart showed great interest in the idea of concertos for more than one soloist. In Paris in 1778 he had written a concerto for four wind instruments, and later that year had begun a concerto for piano and violin. From early in 1779 comes the Concerto in E flat for two pianos, and from around the period of the Sinfonia concertante there is a tantalising 134-bar fragment of a triple concerto for violin, viola and cello.

The main problem in writing a double concerto for two different instruments is that of balancing the soloists. The violin and viola, though closely related, have very different acoustic characters. This is chiefly because the viola, though pitched only a fifth lower than the violin, would have to be unmanageably large if the length and tension of its strings were to allow it to match the brilliance and penetration of the violin. A pairing of violin and viola will naturally favour the violin, casting its softer-toned and less agile partner into a secondary role.

Mozart's solution to the problem was to write the viola part in D major, and then instruct the viola player to tune the strings of his instrument a semitone higher so that it actually sounds in E flat. This favours the viola in three ways: by increasing the tension of the strings, the viola speaks more penetratingly; D major is a more grateful key for the viola to play in, both technically and acoustically; and so, correspondingly, the violin is slightly handicapped by playing in the less brilliant and technically more difficult key of E flat (there are no great violin concertos in this key).

The first appearance of the soloists, emerging magically from out of the orchestra's cadential figures with a high, held E flat, is one of the great dramatic solo entries in Mozart. It is also the only passage in the work (apart from the corresponding moment in the recapitulation) where the violin and viola play together in octaves; generally when they are paired together it is in thirds, sixths or tenths. Throughout the Sinfonia concertante, however, the solo passages consist mainly of alternations, varied imitations and exchanges of phrases, one instrument picking up the discourse where the other leaves off. It is a continuously evolving dialogue which exploits the differences between the instruments while transcending them in a relationship of perfect sympathy and understanding.

Mozart's style of orchestration remains for many musicians the most satisfying ever conceived for its economy, richness and subtlety, and this is nowhere more evident than in this Sinfonia concertante. There are pairs of oboes and horns – both used with consummate imagination, either as soloists within the orchestra, or to colour and point phrases – and strings. Unusually, and to wonderful effect, Mozart divides not only the violins but also the violas into two sections, thus adding to the harmonic richness of the orchestra's middle register and also supporting the lower register of the solo viola from within the orchestra.

In his travels throughout Europe Mozart had absorbed every orchestral style then to be heard. Assimilating and refining what he needed, he not only came to understand everything about the capabilities of instruments, but also became a supreme master of the art of accompaniment. This is particularly evident in the Andante, where the orchestra frames a duet between violin and viola which reaches heights of expression that the twenty-three-year-old composer had hitherto rarely approached. The key is C minor, always a key of deep seriousness for Mozart. The impassioned solo lines unfold with vocal eloquence against a veiled orchestral background whose grave beauty anticipates the world of his opera *Idomeneo*, composed the following year.

The orchestra plays a more brilliant role in the outer movements. The opening Allegro maestoso contains a wealth of colour and melody, one inspired idea following another with prodigal invention. As so often in the mature Mozart, however, brilliance is tempered by a frequent tendency towards the minor mode. Particularly notable is the use made of orchestral techniques recently developed by the composers of the Mannheim school: subtle dynamic accents, offbeat pizzicatos, syncopations, trills and crescendos.

Many of these features recur in the finale – for example, the frequent horn and oboe calls. But the movement is shorter, in a quicker tempo and, in the nature of a Mozart finale, more straightforward in form. The minor mode is avoided throughout – quite pointedly in one passage, where the orchestra veers back towards the C minor of the Andante only to be turned aside by the viola with an unexpected entry in A at major. The finale is the only movement in which there is no cadenza for the soloists: perhaps Mozart thought that they had enough opportunity to display their virtuosity without one, particularly as towards the end of the movement first the viola and then the violin are taken up to astonishing heights before the closing tutti.

© Andrew Huth

Francis Poulenc (1899–1963)

Poulenc's first published work, the vocal/ensemble piece *Rapsodie nègre* (1917) established his place in chic avant-garde Parisian circles: there he had met Satie and was drawn into the group that became known as Les Six. After three years' study (1921–4) with Charles Koechlin he scored further success with his Diaghilev ballet *Les biches* (1924). Poulenc's urbane wit triumphed in the *Concert champêtre* (1927–8; a harpsichord concerto written for Wanda Landowska), and the Concerto for Two Pianos (1932). Later in the 1930s, the death of a friend and a visit to the shrine of Notre Dame de Rocamadour inspired a return to Catholicism; the *Litanies à la vierge noire* (1936), Mass (1937) and *Quatre motets pour un temps de pénitence* (1938) followed in close succession. For the rest of Poulenc's life devoutness and ironic wit formed characteristic strands in his work, exemplified by his two full-scale operas, the surreal comedy *Les mamelles de Tirésias* (1939–44) and the religious tragedy *Dialogues des Carmélites* (1953–6). His songs were largely written for the baritone Pierre Bernac, with whom Poulenc collaborated as pianist until the end of his life.

❧ Concerto for Organ, Strings and Timpani in G minor (1938)

> Andante – Allegro giocoso – Andante moderato – Tempo allegro, molto agitato – Très calme, lent – Tempo de l'Allegro initial – Tempo de l'introduction, Largo

Poulenc, never a man for modesty, was proud of his Organ Concerto, dubbing it his 'bestseller'. For several reasons, it's curious that it ever became so famous. First of all, Poulenc was no organist, nor had he much credibility among organ buffs before its composition. Secondly, his allegiances could hardly have been further from the organ loft. As a rebellious teenager trying to get into the Paris Conservatoire, he'd proffered his *Rapsodie nègre*, a delicious oriental spoof, and been threatened with a 'kick in the balls' if he ever darkened their doors again. Satie wrote to console him and he became a paid-up member of Les Six, that group of composers aiming to overthrow the pretensions of Romanticism and Impressionism and simply entertain. He spent the 1920s worshipping Stravinsky, composing the first of many songs and riding on the crest of a wave of ballet-mania.

In the 1930s he underwent a reconversion to Catholicism which brought a change of tone to his music. The death of a fellow composer in a car crash affected him deeply, as did a visit to the extraordinary hillside church at Rocamadour in south-west France. The immediate result was the beautifully simple *Litanies à la vierge noire* of 1936, a piece for female (or children's) voices and organ. Sharing the G minor key of the Organ Concerto of two years later, the two pieces were connected in the composer's mind, not least because he was nervous about his organ-writing, seeking help from Nadia Boulanger.

'This is not the amusing Poulenc,' he wrote to the Princesse Edmond de Polignac, who had commissioned the concerto, 'but rather Poulenc on his way to the cloister, a fifteenth-century Poulenc, if you like.' The piece springs from a similar creative impulse to the Mass in G of 1937: a side of the composer's output that culminated in the *Gloria* of 1959, not to mention his one tragic opera, *Dialogues des Carmélites* (1953–6). Smaller but no less beautiful by-products of a similar vein are the many *a cappella* motets that have established themselves in the repertoire of accomplished church choirs worldwide.

This change of spirit of the late 1930s could be characterised as a new humility after the swagger of the Les Six years. The concerto delights in the full resources of the French *grand orgue*. Inevitably the first chords recall the G minor Fantasia of Bach, and subsequently the piece plunders the Baroque for many of its ideas: ornamental lines, upbeat figures, zigzag fugal ideas and a free, fantasia-like form. Elsewhere effects depend upon the wonderful string effects of the French Romantic organ. The addition of timpani was a masterstroke. Sometimes complementing the almost terrifying power of the full organ, at others they seem to add a heartbeat to prayer. Maurice Duruflé was the first organ soloist when the piece was premiered at the Salle Gaveau in Paris in 1939.

© Richard Langham Smith

∾ Concerto for Two Pianos (1932)

1   Allegro ma non troppo
2   Larghetto
3   Finale: Allegro molto

One of Poulenc's most endearing, accomplished and risqué works, the two-piano concerto had its first performance in 1932 at, of all places, the festival of the International Society for Contemporary Music. Today this concerto would never get through the selection panels; back then, all the great names of the time had a hearing, whether they were Stravinsky or Vaughan Williams. Or Poulenc, who reported after the event (held that year in Venice) that the concerto 'did in fact stun everyone. You will see for yourself,' he wrote to the Belgian musician and promoter Paul Collaer, 'what an enormous step forward it is from my previous work and that I am really entering my great period.'

There is a certain tragic irony in those words. Four years later, with the sudden death of a close friend in a car crash, Poulenc was stunned into a revival of his dormant Catholicism and a new depth of expression that began a further, greater period. As far as the Poulenc of young maturity goes, however, the concerto remains definitive. Poulenc dedicated it to the Princesse Edmond de Polignac, otherwise

Winnaretta Singer, the sewing-machine heiress and a famous patron of young French composers. He and his duo colleague Jacques Février were the first soloists. In subsequent years the music has had some illustrious revivals: twice in London by Poulenc and Benjamin Britten; then by the American duo of Arthur Gold and Robert Fizdale, who recorded it with Leonard Bernstein conducting; memorably at the Proms by Imogen Cooper and Anne Queffélec in the Eighties, and Katia and Marielle Labèque in 1995.

Do not be misled by the violent opening – more about which below. Very soon the pianists start to leap around chromatically and toss thumping chords and pseudo-Baroque bass-lines back and forth. Castanets click, the woodwind play perky tunes. Typically there is a slower, sadder interlude before the gaiety resumes. But it's the slow movement proper that takes the prize for effrontery, a series of poker-faced, totally outrageous cribs from well-known Mozart piano concertos – including the slow movement of K467, once popularised by the film *Elvira Madigan*, kitted out with extra swoons and wonky harmonies, yet still touching in its own right. Post-modern irony was not Poulenc's game, but the music has come to sound ahead of its time. The finale resumes a state of general frolic. Again typically, it turns slightly sour later, as though in devastation that the good times have to come to an end.

And the concerto's opening? Unexpectedly, it gives an insight into the way real (as opposed to textbook) musical history works. Its distinctive sound is based on a Balinese gamelan scale – just as a number of Debussy's pieces had evoked a Javanese gamelan – and was similarly inspired by the appearance of a visiting group at a Paris exhibition. The concerto returns to Bali at a few other points, particularly the end of the first movement, without making much fuss about the matter. But it would have been noticed immediately by Britten. His performances of the work in 1945 and 1955 predate his own ballet *The Prince of the Pagodas*, which includes some elaborate gamelan pastiche. Britten had already heard Indonesian music, and even recorded piano-duet arrangements of it with the Canadian-born composer Colin McPhee, but there's nothing like a memory jog.

The repercussions went further. Britten was, of course, to return to the sound to invoke the allure of the beautiful boy Tadzio in the beach games of his last opera, *Death in Venice* (1971–3). Following these links, some American composers now use gamelan references as a kind of coded gay message. So, without any conscious intention, thanks to a detail as casual as the castanets, this concerto takes on an iconic meaning beyond its composer's dreams, but surely close to its spirit.

© Robert Maycock

Sergey Prokofiev (1891–1953)

An *enfant terrible* in his earlier years, Prokofiev entered the St Petersburg Conservatory aged thirteen, creating a stir with his early taste for rhythmic energy and grating dissonance. A rich period around the time of the Revolution brought the lyrical First Violin Concerto and the 'Classical' Symphony, before a spell in the USA, where his ballet *The Love for Three Oranges* and the Third Piano Concerto were badly received. He went on to Paris, drawn to the epicentre of the avant-garde, before moving his family to the USSR in 1936. Adopting a more direct, lyrical style in line with prevailing socialist-realist ideals, he produced the ballet *Romeo and Juliet* and the children's tale *Peter and the Wolf* (both 1936), the film music for Eisenstein's *Alexander Nevsky* (1938) and *Ivan the Terrible* (1945), and the epic opera based on Tolstoy's *War and Peace* (1943). Despite his compliant efforts, Prokofiev was denounced by Communist officials in 1948 ('the unfeeling essence of his music is alien to our reality'), though he had managed to placate them by 1951, when he won the Stalin Prize.

∾ Piano Concerto No. 1 in D flat major, Op. 10 (1911–12)

Allegro brioso – Andante assai – Allegro scherzando

The songwriter Vernon Duke (né Vladimir Dukelsky) remembered being taken to hear Prokofiev play his First Piano Concerto in 1914, some two years after its first performance, also given by the composer when he was still only twenty-one. This was combative stuff, 'young man's music', like 'the onrushing forwards in my one unfortunate soccer experience – nothing but unrelenting energy and athletic joy of living. No wonder the first four notes of the concerto, oft-repeated, were later nicknamed *po cherepoo* (hit on the head), which was Prokofiev's exact intention.'

Quite apart from its exuberance, which marks it out at once as 'young man's music', the concerto is much more individual in point of style than the student works Prokofiev had had performed in July 1911. These included the symphonic poems *Dreams* ('rather limp' according to the composer) and the Rakhmaninov-derived *Autumnal* (excessively 'pensive and sombre'). A contemporaneous opera, *Maddalena*, had to wait until 1979 for a first performance, given on BBC Radio 3 under the direction of Edward Downes (who orchestrated most of the score).

Prokofiev was on surer ground with the First Piano Concerto. He had been among the very first to discover the percussive use of the piano and, as one of its more precocious technicians, was able to exploit these stylistic possibilities while not yet out of his teens. Without being as iconoclastic as Schoenberg – some of whose piano music he introduced to sceptical Russian audiences in this period – Prokofiev could lay claim to a unique place in modern keyboard literature, pre-empting even Bartók with the innovative savagery of his *Suggestion diabolique* in 1908. Nevertheless, it was the Piano Concerto No. 1 which marked the crucial step forward into larger musical forms and forces: 'my first more or less mature composition as regards the conception and its fulfilment,' said Prokofiev.

Trenchant, witty and precise, the work condenses the traditional three movements into a continuous (if episodic) structure. Prokofiev saw it as a modified sonata design: 'a sonata allegro with the introduction repeated after the exposition and again at the end, and with a short andante before the development, the development taking the form of a scherzo and cadenza introducing the recapitulation'. Thus the obstinately memorable introductory theme functions as a kind of ritornello, returning to round off the piece with terrific aplomb.

The central Andante assai, by contrast, reveals a continuing debt to Rakhmaninov, although the tone is somehow fresher, more 'objective'. Already we have Prokofiev feeling for his own brand of neo-classicism – that combination of intense vitality and simple lyricism which conveys a nostalgia for tradition in peculiarly twentieth-century fashion, and is finally a reinterpretation of that tradition.

Taken as a whole, the concerto gives us a good idea of the strengths of Prokofiev's own performing style, alternating the massive texture of chords and octaves with giddy acrobatic leaps and softer-grained, étude-like runs. For Francis Poulenc, a great friend of the composer during his years abroad, the concerto placed its author among the ranks of the musically great, as surely as the First Concerto of Beethoven prefigured *his* mature work. This may be overstating the case. But the concerto seldom fails to impress an audience head-butted by those opening bars.

© David Gutman

∾ Piano Concerto No. 2 in G minor, Op. 16 (1913; rev. 1923)

1 Andantino
2 Scherzo: Vivace
3 Intermezzo: Allegro moderato
4 Finale: Allegro tempestoso

The rather stuffy musical world of St Petersburg was startled when it heard Prokofiev's First Piano Concerto in July 1912, the same year as Vladimir Mayakovsky's Futurist manifesto *A Slap in the Face of Public Taste*. Conservative musicians felt that Prokofiev, too, was slapping the public's face. The young composer certainly enjoyed being naughty, but sympathetic listeners also appreciated his tremendous vitality, his strong lyrical impulse and rare prodigality of ideas.

With the Second Piano Concerto, composed during the following year, Prokofiev clearly wanted to expand on the achievements of the First, both in style and in dimensions. In the summer of 1913 he went on a European holiday with his mother, practising the new concerto whenever possible, and confessing that it 'has turned out to be incredibly difficult and mercilessly tiring'. He gave the first performance on 23 August 1913 at a concert in the grounds of the eighteenth-century palace of Pavlovsk near St Petersburg. The audience was expecting soothing entertainment for a summer evening, and was unpleasantly shaken by what it heard.

When Prokofiev abandoned Russia for America in 1918 the orchestral score of the concerto was left behind, and in 1923 he learned that it had been destroyed – apparently the new tenants in his apartment had burned it 'to cook an omelette' – probably not thoughtless vandalism, but evidence of the terrible conditions in Petrograd during the Civil War, when people were dying of cold and hunger. Prokofiev reconstructed the orchestral score and took the opportunity to revise the whole concerto. In this new form, he introduced it in Paris on 8 May 1924. The conductor was Serge Koussevitzky, a great champion of his music, both as conductor and publisher.

Prokofiev himself admitted that the Second Concerto was 'more interesting for the soloist, less for the orchestra' than the First. By 'interesting', perhaps he meant difficult – its length alone requires great stamina, and the piano writing is as demanding as anything in the repertory. Prokofiev had absorbed the virtuoso techniques of Rakhmaninov and Skryabin (though he soon outgrew the influence of their musical styles) and to these he added his own brilliant, sharp-edged virtuosity, marked by a keen dramatic contrast between lyrical and percussive styles.

The sequence of movements is highly unusual. The first is only moderately paced. It is followed by the quick, short scherzo, a moto perpetuo where the soloist's left and right hands scamper away in semiquavers, in octaves throughout, without a single moment's rest. The third movement is a sort of brutal march, though leavened by lyricism from the soloist. There is a foreshadowing of Prokofiev's mechanistic music of the 1920s here, and this was probably the movement that caused most offence at the concerto's premiere. The Finale, after a big piano-and-orchestra flourish, launches into a percussive, leaping texture for piano. But in the centre of the movement there appears a theme which is very Russian in its limited compass and repeated phrases – an acknowledgement of the tradition which is the backbone of Prokofiev's art.

© Andrew Huth

Piano Concerto No. 3 in C major (1917–21)

1 Andante – Allegro
2 Theme and Variations
3 Allegro, ma non troppo

Prokofiev spent the summer of 1921 on the French Channel coast. He was entering the fourth year of his self-imposed exile from Soviet Russia in upbeat mood. His ballet *Chout* (or *The Buffoon*) had been the novelty of Diaghilev's Ballets Russes season in Paris, and had also created a minor scandal in London. Now he could resume work on something strictly for himself – a third piano concerto.

Prokofiev was one of the few composers of recent times to write really extensively for the piano. As far as the piano concertos are concerned, he might be said to present certain parallels with Beethoven. Both completed five such works in the earlier part of their careers. Both ceased writing in the medium once they had given up playing on the concert platform, while continuing to produce sonatas for the instrument. Prokofiev's compositional approach was, of course, very different. Like Beethoven, he kept a notebook close to hand, jotting down ideas as they occurred to him (all his life he hated to let a good tune go to waste); but in symphonic writing, good lyrical invention takes second place to the creation of material designed to generate further musical development. For many years Prokofiev had had to be something of an illusionist in this respect: his own structural method had more to do with the skilful joining of disparate ideas, reinforcing the familiar tendency to 'step on the throat of his own song', to counter lyricism with irony.

The Third Piano Concerto is an excellent example of this practice – one which, unlike, say, the Fourth Symphony (stitched together from the music for the ballet *The Prodigal Son*), belies its patchwork origins. The passage of parallel ascending triads towards the end of the first movement was actually composed as far back as 1911 during work on the First Piano Concerto. The sharp-witted idea on which the second movement is based dates from 1913. The beginning of the whole work (two themes) followed in 1916–17, while the first and second themes of the finale stem from a string quartet Prokofiev sweated over in St Petersburg, Japan and America without managing to finish. 'Thus, when I began working,' said Prokofiev, 'I already had the entire thematic material with the exception of the subordinate theme of the first movement and the third theme of the finale.' The result was in fact a conventional three-movement design.

First performed in Chicago on 16 December 1921, with Prokofiev as soloist and Frederick Stock conducting, the Third Piano Concerto quickly achieved international acceptance and has remained one of the composer's most popular scores. Certainly it must be considered the most successful of his five piano concertos. Its solo part bristles with the customary pianistic innovations, but this time the orchestra emerges as an active and responsive partner.

The first movement is a compressed sonata form, vital and lucid, in which the nostalgic Russian-ness of the opening clarinet theme is confined thereafter to the dreamy central episode which replaces the usual development.

The second movement is a sparkling theme with five variations. Prokofiev has particular fun with a repeated plagal cadence here. The classical cadence is always important in his style: he uses it as a (not invariably ironic) point of reference, a local articulation to clarify the constant side-slips into alien keys. In the coda, the original theme returns in orchestral dress, gently guyed by the clipped staccato chords of the piano. Prokofiev's orchestration maintains an acute sense of balance and imaginative texture throughout.

As for the finale, its combination of bracing dynamism and soft-centred lyricism can hardly fail. The 'big tune' at its heart is certainly ripe, but this gives way to a clangorous restatement of the opening material which generates enormous cumulative tension – not least for the soloist! As Hugh Ottaway has remarked, the concerto 'accommodates nearly all the Prokofievs we have ever known'.

Prokofiev dedicated his Third Piano Concerto to the émigré poet Konstantin Balmont, who returned the compliment in the form of a sonnet:

An exultant flame of a crimson flower,
A verbal keyboard sparkling with flames
That suddenly leap forth in fiery tongues.
A raging stream of molten ore.
The moments dance a waltz, the ages a gavotte.
Suddenly a wild bull, startled by foes,
Bursts his chains, halts, his horns poised to strike.
But once again the tender sounds call from afar.
From tiny shells children fashion a castle.
An opaline balcony, beautiful, finely wrought.
But all is dashed by a foaming wave.
Prokofiev! Music and youth in bloom,
In you the orchestra yearns for summer's ecstasies
And the indomitable Scyth strikes the tambourine-sun.

© David Gutman

∾ Violin Concerto No. 1 in D major, Op. 19 (1916–17)

1   Andantino – Andante assai
2   Scherzo: Vivacissimo
3   Finale: Moderato – Allegro moderato – Moderato –
    Più tranquillo

The year 1917 was perhaps the most productive in Sergey Prokofiev's career. Revolutionary turmoil notwithstanding, he made a start on a new opera, *The Love for Three Oranges*, resumed work on a new (third) piano concerto, and completed a whole series of disparate compositions, including the Third and Fourth Piano Sonatas, the 'Chaldean invocation' *Seven, They Are Seven*, the set of *Visions fugitives* and the 'Classical' Symphony. Also among these works was a Violin Concerto in D major that had begun life as a modest *Concertino* in 1915. As so often, his work in this period can seem like a perpetual zigzag between incompatible means and conflicting goals. The aggressive innovator, who delighted to offend, was also a traditionalist who hankered after simpler, clearer melodies, especially when writing away from the demands of the concert platform and the clamour of city life.

Music decidedly out of sync with the spirit of the age, the concerto was not an immediate success at its belated premiere in Paris on 18 October 1923. Its peerless lucidity was found insufficiently novel, though Igor Stravinsky, whose Octet was on the same programme, had a soft spot for it, perhaps precisely because of this 'disconnected' quality. Other commentators were more inclined to sneer: Georges Auric chided the composer for traces of artificiality and 'Mendelssohnism'. Not until the piece was taken up by Joseph Szigeti did it begin to win the fame it deserved – his many performances included one at the 1946 Proms. Subsequently, it was closely associated with David Oistrakh. Today, the First Violin Concerto is core repertoire and, on purely musical grounds, may be regarded as superior to the five concertos Prokofiev composed for his own instrument, the piano.

Lyrical and virtuoso qualities apart, the score is remarkable for an expressive character at odds with conventional notions of Romantic display. While one might draw comparisons with the fairy-tale unreality of Ravel, Prokofiev is always his own man, creating an individual, pristine sound-world with a precise economy of means. The exotic luminosity of Karol Szymanowski's First Violin Concerto (1916) may be a better parallel: Prokofiev took advice on technical points from the Polish violinist Pawel Kochánski, Szymanowski's friend and champion, then based in Russia. Prokofiev includes a surprisingly prominent part for tuba, but there are no trombones, and otherwise lean, translucent textures predominate.

The work is cast in the traditional three movements, and only the sequence is unusual: the fastest music comes in the central panel, a mocking Scherzo. Prokofiev begins not with some bustling Allegro but with one of his most haunting melodies. And as if this idea were not exquisite enough, its recapitulation on solo flute (*pp*, dolcissimo) with harp, muted strings and lightly running tracery from the soloist is quite ravishing – matched by the more elaborate return as the mists close in at the very end of the concerto. Another key to the atmosphere of the opening movement is the presence of such markings as 'sognando' for the 'dreamy' opening, and 'narrante' for the second section in which the violin's skittish 'storytelling' veers towards the grotesque.

The second movement feels more like a modern take on the conventional display piece, though devoid of nineteenth-century rhetoric. It is a miniaturised version of the sort of rondo that usually comes last. The main theme is sparkling and mercurial, the contrasting episodes more combative in tone and innovative in technique. While there is no big solo cadenza here or anywhere else in the concerto, the soloist is given ample opportunities for high jinks.

The Finale opens with another typical device, a clockwork staccato effect against which Prokofiev introduces a seemingly jokey idea on bassoons, whereupon the soloist takes it up and transforms it into a gloriously lyrical paragraph. This is a perfect demonstration of the way a Prokofiev tune can set out in one fashion only to 'slip' into quite another mode. Whether negotiating the pitfalls of sentimentality or simply avoiding the obvious, the composer will often stretch his melodic line into a harmonic frame that seems arbitrary or disconnected on the page but actually produces, as here, the feeling that his theme has been 'refreshed'. As throughout, the flow of ideas is so spontaneous that the music seems to be creating its own form, an alloy of innocence and sophistication that served as a model for the concertos of William Walton even as Prokofiev himself moved on inscrutably to pastures new. The coda ties the threads in the most magical way imaginable.

© David Gutman

∾ Violin Concerto No. 2 in G minor, Op. 63 (1934–5)

1 Allegro moderato
2 Andante assai
3 Allegro, ben marcato

The gap of eighteen years that separates the composition of Prokofiev's two violin concertos coincides almost exactly with his period of residence outside his native Russia.

The First Violin Concerto (composed 1916–17, but not performed till 1923) had come as something of a surprise to those listeners who had not penetrated the brash modernistic façade of Prokofiev's music to the essentially simple lyrical impulse that so often lay beneath. Furthermore, although Prokofiev was a performing virtuoso, it was not as a violinist but as a pianist. His performance style, in common with much of the music he composed in his twenties and thirties, was brittle, percussive, abrasive – the very qualities that are traditionally foreign to the character of the violin, at least as a solo instrument. The First Concerto, however, revealed a deep understanding of the violin, together with an unselfconscious lyricism that many people welcomed at the time, but that was rarely to be given full scope in the unsettled years that followed the composer's departure from Russia.

The Second Violin Concerto dates from 1934–5, the period when Prokofiev, after several extended visits, was about to commit himself to returning permanently to the USSR, and indeed it was the last commission he was to accept from Western Europe. He wrote it at the request of a group of admirers of the French violinist Robert Soëtens. As Prokofiev later wrote in his autobiography: 'Reflecting my nomadic concertising existence, the concerto was written in the most diverse places. The main subject of the first movement was written in Paris, the first theme of the second movement in Voronezh, the instrumentation was completed in Baku, and the premiere took place in December 1935 in Madrid.'

Just as the First Concerto had seemed at the time to stand at the opposite pole from such dissonant works as the *Scythian Suite*, so the Second Violin Concerto was a landmark in Prokofiev's search for a 'new simplicity'. He was turning his back on the search for novelty and the pleasure of shocking his conservative elders. From now on there was to be a directness of expression in his language and a genuine desire to write the sort of music that he thought a Soviet public wanted. Most of his work on the concerto coincided with the completion of his first stage work for the USSR, the ballet *Romeo and Juliet*, and both works appeal through very much the same characteristics.

Simplicity and directness, however, were on no account to be taken as excuses for banality or a lack of invention, and least of all as a capitulation to the demands of officialdom. In a 1934 *Izvestiya* article Prokofiev set out his aims:

> Finding the right language for our music is not easy. It should first of all be melodic, but the melody, though simple and accessible, shouldn't become a refrain or a

trivial turn of phrase. Many composers have difficulty in composing melody in general – no matter what kind – and composing a melody for definitely stated goals is even more difficult. The same holds true for compositional technique and how it is set forth; it must be clear and simple, but not hackneyed. Its simplicity must not be old-fashioned.

Prokofiev's Second Violin Concerto is laid out in the traditional three movements: a sonata Allegro and Andante of roughly equal length, and a shorter, fast rondo finale. Although the solo part is extremely challenging, there is little overt display of virtuosity: there is, for example, no solo cadenza, and the violin and orchestra are hardly ever set in competitive opposition to one another. While planning the piece, Prokofiev thought at first in terms of a 'concertante sonata for violin and orchestra' – in other words, something more modest in scale than the big nineteenth-century concertos, and avoiding Romantic pathos or psychological conflict. Rather than relying on wide expressive contrasts, this is a work that unfolds with an almost narrative character.

The concerto opens with the unaccompanied soloist playing a theme which, with its minor mode and irregular phrasing, has a distinctly Russian quality; and the major-mode and more regularly phrased second principal theme (reached after an animated transition) is closely related to it. Subtle changes of tempo play an important expressive role in this movement. The subsidiary sections tend to be at a quicker tempo, so that the frequent returns to the moderate tempo of the two principal themes reinforce their introspective, dreamy character. This is further stressed in the second part of the movement, where the first main theme is not played at all by the soloist until the coda, and then fades out in a series of ghostly pizzicatos.

The beautifully conceived texture of the opening of the slow movement – a long-breathed violin cantilena against a steady accompaniment of triplets from clarinets and pizzicato strings – evokes the poised gravity of some Baroque aria; but the expressive harmonies ensure that this is no dry neo-classical stylisation of the sort produced in such quantities in the 1930s by composers who had failed to understand Stravinsky. The concerto's kinship with Prokofiev's *Romeo and Juliet* ballet is nowhere more evident than in this movement. The outer sections recall the fervent love music of the ballet, while the more animated inner sections have the innocent grace of Prokofiev's portrayal of Juliet as a young girl.

The lyricism of the first two movements is left behind in the finale, which displays a different but equally important side of Prokofiev's musical nature. It is a quick sonata rondo whose main theme, introduced by the soloist in double- and triple-stopping, could be described as a sort of sharp-edged waltz. The level of dissonance is higher than before, and this, together with a teasing rhythmic irregularity, gives the music a new pungency. Prokofiev's 'new simplicity' certainly did not exclude a wry humour and a conscious joy in technical virtuosity that comes close at times to parodying itself.

© Andrew Huth

Sergey Rakhmaninov (1873–1943)

For most of his life, Rakhmaninov led a dual career as pianist and composer. He graduated from the Moscow Conservatory with his first opera, *Aleko*, and also took to conducting after the disastrous premiere of his First Symphony in 1897 directed by Glazunov. The resulting three-year compositional silence was overcome by hypnosis, and Rakhmaninov soon wrote his highly successful Second Piano Concerto (1901). He made a lucrative tour of America in 1909 (for which he wrote his Third Piano Concerto), and after the Revolution in 1917 he lived in self-imposed exile, largely in the USA. His richly chromatic, broadly lyrical and unashamedly nostalgic style has found many critics, but has ensured his music's popularity among audiences. In addition to his three symphonies and two piano sonatas, he wrote two sets of *Études-tableaux* and *Préludes* for piano, a mighty Cello Sonata, three evocative symphonic poems and a rich setting of the Vespers (*All-Night Vigil*, 1915).

◎ Piano Concerto No. 1 in F sharp minor, Op. 1 (1890–1; rev. 1917)

1   Vivace – Moderato
2   Andante
3   Allegro vivace

The Piano Concerto No. 1 was Rakhmaninov's first major work, and was completed when he was eighteen. He performed the opening movement at the Moscow Conservatory just three days before his nineteenth birthday, with the Director of the Conservatoire, Vasily Safonov, conducting. The whole concerto was published, along with several other early pieces, including the C sharp minor Prelude, through the influence of Tchaikovsky. As Rakhmaninov matured, he began to find the concerto unsatisfactory, and when he was invited to play it at the Proms in London in 1900, he declined – a pianist called Evelyn Suart took his place. But it was not until 1917, when Rakhmaninov had time on his hands following the Revolution, that he got down to a thorough revision.

By then he had written both his Second and Third Piano Concertos and acquired a good deal of conducting experience. It is instructive to hear an occasional revival of the original version, just to learn how much Rakhmaninov's style had developed beyond the relatively crude orchestration and thick keyboard layout. He still believed in the music itself, and after revising it boasted that its 'youthful freshness' was still there. A comparison of the two versions also shows how his sense of narrative pace refined itself, for he made big changes – all for the better – to the course the music takes, the most drastic being in the finale.

Originality is by definition mysterious. Some of Rakhmaninov's inspiration for the concerto came from Grieg, whose Piano Concerto he admired, though (oddly enough) never played. The First Concerto is Rakhmaninov's only concerto to begin with a flourish – a cascade of descending octaves and chords, like the beginning of Grieg's concerto. Yet only the bare formula is similar: Rakhmaninov's contour is more elaborate and chromatic. Then the bare-breasted soul-sickness of Rakhmaninov's main theme is worlds away from Grieg's terse little first subject. It is the best tune in the first movement (though certainly not in the whole work), and compared with it the second main theme is almost neutral, simply a rising figure stressing the penultimate semitone.

The middle movement starts with a similar ascending shape and a sense of exploratory transition, until the piano improvises its way to D major and a glamorous new tune which passes to the orchestra while the piano chirrups contentedly in triplets.

The finale is launched with a bang and the pianist competing with the orchestra in great leaps of joy. This is only by way of preparation for the capricious rhythmic intricacies of the main theme, in which the piano and orchestra seem to be catching each other out. There is a second theme, which by contrast is straightforward, based on four descending notes, the piano bubbling away while the strings add a suave new counter-theme. But the main contrast comes with a relaxation of tempo and a luscious theme in the remote key of E flat major: the violins play it while the piano punctuates rather frivolously with speeded-up echoes. Rakhmaninov inserted these during the revision, and he also took the daring step of changing the key from D major. But the most striking change of all came later. In the original version Rakhmaninov brought back the theme of the slow section in a slightly weak attempt at a grandiose peroration, but perhaps he thought that sentimental, because he replaced it, in the revision, with an altogether more bracing conclusion.

© Adrian Jack

✍ Piano Concerto No. 2 in C minor, Op. 18 (1900–1)

1   Moderato
2   Adagio sostenuto
3   Allegro scherzando

With this concerto Rakhmaninov proved that he could write a large-scale work after the failure of his First Symphony. (The symphony had merely been the victim of a bad first performance, but the public humiliation was enough to make Rakhmaninov withdraw it and the work was not played again or appreciated until after his death.) The concerto is the touchstone of Rakhmaninov's mature style, and close to the preludes he wrote for solo piano during the following decade. His very first prelude, the famous and monumental piece in C sharp minor, was composed ten years earlier than the concerto, however, and shared its feature of massive chords in both hands. Rakhmaninov had an exceptionally wide stretch, though no one seems quite certain how wide it was, and in his

1929 recording of the concerto he played the opening chords with the lowest note of each touched in, almost casually, just before the rest, even though he didn't need to.

Massive weight is less of a priority in the concerto than in the early prelude, though weight has its due importance. Much of the piano writing has a feline grace, or achieves sonorous richness by Rakhmaninov's canny spacing of notes and use of a wide range – for instance, in a poignant 'fading sunset' sort of passage towards the end of the first movement, as it winds down before a final acceleration. Some of the middle movement has the soloist spinning a single line, whether completely unsupported, with slower chords or with an ornamental accompaniment. The first main theme of the finale is an example of particularly intricate piano writing, with sharply accented chords connected by a continuous stream of triplets alternating between hands: the effect is glittering.

Rakhmaninov was acutely sensitive to texture and the interplay of soloist and orchestra. The concerto from which he may have learnt most was Schumann's, because of its consistent integration of the two: the pianist is almost another member of the orchestra, or rather, it counts as a few more members. Yet the stealthy opening of this concerto owes nothing to earlier composers and is a unique stroke of inspiration, in which the soloist creates a mood of mysterious promise, only to retire into the role of accompanist to the first big tune, at least for the time being.

The slow movement opens off-centre, with the orchestra moving deftly from the first movement's home key to the remote region of E major. And the remoteness of the key is matched by a sense of dreaminess as the main melodies float on a constant motion of triplets, with cross-accents (after every fourth note) contributing an essential ambiguity; we are not sure where the beat comes.

From E major, the brisk, slightly military opening of the finale turns a corner onto the dominant of C minor and the soloist bursts in with a flourish. The big contrasting tune, when it arrives, has a sort of parallel character, or family likeness, to the second subject of the first movement, even though the context is quite different. This isn't a deliberate attempt to unify, for after all a good contrast does as well as, if not better than, a resemblance; but it shows how fertile, and at the same time how consistent, were Rakhmaninov's sources of melodic invention.

The amazing fact is that Rakhmaninov actually wrote, and performed, the second and third movements before adding the first. Nor, once the whole work was complete, did he feel the need to revise, as he did with both his First and Fourth Concertos, or even to cut, as he did in the case of the much longer Third Concerto.

© Adrian Jack

ॐ Piano Concerto No. 3 in D minor, Op. 30 (1909)

1 Allegro ma non tanto
2 Intermezzo: Adagio – poco più mosso –
3 Finale: Alla breve

The period leading up to the composition of the Third Piano Concerto was a high point in Rakhmaninov's career as composer, conductor and pianist. The success of his Second Symphony in 1908 did much to banish the ghosts of the First's failure a decade earlier, and between the death of Rimsky-Korsakov in 1908 and the emergence a few years later of Stravinsky and Prokofiev, Rakhmaninov was recognised as one of the most important figures in Russian music. He had also become widely known in Western Europe and hoped to extend his reputation with a tour of the USA (America, as well as fame, also meant fortune: Rakhmaninov dreamed happily of such luxuries as buying a motor car).

Negotiations with an American concert agency had begun as early as 1906, but only in July 1909 were all the contractual problems sorted out, and by then the composition of the Third Concerto, his major new work for the tour, was well under way.

He completed it on 23 September and played it on 28 and 30 November with the New York Symphony Orchestra under Walter Damrosch, and then again in January 1910 with Gustav Mahler conducting the New York Philharmonic.

After the first Russian performance in Moscow that April, the critic Grigoriy Prokofiev (no relation to the composer) wrote of the concerto's 'sincerity, simplicity and clarity of musical thought . . . it has a sharp and concise form as well as simple and brilliant orchestration, qualities that will secure both outer success and enduring love by musicians and public alike' – an acute judgement, but one that took a long time to meet with general agreement. Indeed, the young Sergey Prokofiev (the composer) thought that the work was 'dry, difficult and unappealing', although he found Rakhmaninov's first two piano concertos 'wonderfully charming'.

Rakhmaninov performed the Third Piano Concerto a total of eighty-six times over the next three decades (as opposed to 143 performances of the Second), but it only achieved real popularity when it was taken up by Vladimir Horowitz in the 1930s. Horowitz's earlier recordings, as well as the composer's own recording (made in 1939 with Eugene Ormandy and the Philadelphia Orchestra) are sadly marred by unnecessary cuts, particularly in the Finale, and until the 1960s it was standard practice among pianists to observe these. Only Rakhmaninov's chronic lack of self-confidence (and perhaps his distrust of American audiences' attention spans) could have allowed him to sanction them, for they are as damaging to the work's proportions as those he also made in the Second Symphony.

The Third has long been acknowledged as among the most technically challenging of Romantic piano concertos. Its length, at around forty-five minutes, is a formidable challenge and it demands enormous reserves of power and endurance from the soloist. As well as these, it requires those characteristics that are essential for all of Rakhmaninov's longer works: just the right mixture of precision and passion, of rigour and flexibility to shape the long melodic lines and illuminate the texture of even the most unobtrusive inner parts.

Rakhmaninov maintained that the concerto's opening melody, unfolded by the soloist in simple octaves over a pulsing accompaniment, was derived neither from folk music nor from liturgical chant, but simply 'wrote itself'. The way in which it develops is typical of his approach to composing: he begins with an immediately appealing tune, elaborates it, then travels further and further afield with contrasting material, but again and again returns to some form of the opening idea. The impression is that, for all the concerto's variety, it springs from one single idea, one particular and perhaps obsessive emotional experience that can be viewed from different angles but that underlies every aspect of the music.

The Intermezzo provides an expected and necessary contrast of key, tempo and texture, but towards the end there is a faster episode, a sort of shadowy waltz, which refers back directly to the first movement's opening melody. This unity of experience is also reinforced by the way in which the slow movement leads directly into the Finale, as though the Intermezzo's melancholy song and the Finale's more extrovert gestures are related aspects of the same experience. In the course of the Finale, too, the main themes of the first movement reappear in new shapes, but emotionally they are never far away from that melody which, as the composer said, 'wrote itself'.

© Andrew Huth

✎ Piano Concerto No. 4 in G minor, Op. 40 (1926; rev. 1941)

1   Allegro vivace (Alla breve)
2   Largo –
3   Allegro vivace

The Fourth Piano Concerto marked Rakhmaninov's return to composition after a gap of several years during which he had been forced to come to terms with the greatest upheaval in his own and in his country's life. The outbreak of the First World War in 1914 had been a severe shock to him. Although intensely Russian in culture and temperament, he was nevertheless broadly cosmopolitan in outlook, but now found himself confined to a Russia where musical life could only continue on the most limited scale, progressively reduced by the social turmoil that eventually led to the revolutions of 1917. When conditions became intolerable, Rakhmaninov and his family hurriedly left Russia, abandoning the greater part of their money and almost all their possessions. He now found himself in a shattered world, obliged to pick up his career from the beginning.

Years of arduous concert tours in Europe and the USA followed his emigration, and it was not until 1926 that Rakhmaninov felt that he could spare the time for a major composition. He arranged for a year's freedom from concert engagements, and resumed composition of the Fourth Piano Concerto that he had been planning before the Revolution. It was first performed in Philadelphia on 18 March 1927. Rakhmaninov, of course, played the solo part and the Philadelphia Orchestra was conducted by Leopold Stokowski.

To Rakhmaninov's disappointment, it was not well received, either then in America or later in Europe, and he determined to revise the score after a period of reflection. Fourteen years later, in 1941, he prepared the version which is invariably heard today. Much of the orchestration was altered, the proportions adjusted, and the last movement, in particular, largely recast.

It is hard to understand what prevented the immediate success of the concerto, but it was probably something to do with the attitude that dogged Rakhmaninov's later years – that he was writing the wrong sort of music at the wrong time: too conservative in style for the 1920s modernists, too advanced in ideas for those audiences who made Rakhmaninov's concert life a misery by insisting on hearing the early C sharp minor Prelude as an encore to every recital programme.

Audiences in 1927 may well have been bewildered by the development that had taken place in his musical language over the eighteen years since his Third Concerto. The sharp, brittle sounds of the orchestra and the often acerbic harmonies were startling to those people familiar with the lavish, sensual opulence of his pre-war orchestra in such works as the Second and Third Concertos, the Second Symphony or *The Isle of the Dead*. The Fourth Concerto, however, inhabits a more complex and ambiguous world than these pieces. Perhaps this world is becoming more accessible in our own day, now that the Third Symphony and *Symphonic Dances* are becoming more widely known: these two great works from the last years of the composer's life develop such ambiguities of meaning and language even further than the concerto and their constantly shifting surfaces reveal depths which seem stranger and more unexpected at each performance.

The first movement of the concerto is one of wide contrasts. The broad chordal theme announced by the piano at the opening promises grand rhetoric, but the overall character of the movement is more truly to be found in the harmonic side-slips and the agitated wind triplets which accompany the theme. This is music more questioning and nervous than anything Rakhmaninov had yet written. The harmonic range is unexpectedly wide, so that discord and consonance greatly enhance one another's effect, as do constant shifts between major and minor modes, or between passages of intimate reflection and virtuoso brilliance. The thematic material is abundant, and there are many passages of great beauty which the pre-war Rakhmaninov would certainly have lingered over; but nothing here is overstated, there are few extended repetitions, and recapitulations are generally much abbreviated – in short, the movement's changes of mood demand a quickness of response from the listener which early audiences were perhaps not prepared for.

The second movement, by contrast, is almost obsessively static. The descending three-note pattern which emerges from the piano's introductory bars appears in many different guises, with varied harmonies, textures and rhythmic forms, but the music scarcely departs from the mood established at the opening; a single agitated outburst soon falls back into the prevailing stillness. The finale follows without a break. It is full of glittering virtuosity, and although more stable in its course than the first movement, still contains several unexpected turns. Here again there is no lingering over details, and the rhythmic energy creates a sense of rushed excitement. The brilliant piano writing is matched by a fantastically coloured orchestral invention.

In common with the other works he wrote for his own instrument, the Fourth Concerto naturally exploits to the full Rakhmaninov's own outstanding qualities as a pianist: his insistence that his formidable technique must be placed at the service of large-scale form and meaning; extreme rhythmic precision and clarity even in the most complex textures, and a vocally breathed sense of phrasing (his stature as a song composer is still not fully appreciated).

Rakhmaninov was apparently anxious about the concerto's length, and made several cuts even before its first performance. This was an unfounded worry. The 1926 version of the Fourth Concerto was indeed significantly longer than what we hear today, but still nothing like as long as the Second or Third Concertos. The variety contained in the work and the consequent fear of seeming diffuse were probably at the root of Rakhmaninov's anxiety to revise the concerto and make it more compact. But perhaps this waywardness is in itself a reflection of Rakhmaninov's own musical personality. A perfectly balanced well-proportioned form presupposes a world ruled by balance and proportion (even if only an ideal, inner world of the spirit). But Rakhmaninov's world – both inner and outer – was altogether more precarious. Essentially an aristocratic, melancholy, withdrawn man, he performed in front of a public whose taste he must often have found questionable; his personal and musical formation were conditioned by late-nineteenth-century Russia, and he now found himself exiled into the turbulence of post-war Europe and America; his awareness of the variety and fragility of life included an acute sense of irony and the humour of precise observation, with all the contradictions that these involve. Rakhmaninov was always glad when a work of his achieved popularity, but he was too great a musician to court that popularity by clinging to certainties that he knew had disappeared for ever.

© Andrew Huth

ꙮ *Rhapsody on a Theme of Paganini*, Op. 43 (1934)

In 1933 a newspaper interviewer asked the sixty-year-old Rakhmaninov if he had given up composing. 'Not entirely,' he replied. 'During my summer rests from the fatigue of my tours as pianist, I return to composition. My last works were transcriptions . . .' But the question must have rankled, for the years between 1917 and 1926 had been completely barren of new music; and since the first performances in 1927 of the Fourth Piano Concerto and the *Three Russian Songs* for chorus and orchestra there had been only the *Variations on a Theme of Corelli*, for solo piano, composed and first performed in 1931.

In the summer of 1934, however, Rakhmaninov and his family settled into a new villa he had been building on the shores of Lake Lucerne (near the villa Tribschen, where Wagner wrote *Tristan*), and in about seven weeks he wrote down a major new work. On 19 August, the day after its completion, he wrote to his sister-in-law: 'This work is rather a large one, and only yesterday, late at night, I finished it . . . This piece is written for piano and orchestra, about twenty to twenty-five minutes in length. But it is no "concerto"! It is called *Symphonic Variations on a Theme by Paganini*.' Three weeks later, he was referring to it as a 'Fantasia for piano and orchestra in the form of variations on a theme of Paganini'.

The premiere was given by the composer with the Philadelphia Orchestra and Leopold Stokowski on 7 November 1934 in Baltimore. It was an immediate success and indeed became so popular that Rakhmaninov – always so fastidious and self-critical – began to have doubts about it: if it was so popular, he felt, might there be something wrong with it?

The theme comes from the last of the twenty-four Caprices for solo violin published in 1820 by Niccolò Paganini (1782–1840), and has attracted many other composers besides Rakhmaninov, among them Schumann, Liszt, Brahms and Lutosławski. Paganini's Caprice itself consists of a theme followed by variations that put the violin through all its technical possibilities and display the fiendish virtuosity that led to the rumour that the demonic violinist had sold his soul to the Devil. The theme is ideal for variation: it has simple harmony, a memorable melodic shape, crisp and characteristic rhythms and regular phrasing. Any of these features can be varied, leaving the other elements clearly recognisable; and after several hearings, it can be varied very freely but still remain in the background of the listener's mind.

Rakhmaninov's *Rhapsody* consists of twenty-four continuous variations on the Paganini theme, but the work also falls into four broad sections, rather like a symphonic first movement, scherzo, slow movement and finale, although the comparison should not be stretched too far. The orchestra is at times pared down to a minimum but makes an enormous impact when used in tutti.

Variation 1 precedes the theme, outlining just its skeleton before the full theme is given by the violins, with the main notes picked out by the piano. Variations 2 to 10 are all in a quick tempo, apart from No. 7 where the solo piano introduces another theme – the *Dies irae*, that famous medieval chant which in works such as Berlioz's *Symphonie fantastique* has symbolised death and mortality, and which pervades so much of Rakhmaninov's music. It reappears in the march-like Variation 10, at first in the piano, then as a brass fanfare.

Variation 11 is a slow, reflective piano cadenza. Variations 12 to 15 are all in triple time, beginning with a melancholy, slow minuet, while Variations 16 to 18 form a sort of slow movement, culminating in the 'big tune' of No. 18, which consists of Paganini's theme slowed down and turned upside down. The final section resumes the quick tempo and begins a gradual acceleration to the final Variation 24, with its last reference to the *Dies irae* in the brass.

© Andrew Huth

Maurice Ravel (1875–1937)

Ravel was a fastidious, perfectionist composer who produced some of the most enduring music of the early twentieth century. Born in the Basque region to a Swiss father and a Basque mother, Ravel studied at the Paris Conservatoire, where he consistently and controversially failed to win the prestigious Prix de Rome. Yet by the time of his final failure, in 1905, he had written impressive works such as *Jeux d'eau* (1901), the String Quartet (1902–3) and the orchestral song-cycle *Shéhérazade* (1903). Often cast as an Impressionist alongside Debussy, he was also drawn to the simplicity of classical dance forms (*Sonatine*, *Le tombeau de Couperin*), and other dances figure prominently in his output: waltzes (*La valse*, *Valses nobles et sentimentales*), and the *Boléro* (one of many works showing an Iberian influence). Always reclusive, he was deeply affected by the death of his mother, after which he seemed to abandon all close human contact. He conjured up a world of childhood innocence in the ballet *Mother Goose* and the opera *L'enfant et les sortilèges*. He wrote little after his two piano concertos (1929–31), and died a week after a brain operation in December 1937.

∾ Piano Concerto in G major (1929–31)

1 Allegramente
2 Adagio assai
3 Presto

In 1928 Ravel went on a four-month concert tour of North America during which he played his *Sonatine* and excerpts from *Miroirs* and was generally fêted at performances of his music by other musicians. In Hollywood he posed for pictures with Douglas Fairbanks and Mary Pickford, and he spent several evenings in Harlem listening to jazz with

George Gershwin and Paul Whiteman. Jazz was not new to Ravel, but after his American tour he absorbed it more deeply than before and found an outlet for his enthusiasm in two very different works, both piano concertos.

He began the Piano Concerto in G major in 1929, but interrupted work on it when commissioned to compose a second concerto, for left hand only, by the Austrian pianist Paul Wittgenstein (brother of the philosopher, Ludwig), who had lost his right arm in the First World War. Ravel deliberately made that a grander, heavier piece to compensate for its technical limitation, whereas he described the G major Concerto as written in the spirit of Mozart and Saint-Saëns, and even thought of calling it a 'divertissement'. Yet despite the transparency of the piano part and the small number of players required in the orchestra, the G major Concerto is far from easy, and the first and last movements call for spectacular agility not only from the pianist but also from the woodwind and brass players.

Ravel caused his friends and colleagues considerable anxiety by announcing that he intended to play the solo part himself and wanted to take the concerto on a world tour. Declining health modified his ambitions, and he conducted the first performance, in Paris in January 1932, with Marguérite Long as soloist, after which they played the work in some twenty European cities, including London.

A crack of a whip sets the brilliant first movement spinning – the piccolo playing a jaunty tune against the piano's glittering accompaniment, right hand on white notes, left on black. The circus atmosphere is well and truly clinched when sprays of piano glissandos cue in the trumpet, which takes over the tune from the piccolo. Abruptly, the buoyant mood collapses and the pace slackens in a sultry jazz style, with blue notes and swoons. But just as Ravel starts getting tender, he recovers his wits and the brittle, syncopated activity of the opening. The entire movement is a dialogue of these contrasts, alternating fast and slow, and brimming with melodies. The solo cadenza is short and fully written out, continuous trills in the right hand slithering around in imitation of a flexatone or musical saw, and leading to the grandest moment, when the piano decks out one of the slow themes in sonorous textures – the closest Ravel gets to the Romantic style of concerto.

There's none of that in the slow movement, but a sober reconstruction of the classical style – although no eighteenth-century composer would have composed such a seemingly endless melody as the piano's opening solo. (Ravel said his model was Mozart's Clarinet Quintet.) Its purity is then gradually sullied until the tune is recovered by the cor anglais.

The finale returns to the spirit of entertainment, framed by four cheeky, emphatic chords, and punctuated throughout with throwaway fanfares, shrieks and cackles in the wood-wind and brass, partly inspired by the example of jazz bands, while the piano races on, challenged at one point by two very fit bassoons.

© Adrian Jack

✥ Piano Concerto for the Left Hand
(1929–30)

Ravel's Left-Hand Concerto is one of his 'grand' works; his biographer Arbie Orenstein calls it Ravel's most dramatic. It's an amusing game, perhaps no more, to divide Ravel's music into 'dark' and 'light'. The dark works share qualities of mystery, exoticism (whether oriental or Spanish) and even thoughts of death, like the song-cycle *Shéhérazade*, the symphonic dance works *Daphnis and Chloë* and *La valse*, and the heavier piano cycles *Miroirs* and *Gaspard de la nuit*. The light works are more neo-classical, objective, like the *Sonatine*, *Le tombeau de Couperin* and the G major Piano Concerto (for two hands). But these are only the poles of Ravel's musical world, and there are many works it would be hard to confine to either category. The contrast is most striking in the two piano concertos, which Ravel wrote at the same time, although both were influenced by Spanish music and jazz. They were his last orchestral works.

He had already started on the G major Concerto (which he intended to play himself but conducted instead) when he received a commission from the Austrian pianist Paul Wittgenstein, brother of the philosopher Ludwig. Wittgenstein had lost his right arm in the First World War and, being rich, commissioned works from Richard Strauss, Britten and Prokofiev, as well as many others. He was a difficult customer and, when he got the score of Prokofiev's Fourth Piano Concerto, he wrote to the composer saying he didn't like it so wouldn't play it. Ravel fared a bit better, and although Wittgenstein had doubts at first, he came to acknowledge the Left-Hand Concerto's qualities. He did, however, try to rewrite, or rearrange, parts of it, which led to the famous exchange between pianist and composer: 'Performers must not be slaves!' – 'Performers are slaves!' Despite that, Wittgenstein gave the first performance in Vienna in January 1932 and (with Ravel conducting) the Paris premiere almost exactly a year later. Critics were enthusiastic.

Ravel agonised over the G major Piano Concerto, that transparent, polished work, for some two years, whereas he completed the Left-Hand Concerto in nine months. His relative speed in writing is reflected in the sweep of the work's single movement, made up of an imposing introduction, march-like *danse macabre*, and apotheosis of the introduction, shortened.

The concerto begins in the depths, quietly, a contra-bassoon weaving through and above cellos and double basses; horns intone a bluesy theme beginning with three descending notes, and the orchestra slowly awakens. After some two minutes the soloist enters with a grandiose flourish – Ravel was determined to make one hand sound like two – and then introduces a slinky, though proud, melody, self-accompanied. The orchestra takes it up, dressed rather tawdrily (trumpet doubling violins) before the soloist brings in a tender, slower contrast. Tension builds up with cor anglais (playing the slinky melody) leading a series of wind solos against piano arpeggios, and suddenly we are out of the introduction and into march tempo, triads skidding jazzily. Against the relentless two-time beat the soloist dances in triplets, tracing a lean line reinforced, now and then, by chords, octaves or bare fifths. Tripping flutes and piccolo against piano arpeggios lead back to the bluesy theme from the introduction, now on bassoon and thereafter dominating a second crescendo while the piano dances like a mischievous demon. A brief acceleration (wicked jumps for the pianist) leads into a return of the slinky tempo of the introduction on full orchestra and the final, decisive cadenza in which the piano collects the important themes. The end is swift.

© Adrian Jack

Joaquín Rodrigo (1901–99)

Though he lost almost all his sight in childhood through diptheria, Rodrigo nevertheless studied violin and piano from the age of eight, and harmony and counterpoint at the Valencia Conservatoire from sixteen. His first orchestral work, *Juglares*, was premiered in 1924, three years before he set out for Paris (following Falla and Granados before him) where he was a pupil of Dukas from 1927 to 1932. In 1933 he married the Turkish pianist Victoria Kamhi, who devoted herself to her husband's career. He returned to Spain in 1939 after the Civil War, a year before the premiere of the *Concierto de Aranjuez*, with which his reputation soared. Further guitar concertos, including the *Fantasía para un gentil-hombre* (1954) and concertos for two and for four guitars, followed up the success. Rodrigo became a professor at Complutense University, Madrid, and Head of Music Broadcasts for Spanish Radio. His compositional style remained largely conservative, but his espousal of Spanish idioms won him continuing popularity until his death, in addition to a plethora of honours and awards.

❧ *Concierto de Aranjuez*: for guitar and orchestra (1939)

1 Allegro con spirito
2 Adagio
3 Allegro gentile

Rodrigo's most famous concerto, one of the quintessential popular evocations of Spain in the concert repertoire, was not composed in that country but – like so much great Spanish music – in Paris. Rodrigo had lived chiefly there and in Freiburg during the years of the Spanish Civil War, and he wrote the concerto (at the suggestion of the guitarist Regino

Sainz de la Maza) early in 1939, as that war was coming to a close. When Rodrigo made his permanent return to Spain on 1 September – two days before the official outbreak of World War II, which actually began with the German operations against Poland that very day – he carried the manuscript of the concerto with him. Though many sources suggest that the premiere occurred in Madrid, where Rodrigo settled, it was actually given in Barcelona – the other great centre of resistance to Franco's forces, alongside the capital – on 9 November 1940, with Regino Sainz de la Maza taking the solo part, and the Barcelona Philharmonic Orchestra conducted by César Mendoza Lassalle. The Madrid performance followed a month later. From the first the work was an outstanding success, and consolidated the composer's reputation both within Spain and outside it.

Rodrigo did not play the guitar himself, but he was intimately acquainted with its literature, both folk and classical, and with its greatest modern exponents. There had been guitar concertos before, going back to the classical era, but certainly none in the early twentieth century had so elegantly solved the problems of balance between the modern orchestra and the solo guitar, inspiring many other composers to add to the genre.

Rodrigo was prone to ask 'whether there was such a thing as classicism in music' – he, for his part, was seeking 'a new purity'. If the forms of the *Concierto de Aranjuez* and his other concertos appear classical, then this is more because of his concern with clarity than from any neo-classicising impulse. Rodrigo always favoured broad, simple forms, very clearly laid out, their component parts strongly characterised by melody and colour – one reason for his music's immediate mass appeal. Another is the flamboyant virtuosity he requires of the soloist: this is certainly a work which seems to penetrate to the very soul of the Spanish guitar. The title *Aranjuez* relates the concerto to the Madrid region: Aranjuez is the name of the royal palace near the city, favoured as the summer residence of the Bourbon kings of Spain. Yet the music is not a pastiche of any historical style, though its general clarity alludes to the Baroque, perhaps especially in the Adagio, which seems rather a modern re-creation of rococo discourse and gesture.

The first movement, in a clear sonata form, opens with the guitar's *rasgueado*-like strumming against a pedal point in the double basses; the rhythms of this introduction dominate the movement and seem always to carry the various melodic elements, while the guitar is resourcefully contrasted against the characteristic timbres of other solo instruments such as cello, clarinet, flute and oboe.

It is, however, the soulful central Adagio that has become classical music's equivalent of a 'greatest hit'. The guitar's opening chords become the accompaniment to the exquisitely dolorous florid melody on cor anglais which evokes the sound of a *saeta*, the traditional song to the Virgin heard during Holy Week festivities in Seville. The guitar and then other instruments take up the long tune, weaving a seamless tapestry threaded upon the main melodic line, enriched by intricate decoration and embellishment. Towards the end the guitar has an essentially meditative cadenza whose rising tensions precipitate the orchestra's only tutti before the gentle conclusion.

The finale is based on a single blithe, pert theme, like a children's rhyme, in alternating 2/4 and 3/4 time. Stated first by the guitar, which here has its most bravura writing in the whole concerto, it appears in many guises and keys, in ever-changing orchestration, before the soloist ends the concerto with a witty descent into silence.

Malcolm MacDonald © BBC

Camille Saint-Saëns (1835–1921)

The classical simplicity of Saint-Saëns's music, and the fluency with which he produced it, belies his more overtly intellectual pursuits as a scholar, editor, student of archaeology and natural history, and writer of poems, plays and criticism. A prodigy of Mozartian facility (aged ten, he gave a concert in Paris which included piano concertos by Mozart and Beethoven) he studied at the Paris Conservatoire before winning the post of organist at La Madeleine in 1857. He taught piano at the École Niedermeyer, where Fauré was among his students. A predilection for travel, especially to North Africa, influenced a number of musical references, as in his first opera *La princesse jaune* (1871), the 'Egyptian' Piano Concerto (No. 5), Persian songs and the *Suite algérienne*. Of his thirteen operas, only *Samson et Dalila* is regularly staged. In a bid to preserve his reputation as a serious composer, Saint-Saëns banned the publication of his *Carnival of the Animals* (1886) until after his death.

❧ Cello Concerto No. 1 in A minor, Op. 33 (1872)

By the age of twenty-five, Saint-Saëns's formidable abilities as a composer and virtuoso pianist had brought him to public notice. 'I live in music like a fish in water,' he said, adding that he could produce music 'as a tree produces apples'. By the late 1860s he had already written three piano concertos (including the popular No. 2, much praised by Liszt), together with two violin concertos and the sparkling *Introduction and Rondo Capriccioso*, inspired by the playing of the brilliant Spanish virtuoso violinist Sarasate. But while Saint-Saëns enjoyed professional success and esteem, his personal life was not so fortunate. Until he was forty – when he suddenly and unwisely married a girl twenty-one years his junior, only to walk out on her after the tragic deaths of their two young sons – Saint-Saëns lived at home, cosseted and pampered by his adoring mother and her aunt. Saint-Saëns was deeply devoted to both women, and after the death of his great-aunt in 1872, he found an outlet for his grief in the C minor Cello Sonata, Op. 32. The A minor Cello Concerto – another stormy and passionately felt work – followed shortly afterwards. Dedicated to the cellist, gamba player and instrument maker Auguste Tolbecque (1830–1919), one of a distinguished family of Belgian musicians who were closely associated with the Société des Concerts du Conservatoire (France's leading concert society), it was first performed in 1873 at a Conservatoire concert – a mark of the composer's growing acceptance by the French musical establishment.

In the First Cello Concerto, Saint-Saëns showed his willingness to experiment with form, casting it in a single movement, divided into three sections. The turbulent opening Allegro non troppo leads into a brief, but highly original minuet, in which the strings are muted, and which contains a cello cadenza. The finale ('Un peu moins vite') is introduced by a reminiscence of the opening material from the first movement.

© Wendy Thompson

❧ *Introduction and Rondo Capriccioso*, Op. 28 (1863)

Andante (malinconico) – Allegro ma non troppo

Camille Saint-Saëns suffered under a triple misfortune – he was prodigiously prolific, he could write a good tune (think of 'The Swan' from *The Carnival of the Animals*), and he was French – qualities which have ever since caused his relegation by 'musical opinion' to somewhere near the bottom of the second division of the composers' league. Musical opinion has frowned severely on a man who could dissipate his energies on five piano concertos, three violin concertos and two cello concertos while most of his 'greater' contemporaries were busily honing, polishing and refining their single, flawless gems. His detractors – those who unkindly called him a composer of 'bad music well written' – would have done well to remember that many of Saint-Saëns's most characteristic qualities – a natural fluency, a craftsmanlike approach to his art, an incomparable gift for melody and the ability to write accessible music which pleased his audiences – were shared by one W. A. Mozart, whose status in musical history as leader of the first division has rarely been questioned.

Like two of Saint-Saëns's violin concertos, the *Introduction and Rondo Capriccioso* was written for the great Spanish virtuoso Pablo de Sarasate. Many French composers of the time – Bizet, Lalo, Chabrier, the young Debussy and Saint-Saëns himself – were mesmerised by Spain: its turbulent history, colourful traditions and its distinctive musical idioms, with their strong gypsy and Moorish flavours. Sarasate, who began his phenomenally successful career in 1859, having arrived in Paris three years earlier at the age of twelve to study at the Conservatoire with Delphin Alard, provided a direct link with this tradition, and French composers responded by writing concertos and other virtuoso showpieces for him. (In Bizet's case, he returned the compliment with his own *Fantasy on Themes from Carmen*.) Sarasate's playing style was characterised by faultless technique, perfect intonation (especially in the highest register), a sweet and limpid tone, and apparently effortless ease; the one criticism made of his playing was that it sometimes lacked emotional commitment.

Saint-Saëns met Sarasate in the late 1850s: Sarasate was then still a young teenager, and Saint-Saëns about ten years older. The prodigy asked the brilliant young composer for a concerto, and Saint-Saëns immediately obliged with the A major Concerto (No. 1). Four years later, in 1863, he wrote another piece for Sarasate – the brilliant *Introduction and Rondo Capriccioso*, which gained immediate popularity and quickly entered the repertoire as a major violinistic showpiece. In deference to Sarasate's origins, one of the episodes of the rondo has a definite Iberian flavour. Bizet later arranged the piece for violin and piano, and Debussy made an arrangement of it for two pianos.

© Wendy Thompson

∾ Piano Concerto No. 2 in G minor, Op. 22 (1868)

1 Andante sostenuto
2 Allegro scherzando
3 Presto

Saint-Saëns's Second Piano Concerto was written in a mere seventeen days and published within the same year. Late in April 1868, his close friend Anton Rubinstein was seeking to make his Parisian debut as a conductor, and he asked Saint-Saëns to make the necessary arrangements. The next available date at the Salle Pleyel was in three weeks' time, on 13 May, and Saint-Saëns decided there and then to put his creative virtuosity to the test and volunteered to write (and play) a new concerto for the event. Undoubtedly the work had been germinating in his mind for some while before this, though it is also reported that he borrowed the main theme of its first movement from a *Tantum ergo* that his pupil, Gabriel Fauré, brought to show him at the time (this early religious sketch for voice and organ has not survived). In the event the premiere did not go smoothly. 'Not having had the time to practise it sufficiently for performance,' the composer admitted, 'I played very badly, and except for the scherzo, which was an immediate success, it did not go well. The general opinion was that the first part lacked coherence and the finale was a complete failure.'

Since then, however, with proper preparation, this piano concerto has proved the most popular of Saint-Saëns's five, and it shows the mature assimilation of many of the characteristics we have come to associate with him – urbane charm, technical wizardry and sophisticated eloquence – into a personal voice. Indeed, the concerto became a particular favourite of Liszt, who immediately recognised its positive qualities. As he told Saint-Saëns:

> The form is innovative and a most happy choice. The interest builds throughout the three movements, and you take pianistic effects into account without sacrificing any compositional principles, which is a basic rule in this genre . . . At the start, the prelude is very striking and imposing, after this fortunate inspiration, you were wise to reproduce it at the end of the movement and to accompany it this time with some [string] chords . . . I played it again for [the pianist and composer Giovanni] Sgambati two days ago . . . He plans to perform your concerto in public next winter, and it is certain to meet with universal success.

The form of the concerto is certainly novel. Its tempo marking suggests that it begins with a slow movement, though the proliferation of demisemiquaver passagework as it unfolds makes this something of an illusion. Like Beethoven's 'Emperor' Concerto, it begins with a solo cadenza – though, as Liszt observed, this proves integral to the movement at the end. Moreover, it feels more like a Bach Fantasia for organ at the start, and it leads straight into the dominating (Fauréan) idea in the same key, with no real second-subject material. This idea is further developed in the second cadenza, which itself mirrors the whole movement by being in a sort of ternary form. Then the featherweight, Mendelssohnian second movement, with its deft orchestration, is a scherzo with two trio sections using the same memorable material. Perhaps Saints-Saëns had the double trio of Beethoven's Seventh Symphony in mind here, or Schumann's experiments with the form?

While the first movement has two cadenzas, the finale has none at all, and instead of being a rondo, it presents us with the only sonata-form movement in the concerto – and a strict one at that, despite its nonchalant surface. The first subject is a whirlwind tarantella, while the second subject is more imposing and full of trills. Both are skilfully juxtaposed in the development section, and both reappear in the scintillating coda. Here the initial weighty chords are probably meant to recall the first movement but, as the pianist Stojowski wryly observed, the concerto 'begins with Bach and ends with Offenbach', and Saint-Saëns knew his Parisian public too well to introduce anything obviously weighty and cyclic at this juncture.

Overall the emphasis is on pianistic virtuosity and melodious accessibility, and if this concerto has been criticised for the disparity between its opening movement and the others, then this was all part of the stylistic eclecticism that characterises Saint-Saëns at his popular best. Even the first movement is impressive and spectacular rather than profound or soul-searching, and it bears out Berlioz's pointed remark (made a few years earlier) that 'he knows everything but he lacks inexperience'. But as Saint-Saëns the realist observed: 'It is not the absence of defects, but the presence of merits that makes men and Art great.' This concerto has merits in abundance.

© Robert Orledge

Alfred Schnittke (1934–98)

Though born in Russia, where he lived most of his life, Schnittke was greatly influenced by two years spent in Vienna in 1946–8. Here he assimilated the German classical aesthetic, whose forms – concerto, symphony, string quartet – would figure prominently in his output. He entered the Moscow Conservatoire in 1953, producing his First Violin Concerto in 1957, influenced by the premiere of Shostakovich's own First Violin Concerto. On completing postgraduate studies in 1962 he taught at the Conservatoire for ten years. Encouraged by Nono, he produced some serial pieces in the early 1960s, but later established a polystylistic approach noted for its wide borrowings and extremes of consonance and dissonance. He won wide acclaim for his Concerto Grosso No. 1 (1977), championed by Gidon Kremer. In 1985, soon after completing his Viola Concerto and *Concerto for Mixed Choir*, he suffered the first of a series of five strokes. But his output – including three operas and four symphonies – continued to be prolific until his death in 1998. He produced sixty-six film scores between 1962 and 1993, from which he borrowed freely in his concert works.

∾ Viola Concerto (1985)

1 Largo
2 Allegro molto
3 Largo

Eager to accept all that the twentieth century had to offer, Schnittke was as much indebted to Schoenberg's interrelated developments as to the European fringes of his essentially Russian inheritance. So while he wrote fast (and, latterly, as if with a sense of imminent foreboding), his educated awareness of the implicative nature of his own material was far from being haphazardly applied – even though the sheer quantity and variety of his inspiration can often make it appear so.

Take his masterly Viola Concerto, whose entire motivic material derives from the musical letters in the name of the original soloist Yuri Bashmet (which, if spelt in the German manner, yields BASCHmEt); the fact that these notes include the B–A–C–H motif (used by countless composers since Bach himself introduced it getting on for three centuries ago) is a happy coincidence – particularly for Schnittke, whose music abounds with references that may or may not be of the coincidental kind. Add to this the expressive ambiguities that arise at least in part from his ability to perceive quasi-Schubertian relationships between consonance and dissonance, tonality and atonality, as well as the loosely interchangeable modality of major/minor chords, and the motivic cipher B flat–A–E flat–C–B–E can slip easily into the surroundings of other works, other eras, even other contexts within the work itself.

The first movement begins as if in search of its own subject – as a kind of upbeat preparation for the melodic statement of a theme arrived at only with the second entry of the orchestral strings some sixteen bars further on. Heard again at the start of the second movement, the B–A–S–C–H–E motif is quickly revealed as having a passacaglia-like function against which to measure the expanding developments of the theme proper. Melodic transformations and intricate thematic cross-references then begin to gather momentum through a series of waltz-like episodes, arriving first at a more serene interlude, and then at a point where the tonal implications of the passacaglia theme are finally unmasked by a gently rocking piano accompaniment, with one last echo of the passacaglia motif heard low in the bass at the end. The whole of this rondo-like central scherzo is really a gloriously wide-ranging development of material introduced in the first and concluded in the last of the two framing slow movements – with the last movement retrieving the thread of an argument begun in the first, and moving to its eventual close under the gradually receding influence of the second.

Susan Bradshaw © BBC

Robert Schumann (1810–56)

After studying Law in Leipzig, Schumann intended to embark upon a career as a pianist, but an injury to his right hand compelled him to focus his energies on composition. During the 1830s he concentrated on works for the piano: largely character pieces, often literary-inspired, such as *Papillons* (1831), *Carnaval* (1835) and *Kinderszenen* (1838). He founded the influential *Neue Zeitschrift für Musik* in 1834 and by the end of 1835 was in love with Clara Wieck, daughter of his piano teacher, Friedrich Wieck. The year of his marriage to Clara, 1840, saw a blossoming of song composition, including the cycles *Dichterliebe* and *Frauenliebe und -leben*. Encouraged by Clara to explore larger forms, he wrote four symphonies, the concertos for piano (1845) and cello (1850) and the opera *Genoveva* (1852). In the 1840s his mental health declined; after an unsuccessful suicide attempt, he was admitted in 1854 to an asylum near Bonn, where he remained until his death.

❧ Cello Concerto in A minor, Op. 129
(1850)

1 Nicht zu schnell [Not too fast] –
2 Langsam [Slow] –
3 Sehr lebhaft [Very lively]

In 1849 Schumann was living in Dresden, where he was director of the local Liedertafel (an association providing small-scale musical performances) and conductor of the choral society. The year had begun productively with the composition of the *Phantasiestücke* for clarinet and piano, the *Konzertstück* for four horns and orchestra, several sets of part-songs, and other instrumental pieces. But by May the tide of revolutionary fervour that was sweeping Europe – toppling thrones and provoking fierce counter-revolutionary reprisals that forced many intellectuals into hiding – had reached Dresden. The Schumann family – Robert, Clara (who was, as usual, pregnant), their three daughters, and their fifteen-month old son, Ludwig – were forced to flee their home in the middle of the night and take refuge in the country. Despite the upheaval Schumann continued to compose, completing his *Liederalbum für die Jugend* and several more songs, and in June the family was able to return home. Shortly afterwards their next child – a son called Ferdinand – arrived; and Robert completed the first part of his *Scenes from Goethe's Faust*.

But by the autumn he was becoming restless. His conducting post in Dresden offered little scope; while his own technical limitations as a conductor caused major problems with the choirs and orchestras with which he worked. Towards the end of the year he received a proposal that offered a chance to break the routine and restore his morale. Ferdinand Hiller, from whom Schumann had taken over as conductor of the Dresden Liedertafel, offered yet another opportunity to succeed him – this time as Municipal Music Director in Düsseldorf. It took Schumann three months to make up his mind to accept the post. In September 1850 the Schumanns left Dresden for the Rhineland town.

There, although Robert felt depressed and unsettled at first, and their domestic conditions were far from ideal (they had a cramped, noisy apartment which made composition and practice virtually impossible), they were warmly welcomed and the first concerts of the season were an outstanding success. At the end of September Robert and Clara paid a visit to Cologne, where the beauty of the surrounding countryside and the awesome majesty of the great Gothic cathedral made a lasting impression. Schumann returned to Düsseldorf renewed in health and spirits. Three instrumental works were directly inspired by the trip: the 'Rhenish' Symphony, the overture *The Bride of Messina* and the Cello Concerto.

This last, mostly written in the space of just six days, was only Schumann's fourth work for solo instrument and orchestra, the others being the Piano Concerto, begun the year after his marriage and completed in 1845, and two *Konzertstücke* of 1849 – one for piano and orchestra, and the other for four horns. A cello concerto seems an odd choice for a composer to whom orchestral writing did not come naturally, although Schumann had apparently played the instrument himself. Unlike his piano music, which was mostly written for his wife, the Cello Concerto does not seem to have been composed with a specific player in mind, and it was not performed during his lifetime: its first recorded performance was given by Ludwig Ebert at the Leipzig Conservatory on 9 June 1860. Nor was there a precedent of Schumann's own time: the cello had never enjoyed the violin's popularity as a solo instrument, and Schumann's concerto is one of a mere handful of works to bridge the gap of more than a century between the two concertos of Haydn and Dvořák's masterpiece. Clara, however, thought that the new concerto was entirely successful: it pleased her greatly, and seemed to her 'to be particularly suited to the instrument'.

Schumann described his work as a 'Concert Piece for cello with orchestral accompaniment'. The emphasis throughout is on the lyrical and eloquent nature of the solo instrument, with the orchestra playing a subordinate role. As in the *Konzertstück* for four horns, there are no breaks between the three movements, which are linked by transitional passages. The piece shares the Piano Concerto's key of A minor, with a slow movement in F major; and Schumann's characteristic fingerprints are also evident in the lack of an orchestral exposition and the cyclic reappearance of the first movement's main subject in the finale. The slow movement – a compressed, meditative intermezzo similar in mood to that of the Piano Concerto – leads into the energetic finale by way of a recitative-like passage, and the concerto draws to its spirited close via a cadenza with lightly scored accompaniment: a novel idea that was not taken up by another major composer until Elgar.

© Wendy Thompson

∾ Piano Concerto in A minor, Op. 54
(1841–5)

1 Allegro affettuoso – Andante espressivo – Allegro
2 Intermezzo: Andantino grazioso –
3 Allegro vivace

Apart from early attempts that he never completed, Schumann wrote three works for piano and orchestra: the Concerto in A minor; an *Introduction and Allegro appassionato* in G major, Op. 92; and an *Introduction and Concert Allegro* in D minor, Op. 134. Sadly, only the concerto is regularly performed today, though, as Schumann's genius is increasingly appreciated, that might well change. It also began life as a single-movement work, a *Fantasy* which Schumann wrote in 1841, and to which he added the second and third movements in 1845 when he was persuaded that a longer work would stand a better chance of being published. Schumann's wife Clara gave the first performance, in Leipzig, on New Year's Day 1846, and although the response was miserable, the concerto was published the same year.

It seems hard to imagine that Schumann did not plan all three movements of the Piano Concerto from the outset, so naturally do they fit together. Liszt mischievously called it a concerto without piano, while others have called it a piano solo with orchestral accompaniment. Schumann was well aware that he was creating something unique – not a virtuoso showpiece relegating the orchestra to the background, though the solo part is challenging and much more difficult than it sounds; nor a dramatic dialogue between piano and orchestra with a formal framework in the classical tradition of Mozart and Beethoven. Schumann really fused piano and orchestra in a new way and had already described his achievement, prophetically, in an article he wrote in 1839:

> And so we must await the genius who will show us, in a
> newer and more brilliant way, how orchestra and piano

may be combined, how the soloist, dominant at the keyboard, may unfold the wealth of his instrument and his art, while the orchestra, no longer a mere spectator, may interweave its manifold facets into the scene.

The entire first movement grows from the theme first played by woodwinds and horns after the startling opening flourish. In a relaxed episode in A flat major (Andante espressivo) the piano lovingly engages the clarinet in a reverie that broadens out the main theme; when Paderewski played the concerto with Henry Wood, he asked for the clarinettist to sit where he could see him. A volley of exchanges based on the opening flourish and a shower of double octaves lead to a passionately rhapsodic exploration, taking the main theme on new harmonic routes until the recapitulation. The fully composed cadenza for the soloist starts by being toughly determined, then waxes ecstatically lyrical, and it brings the movement to its climax. After that, the coda is brisk and light, discharging all the accumulated tension.

Many modern performers take the middle movement much more slowly than Schumann marked it – each crotchet beat should last exactly a second. The title of 'Intermezzo' shows that he did not think of it as a slow movement, and its little upwards-tripping motif is taken straight from the second bar of the first-movement theme. (Clara Schumann's pupil Fanny Davies came closer to Schumann's wishes in her historic recording with Ernest Ansermet, still available on CD.)

The Intermezzo's light, scherzo-like character is counterbalanced by a long, arching melody on the cellos, whose wooing phrases are encouraged by graceful little responses from the piano. Towards the end, clarinets and bassoons gently propose the opening of the first movement theme – minor or major? – and the soloist springs into life for the finale.

This is a buoyant waltz – continuing in the background, as it were, even when, for contrast, Schumann doubles the beat in tiptoeing syncopation. Out of this the piano emerges bubbling and jumping in an unbroken outpouring of high spirits that must have made the uncomprehending reaction of the very first audience utterly baffling to Schumann and his wife.

© Adrian Jack

Dmitry Shostakovich (1906–75)

Shostakovich won early fame as a pianist and composer at the Petrograd Conservatory, graduating with his First Symphony (1925). His modernist tendencies were halted by Stalin's socialist policy on the arts, and following the damning *Pravda* editorial in 1936 on his opera *Lady Macbeth of Mtsensk*, Shostakovich offered his Fifth Symphony ('A Soviet Artist's creative reply to just criticism') as a rehabilitation piece. He was condemned again (along with Prokofiev) in 1948, and for five years until Stalin's death published only patriotic cantatas and small-scale works. But he continued to compose and completed fifteen symphonies, fifteen string quartets, six concertos (two each for piano, violin and cello), and scores for around thirty films. His final works – such as the last two symphonies, the last four string quartets and the Viola Sonata – are characterised by their sparse textures and their deep intensity and gravity.

∾ Cello Concerto No. 1 in E flat major, Op. 107 (1959)

1 Allegretto
2 Moderato –
3 Cadenza –
4 Allegro con moto

The great Russian cellist Mstislav Rostropovich got to know Shostakovich during the 1950s, when he and the composer performed the latter's Cello Sonata together in Moscow and on a tour of the Soviet Union. Rostropovich was keen to get Shostakovich to write a concerto for him – though wisely he decided to ask the composer's wife first. Her advice was simple: 'If you want [him] to write something for you, the only recipe I can give you is this – never ask him or talk to him about it.' Difficult though it was, Rostropovich managed to restrain himself; and in 1959 his patience was generously rewarded. Shostakovich's First Cello Concerto is one of the summits of the cello repertoire – emotionally and technically challenging, but superbly suited to Rostropovich's exceptional abilities, character and physical stamina.

According to Rostropovich, Shostakovich was partly inspired by his admiration for Prokofiev's *Sinfonia concertante* (1952) for cello and orchestra – another ferociously demanding piece also written for, and dedicated to, the great Russian cellist. But there's one big difference between the Prokofiev and Shostakovich works. Prokofiev – like Dvořák and Elgar in their famous concertos – pits the solo cello against a full symphony orchestra, including trumpets, trombones and tuba (though, also like Dvořák and Elgar, he's careful to score down the accompaniment when the cello is playing). But Shostakovich, realising how difficult it is for the cello to sound clearly through rich orchestral textures, opts for a much smaller orchestra: two of each woodwind, timpani, celesta, full strings, but only a single horn – sometimes used as a second soloist, the cello's more powerful alter ego. And the orchestral writing is starkly economical: every phrase, every detail counts.

It is the cellist who opens the first movement, with a hushed but hard-edged theme that Shostakovich was to quote the following year in his autobiographical Eighth Quartet. After some fiercely energetic writing, timpani and abrasive woodwind introduce the second theme, a high-pitched, impassioned melody for the cello, based on a chant-like figure alternating bars of two and three beats. Only later does the horn appear for the first time, loudly calling out the cello's first theme. The momentum is sustained right to the end – a hint of the second theme, then an abruptly dismissive gesture for horn and cello.

The Moderato is in complete contrast: mostly quiet, meditative, probing. Strings and horn prepare the way for the cello, which enters with a sad, folk-like theme. After the movement's strenuous climax, this theme returns magically on cello (high harmonics) answered by the celesta – the instrument's only appearance in this concerto.

The orchestra falls silent, then the cello begins the unaccompanied Cadenza – at first pondering slowly on themes from the Moderato, but gradually picking up speed and energy, until at its height strings and then woodwind enter savagely with the finale theme. This has the character of a grim dance, punctuated by timpani, fortissimo. After the woodwind have finished the theme, listen out for a brief motif passed rapidly between strings and high woodwind. This is a crafty, and unmistakably sarcastic reference to Stalin's favourite song 'Suliko'. Rostropovich recalls that he didn't recognise this barbed quotation until Shostakovich hummed it to him, then burst out laughing. There is more humour to come, all of it unmistakably black.

Suddenly, the pulse changes from two in a bar to a faster three, and the mood becomes increasingly frenzied. At last, something familiar is heard in woodwind and strings. Horn, fortissimo, confirms that this is the theme which opened the first movement. The theme returns in full, as heard at the beginning of the concerto, and the cello begins the final assault, full of cascading runs and gritty chordal writing. At the end the cello strains its voice to the maximum, with double and triple octaves – then, with another abrupt gesture, the concerto is over.

Stephen Johnson © BBC

∾ Concerto in C minor for Piano, Trumpet and Strings (Piano Concerto No. 1), Op. 35 (1933)

1 Allegretto –
2 Lento –
3 Moderato –
4 Allegro con brio

Shostakovich's six concertos – two each for piano, violin and cello – are nearly all works from the later part of his career, written in the two decades between 1947 and 1967. The single exception is the First Piano Concerto, which was written in 1933 for Shostakovich himself, then aged twenty-seven, to play.

Like Rakhmaninov and Prokofiev, Shostakovich was a formidable pianist: he was taught first by his mother, a professional pianist, and then studied at the Petrograd Conservatory under the great Leonid Nikolayev. He graduated from the piano class in 1923 and four years later received an honourable mention in the first ever Chopin International Piano Competition in Warsaw. But his naturally reticent temperament was unsuited to the tough career of a professional concert pianist, and during the 1930s and early 1940s he tended to stick to performing his own music. Subsequently he gradually withdrew from performing until severe arthritis forced him to give up completely in the mid-1960s.

But thirty years earlier Shostakovich – then a high-spirited young composer with great hopes for the future, and with the apparent support of the official cultural establishment – was working on his opera *Lady Macbeth of Mtsensk*, the notorious piece that would shortly bring down Stalin's wrath on his hapless head. He finished the opera shortly before Christmas 1932, and after a brief break, he began work on the twenty-four preludes for piano, which he finished on 2 March 1933. Just four days later, he began work on the First Piano Concerto, which he finished on 20 July. He gave the score to the Austrian-born conductor Fritz Stiedry, a refugee from Nazism who became Principal Conductor of the Leningrad Philharmonic in the mid-1930s. Stiedry put the work into rehearsal in late September, and on 15 October 1933 it was first heard in public in the Great Hall of the Leningrad Philharmonia, with Shostakovich at the piano and Alexander Schmidt, the orchestra's principal trumpet, playing the substantial trumpet part. In December the work received its Moscow premiere, and just over two years later it was first heard in Britain at a Winter Prom given by the BBC

Symphony Orchestra under Henry Wood at the Queen's Hall in London. The pianist was Eileen Joyce. Shostakovich later recorded the work twice as soloist, once with the Moscow Philharmonic in 1957, and a year later with the French National Radio Orchestra under André Cluytens.

In December 1933 Shostakovich gave an interview in which he said that this work was his first attempt at

> . . . filling an important gap in Soviet instrumental music, which lacks full-scale concerto-type works. What is the basic artistic theme of this concerto? . . . I am a Soviet composer. Our age, as I perceive it, is heroic, spirited and joyful. This is what I wanted to convey in my Concerto. It is for the audience, and possibly the music critics, to judge whether or not I succeeded.

Like many of Shostakovich's public pronouncements, however, this isn't quite the whole story. Shostakovich's music may pretend to be heroic and joyful, but underneath it is usually savage, biting and sardonic – a commentary on the Kafkaesque society in which the composer lived. This may explain the presence of the trumpet as a second soloist: the timbres of the two solo instruments are incongruous, not complementary, and the work's ironic humour derives from their power struggle. This is particularly evident in the rondo finale, in which a long trumpet solo in the central section (quoting a popular street song) is brought to an abrupt halt by a caricature of a piano cadenza. And when the trumpet launches a triumphant coda punctuated with fanfares, its valiant attempts to bring the piece to an end are twice frustrated by the piano, the second time with a crazy, drunken polka.

The finale is also peppered with quotations: the main string theme is based on a variant of Beethoven's *Rondo a capriccio* (also known as 'Rage over a Lost Penny'), while the trumpet briefly alludes to the opening of a Haydn piano sonata in D major.

© Wendy Thompson

∾ Piano Concerto No. 2 in F, Op. 102 (1956–7)

1 Allegro
2 Andante –
3 Allegro

Shostakovich's concertos for his own instrument are among his most sheerly enjoyable, least demanding works, snappily neo-classical in manner but with a not-quite-concealed vein of poetic feeling. The Second Piano Concerto was composed in 1956–7 immediately before Shostakovich began work on the mammoth Eleventh Symphony. Intended for his teenage son Maxim, it was caustically dismissed as having 'no artistic value' by the composer himself in a letter to Edison Denisov, but might more fairly be seen as a relaxation from more serious artistic preoccupations.

Written not long after Shostakovich had released a number of the highly intense works he had concealed during the last years of Stalin's dictatorship, it is tempting to read into the music the optimism and sense of freedom that followed Stalin's death. But in point of fact these were sad times for Shostakovich: his first wife, Nina, had recently died and he had got himself entangled in an unsuitable and short-lived second marriage. With its plentiful stock of first-rate melodic material, the concerto reflects rather Shostakovich's closeness to (and involvement with the musical education of) his son. It was Maxim who premiered the work in Moscow on 10 May 1957; the composer himself recorded it in Paris, and Leonard Bernstein soon introduced it to American audiences, directing performances from the keyboard.

There are the usual three movements. The first begins with a pungent idea for bassoon that sets the scene for the soloist's entry – a delightfully cheeky theme sparely set as a single line doubled in the two hands. This octave doubling is a characteristic feature of Shostakovich's keyboard writing, which also exploits the extremities of the instrument. While momentum is maintained throughout, the texture is always light and airy, with plenty of perky contributions from the wind. The Andante is again wholly straightforward but affecting too, with a dreamy atmosphere that taps into a range of archetypes from Grieg to Rakhmaninov. Some have dismissed it as pure kitsch, which is to belittle Shostakovich's skill, even if he appears here as the adaptable (and genuinely popular) composer of movie music rather than the granitic titan of Soviet symphonism.

The finale (which follows the second movement without a break) returns to the style of the opening – sparkling and brilliant, addressing a younger audience, maybe, but quite without the patronising overtones which that can imply. The movement is in the form of a rondo with the first, dance-like theme contrasted with a second, more demonstrative idea in 7/8, plus some ironic allusions to the didactic exercises – all too familiar to countless piano students – of Charles-Louis Hanon.

© David Gutman

∾ Violin Concerto No. 1 in A minor, Op. 77 (1947–8; rev. 1955)

1 Nocturne: Moderato
2 Scherzo: Allegro
3 Passacaglia: Andante – Cadenza –
4 Burlesque: Allegro con brio – Presto

'It is only under the highest pressure that diamonds are formed.' So Boris Tishchenko, one of Shostakovich's favourite pupils of the 1960s, has described his teacher's striking ability to produce masterpieces such as the First Violin Concerto at times of extreme personal and professional adversity.

After the relative creative freedoms of wartime, Stalin was determined to reassert Party control over the Arts, as over every aspect of life in the Soviet Union. He appointed as his henchman Andrey Zhdanov, who carried out the task with exemplary efficiency. Zhdanov's first priority was to bring writers and film-makers to heel. Then in 1948 it was the turn of composers. On 10 February, while Shostakovich was in the middle of composing the finale of his First Violin Concerto, he and a clutch of his most distinguished colleagues were at the receiving end of a resolution of the Central Committee of the Communist Party castigating them for 'formalist distortions and anti-democratic tendencies'. For the rest of the year a torrent of abuse descended upon him, and he was dismissed from his teaching posts at the Leningrad and Moscow Conservatoires.

His work on the Violin Concerto, however, continued without obvious hitch. Asked where he had got to in the composition when the resolution was published, Shostakovich pointed out the place in the score. As the eyewitness commented many years later: 'The violin played semiquavers before and after it. There was no change evident in the music.'

Completed in March 1948, the concerto had to join a long list of effectively banned works (though it did not feature on the official list of the Committee for Artistic Affairs, which included the Sixth, Eighth and Ninth Symphonies and the First Piano Concerto). The work had not been written 'for the drawer', in the manner of some non-conformist literature of the time, but it had to be kept there until its belated premiere in October 1955, two and a half years after the death of Stalin.

The soloist on that occasion was David Oistrakh, doyen of Soviet violinists, for whom the piece had been written. The composer and violinist had first met on a visit to Turkey in 1935, after which they had performed Mozart and Beethoven sonatas together. But the immediate stimulus for the First Violin Concerto seems to have been Oistrakh's extraordinary concert series in the 1947–8 season: 'The Development of the Violin'.

Despite the movement titles, which might suggest something akin to a suite, this is one of the most symphonic of concertos by any composer for any instrument. Only the opening Nocturne lacks the weight of a symphonic first movement, though it is certainly profound and passionate enough in expression; essentially this is an accompanied meditation for the soloist, whose angular but always singing lines continually aspire from darkness to light.

The Scherzo is a grimly determined affair, and just as concentrated and intense as the Nocturne; at its apex is a characteristic dance of death, marked by the appearance of the xylophone.

The Passacaglia is one of Shostakovich's most profound slow movements; its main theme, initially on timpani, cellos and double basses, picks up one of the numerous ideas thrown off in the course of the preceding Scherzo, while the stern horn call above it will prove to be the seed for the following Cadenza.

So exhausting did Oistrakh find this Cadenza that he had to plead with the composer to give him some respite at the beginning of the finale. This Shostakovich eventually agreed to do, by giving the finale's opening bars to orchestra alone, although the original continuous version is extant and is sometimes performed. Despite the heading Burlesque, this finale is another single-minded and determinedly serious movement, a worthy conclusion to one of Shostakovich's most exciting, yet most carefully composed scores.

© David Fanning

Jean Sibelius (1865–1957)

Sibelius established himself early in his career as Finland's national composer, helped by his ability to convey the austere beauty of his country, his passionate adoption of themes from the Finnish folk epic the *Kalevala*, and his patriotic music such as *Finlandia* (1900). Born north of Helsinki, he initially intended to become a violinist, but studied composition in Vienna and Berlin between 1889 and 1891. His choral *Kullervo* Symphony and the tone poem *En Saga* (1892, both inspired by the *Kalevala*) preceded seven purely orchestral symphonies, ranging from the Tchaikovsky-influenced First (1900) to the enigmatically brief Seventh (1924). Supported by a government pension from the age of thirty-two, he effectively retired for the last thirty years of his life, writing no major works (though he started an eighth symphony, which he destroyed). His Violin Concerto, by turns introverted and highly virtuosic, remains among the most popular in the repertory.

❧ Violin Concerto in D minor, Op. 47 (1903; rev. 1905)

1   Allegro moderato
2   Adagio di molto
3   Allegro

'Dreamt I was twelve years old and a virtuoso.' So Sibelius noted, wistfully, in his diary in 1915. To those of us who aren't geniuses, it may be hard to understand how a man with five magnificent symphonies, a growingly popular violin concerto and a sequence of superbly imaginative tone poems to his credit should feel in any way an artistic failure. But as that poignant little diary entry shows, Sibelius at fifty could still smart inwardly at the thought of what might have been.

For there had been a time when a career as a violin virtuoso had been a real possibility. Sibelius's violin teacher at the
Helsinki University, Mitrofan Vasiliev, had pronounced him
a 'genius'. Others were more cautious, but on the whole
encouraging. Yet something seems to have gone wrong with
Sibelius's confidence, and his technique suffered. Eventually
came the moment of decision. He thought of renouncing
music altogether – 'and living the life of an idiot, for which
I'm well qualified'. But while he was able to give up the violin, the urge to compose was too strong. Sibelius bowed to
what he believed to be the ruling of Fate – he was to be a
composer, not a violinist – but not without lasting regret.

Then, at the turn of the century, Sibelius met the man who
was to become one of his closest and most influential friends,
Axel Carpelan. Carpelan was bursting with ideas: Sibelius
should go to Italy for inspiration, he should write another
symphony, music for Shakespeare's plays, a violin concerto
. . . Sibelius did all these things; but one can imagine how
mixed his feelings must have been when he came to tackle the
concerto project.

It may be significant that the time immediately before and
during Sibelius's work on the Violin Concerto was marked by
one of his worst periods of alcoholism. His heroically patient
wife Aino frequently went out to search Helsinki's fashionable clubs, bars and restaurants for him, hoping against hope
that he might just sober up enough to complete the work.
The slow movement of the concerto was apparently sketched
out during a colossal three-day hangover. Sibelius's brother,
Christian (a clinical psychiatrist), begged him to stop drink-
ing. But Sibelius replied that he was just too weak. 'When I
am standing in front of a grand orchestra and have drunk a
half-bottle of champagne, then I conduct like a young god.
Otherwise I am nervous and tremble, feel unsure of myself,
and then everything is lost. The same is true of my visits to
the bank manager.'

Given all this, it is surprising how little evidence there is of
'weakness' – either intellectual or spiritual – in the Violin

Concerto. True, we are hearing a revised version, made the year after the work's premiere (in Helsinki on 8 February 1904), in which the original score was cut and the violin part somewhat simplified. And yet nowhere is this the kind of music one would describe as self-indulgent or loose-limbed. The violin writing is masterly – an indication of how thoroughly Sibelius understood his instrument. Some of it is ferociously difficult – even in the 'simplified' revised version – but on the whole it presents the kind of challenges that excite rather than intimidate virtuosos. Still, there are moments which can bring the most expert player out in a cold sweat – and they're not always the passages that sound the most difficult to the audience. After the first big climax in the slow movement, there's a sudden hush from the orchestra, while the soloist, still forte, plays two rhythms simultaneously: a syncopated high figure accompanied by crotchet triplets. It's hard enough on a keyboard, with two hands; with just one bow, five fingers and four strings it's very nearly impossible.

The idea of mastery extends to every dimension of the Violin Concerto. Construction is taut, emotions are powerful but not uncontrolled, the long lyrical paragraphs (like the floating, soaring violin line at the very beginning) are always beautifully shaped – they never sprawl. There are moments, such as the impassioned second theme of the first movement, or virtually the whole of the central Adagio di molto, where the mood is achingly nostalgic, even pained. But the hand of Sibelius the great symphonist, the master of organic logic, is always in evidence. And after the emotionally probing first and second movements comes an energetic, resolute finale, with a theme the musician and writer Donald Tovey whimsically dubbed a 'polonaise for polar bears'. The stern, stormy but unambiguously major-key ending suggests inner darkness confronted and defied – the composer very much the captain of his soul. In terms of Sibelius's own life at the time, this may have been wish-fulfilment; but as art it's resoundingly convincing.

Stephen Johnson © BBC

Alexander Skryabin (1872–1915)

A student alongside Rakhmaninov at the Moscow Conservatoire, Skryabin began his career as a pianist. His early compositions were piano miniatures indebted to Chopin, including nocturnes, impromptus and a set of twenty-four *Préludes* (1888–96), as well as the twelve *Études*, Op. 8 (1894). He produced his first orchestral scores around the time of his first marriage, in 1897, to a young pianist, and taught for five years at the Moscow Conservatoire. By 1905 he had left both wife and Conservatoire, and had come under the influence of the theosophy of Madame Blavatsky; after this time his music, including *The Poem of Ecstasy* (1905–8) and the Piano Sonatas Nos 5–10, became increasingly harmonically daring. He was drawn to mysticism and connections between the senses: he proposed the use of a 'colour keyboard' for his *Prometheus: The Poem of Fire*, 1909–10, which would project colours relating to the harmonies on a screen. He also planned a seven-day 'supreme ecstatic mystery', *Mysterium*, to take place in India: a synthesis of all the arts and the senses, which he believed would hasten a cataclysmic world event that would regenerate humanity.

∾ *Prometheus: The Poem of Fire*, Op. 60 (1909–10)

By the age of thirty-seven Skryabin had become the most discussed and controversial of Russian composers, but it was more by reputation than through first-hand knowledge of his recent music, for he had been living in Western Europe for some years. At the beginning of 1909, however, he visited Russia for a series of concerts organised by Serge Koussevitzky, the former double-bass player in the Bolshoy Theatre Orchestra, who had married money, bought an orchestra, founded a publishing house and taken it upon himself to manage the affairs of the hopelessly impractical composer.

The Skryabin concerts at the beginning of 1909 included the premieres of his latest solo piano pieces (played by himself) and of the orchestral *Poem of Ecstasy* which, with its exaltation of the creative ego, marked an early approach to the grandiose vision that was already taking shape in the composer's mind, a gigantic *Mysterium* that would be a fusion of all the arts and require vast numbers of performers who would come together in a hemispherical temple by a lakeside in India.

Skryabin believed that he had actually begun the composition of this project early in 1909, but soon came to realise that the work he had in hand was only a further step towards his vision; as it turned out, *Prometheus* was to be the last orchestral work he completed before his early death. It was composed mainly in Brussels, where Skryabin spent most of the year 1909, and completed early in 1910, soon after he had returned to live permanently in Moscow. The first performances took place in Moscow on 2 March 1911 and in St Petersburg a week later. Koussevitzky conducted, and Skryabin played the solo piano part.

The idea behind *Prometheus* is nothing less than the evolution of the world from formless chaos, through the appearance of mankind, fertilised by the divine spark, towards spiritual liberation and ultimate transcendence. In Greek mythology, the titan Prometheus stole fire from the sparks of Apollo's chariot wheels, and in defiance of the gods of Olympus gave it to mortal men. For this he was punished by the gods: he was chained to a rock and had his entrails repeatedly torn out by a vulture for all eternity. Skryabin further identified this rebel-hero figure with the fallen angel Lucifer, and with two other great sacrificial victims and bringers of enlightenment to mankind – Jesus Christ and himself.

Heady stuff, very much of its period, when so much Russian art found its expression in cloudy abstraction, over-perfumed, decadent excess and esoteric philosophy. Yet Skryabin the musician was a far more hard-headed creature than Skryabin the mystical dreamer. The construction of *Prometheus* is actually very meticulous, almost schematic. Skryabin thought naturally in small units: melodic ideas of a few notes, one-bar rhythmic patterns and tiny decorative figurations. 'There is no difference between melody and harmony,' Skryabin maintained. 'They are one and the same. I have followed this principle strictly in *Prometheus*. There is not a wasted note, not a wedge where a mosquito could get in and bite!'

On close scrutiny his largest pieces, whether for solo piano or for full orchestra, reveal themselves to be a mosaic of contrasts and combinations made up of what are in fact very small elements, so closely woven that they give an effect of an indivisible, organic texture. These separate fragments were invested by the composer with particular philosophical significance, and their blending, and the constant acceleration of pace and incident, express the work's evolutionary programme.

Prometheus opens with an image of formless, shapeless inertia; a quiet theme rising up on the horns represents the creative principle, the solo piano represents mankind fertilised by the divine fire brought by Prometheus. The composer's own lavish directions in the score (in French) give a sort of running commentary on the music's progress: *misty – mysteriously – sparkling – voluptuously, almost painfully – imperiously – with emotion and ecstatic delight – defiantly, warlike, stormy – victorious – sublime – piercing, flashing – with a dazzling burst of sound – in a vertiginous whirl.*

The orchestra is large, with particularly important parts for tuned percussion and harps, and with the solo piano playing a commanding, quasi-concerto role. Towards the end of the score there is also an optional part for a wordless chorus, which Skryabin imagined robed in white. Ideally the audience, too, would be clad in white, for in his dreams of fusing all the arts together, Skryabin placed enormous importance on the relationship between sound and colour. He incorporated into the score of *Prometheus* a *Clavier à lumières*: a sort of 'colour organ' (developed by his friend Alexander Moser, a professor of electronic engineering) that would bathe performers and audience in a play of coloured lights corresponding to the harmonic and philosophical progress of the music. Thus after the final acceleration and wild, fragmented dance, the last bars of *Prometheus* burst through into F sharp major, the first and only tonal resolution in the score, representing mankind's achievement of creative liberation and a dazzling bright blue in colour.

© Andrew Huth

Richard Strauss (1864–1949)

Strauss composed from his early years (his first two published works were written when he was ten), and also developed a conducting career alongside his success in composition: 1886 saw not only the premiere of his First Horn Concerto, but also a conducting post at the Munich Court Opera. In the same year, influenced by Liszt, he produced *Aus Italien*, the first of a string of brilliantly orchestrated tone poems extending through the 1890s, among them *Don Juan*, *Till Eulenspiegel* and *Also sprach Zarathustra*. Strauss was also inspired by Wagner, and went on to write some of the twentieth century's finest operas: in 1905 he shocked the operatic world with *Salome*. *Elektra* (1909, another fiercely powerful portrait) marked his first collaboration with the poet Hugo von Hofmannsthal, a partnership that bore four further operas, including the comedy *Der Rosenkavalier* (1911). His operatic output continued through the turbulence of the Nazi years, and he also wrote successful orchestral works in a generally late-romantic idiom. He died on 8 September 1949, several months before the first performance of his *Four Last Songs*.

∿ Horn Concerto No. 2 in E flat major (1942)

1 Allegro –
2 Andante con moto
3 Rondo: Allegro molto

Had Strauss composed this work one year later, in 1943, he could have used it to mark the sixtieth anniversary of his Horn Concerto No. 1 of 1883. As it is it marks a return, after the completion of his last opera *Capriccio* in 1941, to those more abstract instrumental and orchestral forms tried out in his youth – which would also feature so prominently in his last years, as the two wind sonatinas, the Oboe Concerto and the *Duett-Concertino* confirm.

It is no insult to the Second Horn Concerto to describe it as the triumph of experience – and inspiration – over convention. Strauss, as always, was stimulated by tradition, and so while the ideas in themselves may often be familiar, recalling his own, earlier music and that of other Romantic composers (Mendelssohn, in particular), the ways in which the ideas are organised and explored display a still lively inventiveness, self-questioning rather than self-indulgent.

The first movement begins expansively, with an introduction dominated by the soloist, and a large-scale exposition, launched by the orchestra, in which the second group has particular clear points of contact with Strauss's operatic past. To balance this expansiveness, however, development and recapitulation are much more concentrated, and the coda serves less to round off the Allegro than to prepare for the Andante, a movement whose form could scarcely be more orthodox in its ternary outlines, but whose ideas and textures reveal touches of imagination in every bar.

Convention is transcended with even greater panache in the Rondo finale, a movement of which Strauss himself was particularly proud. It rings the changes on its fanfare-style material with such inimitable flair that the comparisons often made with the final stages of Verdi's *Falstaff* seem far from inappropriate or overstated. Of course this concerto is closer to the world of Strauss's youth, and of his redoubtable horn-playing father, than to the contemporary musical scene of the 1940s, as represented by the most progressive, forward-looking spirits of the time. But with music as vital and good-humoured as this, accusations of sterile conservatism are more than usually beside the point.

© Arnold Whittall

❧ Concerto for Oboe and Small Orchestra (1945)

Allegro moderato – Andante – Vivace – Allegro

After Richard Strauss finished his last opera, *Capriccio*, in 1941, he began to look on his life's work as complete. He told Clemens Krauss, the opera's librettist and first conductor, that henceforth he would compose only for harps. Instead, he lived on for another eight years, into an Indian summer of composition which brought forth a number of instrumental works, including the present concerto, before he said a final farewell with the exquisite *Four Last Songs*. We apparently owe the Oboe Concerto to the suggestion of John de Lancie, who, as an American serviceman with the forces occupying Bavaria, visited Strauss at Garmisch in 1945, and later became principal oboist of the Philadelphia Orchestra.

Writing of his several visits to Strauss at this time, Mr de Lancie has recalled:

> It was on the lovely veranda that I casually mentioned the idea of him composing a piece for oboe. He seemed to like it. Many months later, I learned that a concerto for oboe had been finished. Strauss sent me a handwritten postcard inviting me to attend the world premiere in Zurich [but] . . . my plans did not allow me to attend.

The Zurich premiere was on 26 February 1946, and this and subsequent performances soon revealed that the composer's imagination had looked with affection on an instrument that he had used to eloquent purpose in such works as *Don Juan*, *Don Quixote* and *Der Rosenkavalier*.

Lightness of texture is a consistent feature in all the works of Strauss's old age, and the Oboe Concerto keeps the attention focused on the solo instrument by supporting it with an orchestral ensemble restricted to two flutes, a single cor anglais, and two each of clarinets, bassoons and horns, in addition to strings. The piece follows a conventional classical outline, but its three movements are performed without a break, and are further integrated by themes and phrases common to each of them. A rocking figure for cellos at the outset is a foundation element in the music, its rhythm giving a spur to the soloist's long and lyrical first melody. Part of the theme, together with the rhythmic figure and also the second theme of the opening movement, begun by four repeated notes, recur in the two following movements, and there are cadenzas for the oboe between the second and third movements and before the Allegro coda to the finale. For the rest, the music exists to be enjoyed for its own sake, irrespective of dates and trends, and reflecting the skill and experience of a composer who was content to echo Maillol: '*Je ne travaille pas; je m'amuse*', even though the world around him was far from amusing.

© Noël Goodwin

Igor Stravinsky (1882–1971)

Stravinsky's unrivalled impact on the course of twentieth-century music was originally brought about by the complexity and originality of his first ballets, on Russian themes, for Diaghilev's Ballets Russes: *The Firebird* (1910), *Petrushka* (1911) and *The Rite of Spring* (1913), though we now know how much they owe to the Russian folk-music tradition. With his move to Paris and another ballet, *Pulcinella* (1920), came a shift to the sharp-edged clarity of the neo-classical style, which also characterises the Octet (1923) and Piano Concerto (1924). In the eight months to June 1939, Stravinsky suffered the loss of his daughter, wife and mother in turn and, with war impending, decamped to the USA, where he undertook numerous conducting tours, and composed *The Rake's Progress* (1951). In the 1950s, ever in tune with the times, Stravinsky made another compositional change, in which he embraced serialism (the ballet *Agon*, 1957; the cantata *Threni*, 1958). He made many recordings of his own music, as both conductor and pianist.

∾ Concerto for Piano and Wind Instruments (1923–4)

1 Largo – Allegro
2 Largo
3 Allegro

The Piano Concerto is in many ways the key work of Stravinsky's early neo-classical period. Written between the summer of 1923 and the following April, it encapsulates all the essential features of a style which Stravinsky himself described (while writing the concerto, though he was referring to the immediately preceding Octet for wind) as 'based on objective elements which are sufficient in themselves'.

Nearly all his works of these years are for piano and/or wind, with only a limited role for string instruments. He had composed the *Symphonies of Wind Instruments* (1920), followed by the little opera *Mavra* (1921–2; wind band plus a few solo strings), and the Octet (1922–3); and in between came the *Three Movements from Petrushka* for solo piano (1921), and the definitive version of the ballet *Les noces*, which Diaghilev at last put on in June 1923, with its scoring for four pianos and percussion.

Why was Stravinsky so obsessed with these dry, brittle, seemingly mechanistic sounds? There is no single answer, but a number of separate ones which perhaps belong together. In part, he was certainly responding to a general mood in art at the time: the mood of '*neue Sachlichkeit*' (new objectivity), or of Cocteau's description of art, in the very first sentence of his *Le coq et l'arlequin*, as 'science made flesh'. Out with slushy Romanticism and the artist as hero, in with the hard, the functional, the workmanlike, the artist as craftsman. This might have a political or sociological edge, as in Boris Asaf'yev's dry characterisation of Stravinsky's early 1920s idiom as 'the synthetic instrumental style of contemporary urbanism'. Or it might be a matter of ethics, as in Jacques Maritain's exhortation in 1920 to artists 'to abandon the huge intellectual disarray bequeathed by the nineteenth century and rediscover the spiritual conditions of honest toil'. The idea of a 'recall to order' (Cocteau's phrase again) was obviously in Stravinsky's mind. We know this because in his various essays of the period he explains his concentration on wind instruments as a way of establishing a rigid, un-nuanced, unemotive form. 'The difference of the volume of these instruments,' he wrote (rather obscurely, it now seems), 'renders more evident the musical architecture.'

A big part of this reaction against the Romantic swoon comes out in Stravinsky's fear of the performer. Just at this period he was busy arranging his music for pianola, an instrument which (to oversimplify) plays by itself. And even if he did not compose the Piano Concerto for his own use – having not yet embarked on the solo career which was to dominate his life after 1924 – he quickly accepted Koussevitzky's suggestion that he perform it, and then proceeded to slap an embargo on anyone else doing so for the next five years. Stravinsky was the pianist at the premiere under Koussevitzky at the Paris Opéra in May 1924, and he went on to play it more than forty times before the embargo expired. But by a delicious irony, the machine broke down at the very first performance. 'Just before the Largo, which opens with a passage for solo piano,' Stravinsky wrote in his autobiography, 'I suddenly realised that I had completely forgotten how it started.' Koussevitzky had to hum him the tune before the performance could proceed.

As with many composers of the 1920s, Stravinsky's ideal of architectural rigour and interpretative chastity was Bach. The influence of the great knitting-needle virtuoso is plainly evident in the brilliant outer movements of the Piano Concerto, not only in the Allegro movements, with their identical and unvarying quaver beat ('monometrics', Stravinsky called this), but also in the Largo introduction, with its stern dotted rhythms ('a conscious stylistic reference', the composer admits in his *Conversations*). But as usual the reference is superficial, and in reality the music moves with a purely modern impulse, its spectacular thrown metres responding to the vibrantly dissonant harmony. The slow movement also alludes to Bach, but with a heavy texture and gait which make the reference much less apparent to modern audiences for whom Bach equals Harnoncourt than it probably did in 1924, when Bach equalled Hamilton Harty. But then the 'classicism' in Stravinsky's neo-classicism invariably relays a complicated message about its alleged models, telling us not only that 'his' Bach may not have been ours, but also that in any case the Bach in question is a purely symbolic entity, only incidentally related to its flesh-and-blood namesake.

© Stephen Walsh

∾ Violin Concerto in D (1931)

1 Toccata
2 Aria I
3 Aria II
4 Capriccio

The history of the creation of this work is well documented. In 1931 the violinist Samuel Dushkin asked Stravinsky to write him a concerto. Stravinsky was on tour at the time in Wiesbaden, Germany. He expressed reluctance at first but was persuaded to go along with the idea, perhaps encouraged by the fact that Dushkin had suggested that they share exclusive performance rights for a period. Dushkin was granted a large say in the writing of the solo part and the finished work was given its premiere in Berlin on 23 October 1931.

The partnership turned out to be a personal success as well as a musical one, to the extent that the pair had formed a busy touring duo by the end of 1932. Stravinsky collaborated with Dushkin several times afterwards, on the *Duo concertant* for piano and violin, and on a series of arrangements, including the *Suite italienne* based on music from the ballet *Pulcinella*.

Each of the concerto's four movements is introduced by the same triple-stopped chord that Dushkin had told Stravinsky it was impossible to play when the composer had noted it down on a piece of paper at one of their earliest meetings. Their titles collectively suggest something like a Bach suite, but the new listener should not be deceived: the work is emphatically not a parody of Baroque music. Even though its constituent motivic cells have their roots in the manners of the eighteenth century, this is a different architecture altogether. Angular, colliding and refracted, the music achieves its momentum through constant and sudden change rather than through a process of gradual metamorphosis. A visual analogy might be a stage divided into several sets, each one a different colour, each one illuminated in turn, in unpredictable sequence and for unpredictable periods of time.

If that makes one think of a music that is objective, clever, even dry, again the truth is rather different. The opening Toccata relies not so much upon sheer speed for its effect as upon its dry staccatos, its stabbing chords, its incessant motion, and the manner of its gradual final slowing down, evoking something like the image of the piston action of a steam train. The title of the closing Capriccio might suggest whimsical mischief, but in fact this is bright, kaleidoscopic music, of great rhythmic complexity and of yet more unstoppable impetus, dazzling in its brilliance, its intercutting of ideas. In both movements Stravinsky sometimes resorts to banal circus sounds, oom-pah-pah accompaniments and the rest.

In between are the two Arias, the first basically an A–B–A structure but teeming with ideas and complex changes of mood and pace, from the dark and ripe to the skittish. Certainly there is nothing objective about this music, and neither is there about its successor, subtly orchestrated, founded on a bed of sustained harmonies, yet made uneasy by the alternating pairs of repeated chords that appear some way into the music. Here we are reminded of two important matters often overlooked when discussing Stravinsky's so-called 'neo-classical' music: that he was a Russian who inherited both a Russian sensibility and the musical heritage of Tchaikovsky; and that this concerto is not only for but about the violin and all its inherent characteristics, lyrical as well as percussive.

Stephen Pettitt © BBC

Karol Szymanowski (1882–1937)

Szymanowski was born in the Russian-ruled Ukraine and suffered poor health from an early age. He studied in Warsaw from 1901 to 1904, before absorbing European influences during seven years in Germany, Vienna and Paris; his Second Symphony is from this period. Travels in Italy, Sicily, Algeria and Morocco from 1910 to 1914, together with the influence of Stravinsky and Debussy, led to a more perfumed, exotic style, heard in the Third Symphony *The Song of the Night* (1914–16) and the *Songs of a Fairy Princess* (1915) – written while he was confined in Russia during the war. With his home destroyed by the Bolsheviks in the October Revolution he moved back to Warsaw where he wrote the powerful opera *King Roger* (1920–4). In the early 1920s he began to infuse his sophisticated style with Polish folk song, as in the successful ballet *Harnasie* (1923–31) and the *Stabat mater* (1925–6). He became director of the Warsaw Conservatoire in 1927, then, from 1929 until 1932, rector of the Warsaw Academy of Music. Among his last major works are the *Sinfonia concertante* (1932) and his Second Violin Concerto (1933).

✑ Symphony No. 4 (*Sinfonia concertante*), for Piano and Orchestra, Op. 60 (1932)

1 Moderato. Tempo comodo
2 Andante molto sostenuto –
3 Allegro non troppo, ma agitato ed ansioso

Szymanowski composed this work in three months in the spring of 1932. Some years earlier he had begun to sketch a piano concerto, and now he took up the idea again, this time with a definite practical purpose. By the early 1930s he had no official position and no income. He was desperate for money, and decided to write a work that he could play himself. Although he was too shy and fastidious a man to be suited to a performing career (he never even attempted to conduct an orchestra), he felt that public performances of a new piece in which he could feature as soloist would not only earn him some money but also serve to promote his other music.

He gave the first performance in Poznan on 9 October 1932. The orchestra was conducted by Grzegorz Fitelberg, a close friend of the composer since their student days in Warsaw, who conducted the premieres of much of his music. The *Sinfonia concertante* was one of the few works of Szymanowski to gain some popularity. It received thirty performances in the remaining five years of his life, most of them given by the composer himself. In 1934 he gave the British premiere, conducted by Malcolm Sargent and broadcast by the BBC, then performed it during a tour of Russia and the Balkans, and in 1935 throughout Scandinavia. The *Sinfonia concertante* did indeed bring him some income (though never enough for this hopelessly impractical man), but these tours had a ruinous effect on his already weak health.

The hybrid title indicates the in-between character of the work. It does not have the density of argument associated with a symphony, but neither is it a display concerto (unlike the two violin concertos). Szymanowski was a very fine pianist, though perhaps not in the virtuoso class. The solo piano is very prominent, but so are many instruments of the orchestra, which emerge either in combination with the piano or as soloists in their own right. The orchestral sound is sparser than in many of Szymanowski's earlier works, each instrumental line calculated more tellingly and more audibly. Similarly, there is something of a neo-classical cast to the form, which is clearly sectional, with recognisable developments and reprises.

Szymanowski described the first movement (not altogether helpfully) as being 'close to sonata form, but not quite the same'. It begins with an innocent lyricism, the decorative piano line recalling the rhythms of Chopin (as a Pole and as a pianist, Szymanowski was naturally brought up on Chopin), and almost everything in the movement derives from these opening bars. The music shows a tendency to move from calm towards agitation, with tempos beginning slowly and gradually accelerating.

In the slow movement the solo piano occupies a position that is neither quite background nor foreground. It begins by providing a rich accompaniment to the gorgeous opening flute melody, and although it rarely contributes to the melodic line of the movement, it is an eloquent presence throughout. At the end, flute and piano recall the opening of the first movement before the piano leads directly into the finale.

This is the most folk-influenced of the movements, and the one that most betrays Szymanowski's interest in folk music and in the music of Bartók. Ten years before composing the *Sinfonia concertante* Szymanowski had been captivated by the 'savage, natural native originality' of the folk music from the Tatra mountains in southern Poland. He heard in it a freshness and vigour that showed him the way towards the greater clarity of expression that he was aiming for, after the dense chromaticism and impressionistic textures of his earlier music. Intricate and decorative detail gave way to strong, unbroken melody; the mastery of orchestral colour was directed towards more solid and rhythmically vital textures. These permeate both the *Sinfonia concertante* and the Second Violin Concerto, which he composed a year later. The folk elements in the *Sinfonia concertante* are not in fact particularly obvious on the surface of the first two movements, but come to prominence in the finale, with its ostinato rhythms and strongly marked folk-dance character.

© Andrew Huth

∿ Violin Concerto No. 1, Op. 35 (1916)

Szymanowski wrote the first of his two violin concertos in 1916, during what is usually described as his 'Impressionist' period – the time when he really found himself as a composer. Whether or not the label 'Impressionist' is appropriate, the sound Szymanowski draws from the orchestra is unique, instantly recognisable. By the standards of the early twentieth century, the number of instruments is not remarkable, though they include two harps as well as a piano and several percussion instruments. Yet the effect of spaciousness, rather than weight or loudness, is extraordinary. Szymanowski's melody and harmony are typical of 'advanced' composers of the time in their empirical mix of pentatonic, chromatic, whole-tone and bitonal elements (the very opening may owe something to the black-against-white note clashes of Stravinsky's *Petrushka*); in fact, Szymanowski seems to be able to do anything he likes while consistently achieving an effect of transparency.

As for the solo part, Szymanowski himself claimed that the style of writing that he developed with the help of his friend, the violinist Pawel Kochánski, created a new mode of expression for the instrument, which can be summarised as 'ecstatic'. Pitched mostly (though not invariably) very high, it was intended only for the most accomplished players, preferably with a very sweet tone. All its technical devices are collected in the cadenza which Kochánski wrote near the end of the work.

Kochánski was to have given the first performance in St Petersburg at the beginning of February 1917, with Alexander Siloti conducting: political unrest put paid to that. In the event, the leader of the Warsaw Philharmonic Orchestra, Józef Oziminski, played it, with Emil Mlynarski conducting, in the capital of the new Polish Republic on 1 November 1922. Kochánski introduced it to America in 1924, with Leopold Stokowski, in New York and Philadelphia.

However dazzling the writing for the violin, the concerto is not a vehicle for bravura display: the orchestra is used with restraint, and there is no dramatic confrontation or argument; instead, the relationship between soloist and orchestra recalls Chausson's *Poème*, written twenty years earlier, though that has a very different expressive character.

Szymanowski took his inspiration for this concerto from the poem 'May Night' by Tadeusz Micinski:

> Asses in crowns settle majestically on the grass –
> fireflies are kissing the wild rose –
> and Death shimmers on the pond
> and plays a frivolous song.
> Ephemerids
> Fly into dance –
> oh, flowers of the lakes, Nereids!
> Pan plays his pipes in the oak grove.
> Ephemerids
> fly into dance,
> fly into dance –
> plaited in amorous embrace
> eternally young and holy –
> stabbed with a lethal dart.
> In the twinkling blue water
> golden crucians and roach,
> and patient kingfishers
> gaze with their eyes of steel –
> and on the trees the hammering of the little
>   blacksmiths,
> amid the sorb, red crooked-beaks
> and kestrels with eyes like tinder –
> merrily whistling and chanting
> I fly: here over the water – there under the
>   trees . . .
> In the woods are glades as if appointed
> for these nocturnal revels.
> All the birds pay tribute to me,
> for today I wed a Goddess . . .
> And now we stand by the lake,
> in crimson blossoms,
> in flowing tears of joy, with rapture and fear,
> burning in amorous conflagrations:
> the fire seizes these aged trees

and they shed tears of pitch,
and the familiar gull from the Polar seas
describes a halo over us.

Translation by Sylvia and Benjamin Shoshan, taken from the BBC Music
Guide *Szymanowski* by Christopher Palmer, 1983

The concerto is in a single movement, though constantly
fluctuating – floating, transfixed in reverie, dancing, driven –
but never moving towards a goal, for it is all a dream, from
the first excited fluttering in the orchestra to the soloist's
final disappearance into the stratosphere. Szymanowski
summed up the whole as 'awfully fantastic and unexpected'.
It takes some time for two themes, or rather motifs, to
emerge – a swooning six-note descending phrase, and a
grimly emphatic motif of four notes (two descending semi-
tones followed by a rising minor third); these provide a kind
of structural scaffolding. Midway occurs a still, sublime
moment in which the violin at last reveals its heart then,
coming to its senses, gets busy; it's recalled later, shortly
before the cadenza. Surely Szymanowski intended it all to
remain a beautiful mystery.

© Adrian Jack

❧ Violin Concerto No. 2, Op. 61 (1933)

Moderato – Cadenza – Allegramente – Andantino –
Allegramente

The Second Violin Concerto was Szymanowski's last major
work, the summit of his love affair with the violin and the culmination of his absorption in Polish folk music. His First
Violin Concerto, composed sixteen years earlier, stood at the
centre of a group of works which take an exotic, impressionistic style to the limits of its possibilities. But by the early
1920s Szymanowski felt a need for both renewal and simplifi-
cation in his language. In the winter of 1922–3 he first visited
Zakopane in the Tatra mountains of southern Poland and was

captivated by the 'savage, natural native originality' of the region's folk music.

In this music he heard a freshness and vigour which showed him the way towards the greater clarity of expression which he aimed for. The profusion of intricate and decorative detail in the impressionist works now gave way to strong, unbroken melody; the mastery of orchestral colour was directed towards more solid and rhythmically vital textures. The down-to-earth elements of folk music give the Second Violin Concerto a very different sound from the hedonistic dream-world of the First; but beyond these stylistic differences, the constant aim of Szymanowski's art is unchanged: to conjure up an ideal, often erotically charged world where this passionate but lonely man could live freely, if only in his imagination.

Szymanowski was hopelessly impractical at managing either his personal or professional life. He did, however, have the good fortune to be supported by a group of performers who were devoted to his music. His younger sister Stanislawa (1887–1938) had a notable international career as a soprano and became an ideal interpreter of his songs; Artur Rubinstein (1887–1982) was a lifelong advocate of his piano music; and the orchestral works were vigorously promoted by the conductor Grzegorz Fitelberg (1879–1953). As for Szymanowski's violin works, they owe much of their style to the virtuoso player Pawel Kochánski (1887–1934), whom Szymanowski met in the early years of the century when they were both studying in Warsaw. They embarked on a lifelong personal and artistic friendship: the works Szymanowski composed especially for Kochánski include, as well as both of the violin concertos, the Nocturne and Tarantella and the group of three *Myths* for violin and piano.

'The Second Violin Concerto was squeezed out of me in four weeks by Kochánski,' the composer wrote, exaggerating only slightly. He had already made a rough draft of the concerto when he went to Paris in June 1932 for a two-month stay. There he showed the sketches to Kochánski, who was immediately enthusiastic. In August the two men went together to Szymanowski's house at Zakopane to work together on the concerto for a month. As he had for the First Violin Concerto, Kochánski gave the composer technical advice for the violin part, prepared all the bowings and fingerings and composed the formidable solo cadenza. The first performance took place in Warsaw on 6 October 1933 with Fitelberg conducting the Warsaw Philharmonic. This was the only performance of the work that Kochánski was able to give: already seriously ill, he died three months later in New York. His wife was convinced that work on the concerto had hastened his death and never forgave the composer. Deeply upset, Szymanowski soon developed a superstitious fear of the piece and disliked even speaking of it.

Like the First Violin Concerto, the Second is cast in a single continuous movement; but whereas the earlier work is very complex in form, the Second is formally perhaps his most clearly laid out major work. It falls into two roughly equal parts (the first a sonata-allegro, the second a rondo) which are separated by the cadenza. The exalted, virtuoso playing of the violin is naturally the centre of attention, but there is no question of a simple relationship of a predominant solo and accompanying orchestra. The textures are closely blended, and the relationship between the two is one of stylistic variation rather than opposition, as they share the same musical material but interpret it in their different ways.

The two particular areas of the violin's potential which Szymanowski exploits are extended lyricism (predominant in the concerto's first section), and a sharply rhythmic folk-fiddling style, with much use of double stopping (especially in the second section). This folk-derived style, like certain other features of harmony and texture in the concerto, may sometimes be reminiscent of Bartók, though there was in fact a reciprocal influence: when the Hungarian composer was about to compose his own violin sonatas in 1921, he made a careful study of Szymanowski's violin music.

© Andrew Huth

John Tavener (b. 1944)

John Tavener's extended religious odyssey, which ended with his commitment to Orthodoxy, has taken his music on many varied paths, including major religious works such as *Ultimos ritos* (1969–72). He was inspired to compose by the first broadcast of Stravinsky's *Canticum sacrum* and came to prominence in 1968 with his cantata *The Whale* for the first concert of the London Sinfonietta – featuring a spoken part, amplified percussion and loudhailers for the choir. His conversion to Orthodoxy in 1977 resulted in a profusion of devotional works, some on a large scale – such as *Akathist of Thanksgiving* (1987), for the millennial anniversary of the Russian Orthodox Church; the three-hour oratorio *The Apocalypse*, premiered at the BBC Proms in 1994; *Fall and Resurrection* (1999), premiered at St Paul's Cathedral; and *The Veil of the Temple*, a seven-hour vigil (2002). *The Protecting Veil* for cello and strings has won enormous popularity – as, since its performance at the funeral service of Diana, Princess of Wales in 1997, has the *Song for Athene* (1993), alongside such popular choral works as *The Lamb* and *The Tyger*.

∾ *The Protecting Veil* (1987)

1 The Protecting Veil
2 The Nativity of the Mother of God
3 Annunciation
4 The Incarnation
5 Lament of the Mother of God at the Cross
6 Christ is Risen!
7 The Dormition of the Mother of God
8 The Protecting Veil

Among more than two hundred letters which John Tavener received following the first performance of *The Protecting Veil* at the 1989 BBC Proms, one particularly moved him. Unaware of the religious meaning of the work's title, the writer asked if Tavener's intention was in some kind of way to protect the ancient Platonic concept of truth and beauty. Setting aside the specific ideas which had inspired *The Protecting Veil*, Tavener felt that this had been exactly his purpose, 'to uphold that very unfashionable concept of truth and beauty'.

In the 1980s such ideals became more widespread. The contemplative, mystical spaciousness of Tavener's music seemed in tune with a general revival of spirituality, something which had been largely swept aside by the iconoclastic and intolerant intellectualism of the 1950s and 1960s. Harmony and consonance were re-embraced, as composers turned aside from complexity to what Tavener claims to be music's primordial sacred purpose.

These arguably retrogressive tendencies have their detractors. Yet interestingly, both Tavener and the composers whose styles are close to his – Arvo Pärt and Henryk Górecki – have both served time with the avant-garde. Within the wide variety of current styles, Tavener, like Pärt and Górecki, may represent an extreme, but the lucidity, sincerity and serenity of his music nevertheless clearly answers a need. There can hardly have been a period in history when such diverse styles co-existed, or when music encompassed such a gamut: from the labyrinthine intricacy of Ferneyhough, via the fast machines of later-day minimalism and the colourful pluralism of Henze or Ligeti, to the quiet austerity of Tavener and Górecki. But then, in no other age has mankind been simultaneously so absorbed by a microscopic analysis of the physical world and by the immensity of cosmic space.

Anyone encountering John Tavener's music for the first time should be prepared for its extended time-scale and essentially non-eventful manner. The forty-five minutes of *The Protecting Veil* are, in effect, a single melodic trajectory, a mesmeric 'endless arch', like the ancient music of India and Byzantium which Tavener has found an abiding source of inspiration. *The Protecting Veil* is by no means a conventional

concerto, there being neither virtuoso display nor any polar-
isation of soloist and orchestra. Its most striking feature is the
sustained intensity of the cello playing, at the top of its register, an impassioned melody representing the power of the
Virgin. So prolonged is this elevated chant (whose very duration makes great demands on the soloist) that the cello's eventual descent to its normal register seems like a major event.
The orchestral part throughout the work is confined only to
strings, which surround the cellist with a radiant, resonant
halo of sound.

In *The Protecting Veil* Tavener has tried to capture, as he says,
'some of the cosmic power of the Mother of God, whom the
cello – which never stops singing throughout – represents'. His
starting point was the Orthodox Feast of the Protecting Veil of
the Mother of God, which commemorates the Virgin's appearance in the church at Vlacherni, Constantinople, early in the
tenth century. Tavener explains:

> At a time of grave danger for the Greeks from Saracen
> invasion, Andrew, the 'holy fool', together with his
> disciple Epiphanius, saw the Mother of God during an
> all-night vigil: she was standing high up above them in
> the air, surrounded by a host of saints. She was praying
> earnestly and spreading out her Veil as a protective shelter
> over the Christians. Heartened by this vision, the Greeks
> withstood the Saracen assault and drove away the Saracen
> army. The Feast of the Protecting Veil is kept by the
> Orthodox Church in celebration of this event.

Tavener's music is more reflective than precisely illustra-
tive, but nevertheless follows a loose programme geometri-
cally arranged in eight continuous sections. The first and last
represent the cosmic beauty of the Mother of God and her
power over a shattered world. The second relates to her birth,
the third to her Annunciation, the fourth to the Incarnation,
the fifth (which is totally unaccompanied) to her Lament at the
Foot of the Cross, the sixth to the Resurrection (starting with
a series of high, ethereal string chords) and the seventh to her

Dormition (i.e. her death or 'falling asleep'). After returning to the opening vision, *The Protecting Veil* ends with a musical evocation of the Virgin's tears, an extraordinary passage of glissandi. Overall, the music proceeds strophically like an ancient chant, in which most of the ideas return, perhaps several times. Tavener has described it as 'an attempt to make a lyrical ikon in sound, rather than in wood'.

The Protecting Veil was composed in 1987, after Steven Isserlis had suggested to Tavener that he should write a piece for cello and strings. Tavener had written nothing previously on such a scale without the voice, and in a sense, the extended high cantilena of the solo cello part acts as a substitute voice, almost human in its song-like lyricism. The enormous success of both the premiere of *The Protecting Veil* at the 1989 BBC Proms and its subsequent recording by Isserlis and the London Symphony Orchestra led to its topping the classical charts, and its winning the 1992 *Gramophone* Award for Best Contemporary Recording, among a number of awards and nominations. Can such instant popularity be lasting? In an interview with Andrew Stewart, John Tavener commented: 'If you believe, as I do, that the chant of any culture goes right back to the dawn of civilisation, and comes from the breath of God, although it's an extreme point of view, it might explain why such a piece has proved so attractive.'

© Richard Steinitz

Pyotr Ilyich Tchaikovsky (1840–93)

After study at the School of Jurisprudence and four years working in the Ministry of Justice, Tchaikovsky enrolled at the newly founded St Petersburg Conservatory (1862–5). He came into contact with 'The Five', whose leader, Balakirev, supervised the younger composer's *Romeo and Juliet* overture (1869), which already displayed a gift for tragic lyricism. Despite his homosexuality, he married a young admirer of his music in 1877, which proved disastrous after a matter of weeks. That year also saw the beginning of a fourteen-year relationship with Nadezhda von Meck: though they never met, she acted as Tchaikovsky's benefactress and soulmate by correspondence, and the ballet *Swan Lake*, the Fourth Symphony and the opera *Eugene Onegin* were the results of her support. A fallow period followed the successful Violin Concerto (1878), lasting until the *Manfred* Symphony (1884). Between 1890 and 1892 he wrote two further ballets, *The Sleeping Beauty* and *The Nutcracker*, demonstrating a skill and seriousness of purpose in the medium unusual for a composer principally renowned for his symphonies. He died, possibly through suicide, within ten days of conducting the premiere of his Sixth Symphony.

∿ Piano Concerto No. 1 in B flat minor, Op. 23 (1874–5)

1 Allegro non troppo e molto maestoso – Allegro con spirito
2 Andantino semplice – Prestissimo
3 Allegro con fuoco

The genesis of most of Tchaikovsky's major works is well documented: letters, diaries, anecdotes and reported conversations often pinpoint the inception of a new project. But in the case of his First Piano Concerto, composed during the last two months of 1874, we know nothing. We do, however, know only too well what happened when Tchaikovsky took the newly composed work to his friend and mentor Nikolay Rubinstein, hoping for friendly technical advice on the piano writing. It was Christmas Eve 1874, and what occurred proved to be one of the most humiliating episodes in Tchaikovsky's life. Three years later he recalled:

> I played the first movement. Not a single word, not a single comment! . . . I fortified my patience and played on to the end. Again silence. I got up and asked 'Well?'
>
> It was then that there began to flow from Nikolay Grigoryevich's mouth a stream of words, quiet at first, but subsequently assuming more and more the tone of Jove the Thunderer. It appeared that my concerto was worthless, that it was unplayable, that passages were trite, awkward, and so clumsy that it was impossible to put them right, that as composition it was bad and tawdry, that I had filched this bit from here and that bit from there, that there were only two or three pages that could be retained, and that the rest would have to be scrapped or completely revised . . . In a word, any outsider who chanced to come into the room might have thought that I was an imbecile, an untalented scribbler who understood nothing, who had come to an eminent musician to pester him with his rubbish.

Even if Tchaikovsky exaggerated Rubinstein's reaction, it must have been a frightful scene. All the same, it would be wrong to condemn Rubinstein out of hand. He was certainly no fool, and was particularly well disposed towards Tchaikovsky's music. Tchaikovsky, though a competent pianist, was no virtuoso, and it is unlikely that he was able to give a very convincing account of his own concerto; the highly original structural features may simply have sounded eccentric to Rubinstein in the composer's nervous performance, the piano writing jumbled and unidiomatic. Rubinstein soon changed his opinion, though, for not only did he conduct the first Moscow performance of the work less than a year later, but he then learned the piano part and eventually became one of the concerto's most persuasive advocates.

The concerto has puzzled many people since that Christmas Eve of 1874, among them the English critic who described its opening as 'one of the most baffling solecisms in the music of any great composer'. There were many classical precedents for beginning a work in an apparently misleading key (Haydn's two B minor string quartets, for example, or Beethoven's First and Ninth Symphonies); what is startling about Tchaikovsky's concerto is that the imperious opening horn call is unambiguously in the *right* key, B flat minor, but that the music swings immediately into D flat, the relative major, for a grand, expansive melody which is never heard again in the course of the work.

We so readily associate Tchaikovsky's music with minor-key pathos that it tends to be overlooked just how misleading is the title of one of his most popular works. Even without the long D flat introduction, there is something very tentative about the appearance of B flat minor when the soloist introduces the main body of the movement with a tripping theme which the composer acknowledged to be based on a Ukrainian folk song. The more personal second group of themes tends to avoid minor keys, and at the recapitulation, B flat minor is banished in favour of the major with almost nervous haste.

The slow movement returns to the D flat major of the introduction. It is a nocturne-like meditation, one of Tchaikovsky's great melodic inspirations. At its centre lies another remarkable structural innovation: a prestissimo scherzando section in which, beneath the soloist's figurations, the strings play another borrowed tune. The source was not admitted by the composer, but his brother Modest pointed it out: a French *chansonette* entitled '*Il faut s'amuser, danser et rire*', a great favourite of the Belgian singer Désirée Artôt, with whom Tchaikovsky had for a time fancied himself in love.

The opening of the finale recalls the music vigorously to B flat minor with another acknowledged Ukrainian tune; but it is not the character – still less the key – of this lively folk dance that dominates the movement. That is done by the second theme, heard first in D flat and then in B flat major. This surging melody (which has probably done more than anything else to earn the concerto its huge popularity) provides a perfectly satisfying balance to the first movement's much-disputed 'wrong-key' introduction, and at the same time confirms the concerto as a work of the brightest major-key optimism.

© Andrew Huth

ᴄᴡ Piano Concerto No. 2 in G major, Op. 44
(1879–80)

1 Allegro brillante
2 Andante non troppo
3 Allegro con fuoco

As Mme Larina and the Nurse sing in *Eugene Onegin*, 'Habit is sent to us from above in place of happiness.' For a man as lonely and unsure of himself as Tchaikovsky, inactivity was the greatest enemy. He quite rightly prided himself on his professionalism, and remarked that a commissioned work undertaken out of a sense of duty, or perhaps simply for money, would often turn out better than something he had composed out of an inner sense of artistic compulsion. In October 1879, while staying at his sister's estate in the Ukraine, he found himself free of external obligations for the first time in many months. He wrote to his brother Modest:

These last days I've begun to observe in myself things which I didn't at first understand. I experienced a certain vague dissatisfaction with myself, an over-frequent and almost irresistible desire to sleep, a certain emptiness, and finally boredom. There were times when I didn't know what to do with myself. I had to get on with something: I find myself absolutely incapable of living long without work. Today I began to create something, and the boredom vanished as if by magic.

The 'something' turned out to be a piano concerto, a successor to the work in B flat minor which was now beginning to make its way in the world. Within ten days he had sketched out the first movement; the other two movements were drafted in Paris in November. On 3 December, just before leaving for Rome, he wrote to Mme von Meck: 'The sketch of my concerto is now complete and I am very satisfied with it, especially the second half of the Andante.' Other commitments delayed the orchestration of the work, which was not completed until 28 April 1880, seven weeks after his return to Russia.

At an early stage, Tchaikovsky had decided to dedicate the new concerto to Nikolay Rubinstein – the very man who five years earlier had been so damning in his initial reactions to the First Piano Concerto, but who had in the meantime been won round to become one of its most persuasive champions. In August Tchaikovsky wrote to his publisher Jürgenson:

In the spring I sent Rubinstein the concerto and asked him to give me his comments after he had played it and to let Taneyev [Tchaikovsky's favourite pupil] change as many details of the piano part as he wished without touching the essentials, of which, *no matter how much I was advised, I wouldn't change a single bar*. Taneyev wrote and told me that *there was absolutely nothing to be changed*. In other words, this was Rubinstein's opinion, so now we only have to wait until he has learned it. When is he going to do this?

Rubinstein never did learn the work, for he died in March 1881. It was a severe personal and artistic blow to Tchaikovsky, who dedicated his next major composition, the Piano Trio, to Rubinstein's memory. The concerto had its premiere in New

York in November 1881, and its first Russian performance in Moscow in May 1882.

A year after composing the concerto, Tchaikovsky wrote: 'To my mind, the piano can be effective only in three situations: (1) alone, (2) in a contest with the orchestra, (3) as accompaniment, that is, as the background to a picture.' The presentation of the concerto's big opening theme first by the orchestra, and then by the solo piano, establishes from the beginning an unusual feature of this first movement: the relative separateness of orchestra and soloist. They share the same material, it is true, but Tchaikovsky treats them almost as separate elements in the formal design, working along parallel lines rather than together. In the enormous development section (which occupies almost half of the entire movement) this separation is remarkable. After forty-eight bars for orchestra alone there is a passage of thirteen bars for piano and orchestra; thirty-one bars for piano alone follow; then an eighteen-bar passage for piano and orchestra; then fifty-eight bars for orchestra alone, and finally a 132-bar piano solo – development and cadenza combined – which eventually leads back into the recapitulation.

In the slow movement the orchestra's role is further distanced from that of the piano by the prominence given to two other soloists: a violin and a cello, who singly, together, or with the piano carry much of the burden of the movement's outer sections. The slightly quicker central section ends with short cadenzas for both of the string soloists before the reprise of the main theme in a pure piano-trio texture.

Piano and orchestra achieve integration and a more equal degree of partnership in the finale, whose three themes, all duple-time dance rhythms, are juggled with great formal ingenuity. Considerably shorter than the two previous movements, it is lighter in mood, but unsparing throughout of the soloist's virtuosity.

The popularity of the First Piano Concerto has led to the comparative neglect of the Second; but perhaps another factor contributing to this neglect was the bowdlerised edition in general circulation for many years. Writing to Tchaikovsky some time after the first Moscow performance, Taneyev observed that although the work had been well received, it was generally agreed that the first and second movements were too long, and that too much prominence had been given to the solo violin and cello in the second. Tchaikovsky replied, with justifiable irony:

> I will freely admit that it suffers from being too long, and regret that those people to whom critical examination of the score was entrusted two years ago [i.e. Nikolay Rubinstein and Taneyev himself] did not point out this deficiency at the time. In doing so, they would have rendered me a great service, greater even, perhaps, than performing the concerto so magnificently in its present imperfect state.

In 1888 Tchaikovsky made three very minor cuts, one in the first movement and two in the Andante. The pianist Alexander Siloti had already suggested more sweeping cuts, but Tchaikovsky rejected them out of hand. The matter was raised again five years later, when Jürgenson wished to bring out a new edition of the score. Tchaikovsky wrote: 'I have agreed to certain of Siloti's changes, others I quite definitely cannot accept. He is overdoing it in his desire to make this concerto easy, and wants me literally to mutilate it for the sake of simplicity.' But the new edition only appeared four years after Tchaikovsky's death, and the concerto's reputation had to live down all of Siloti's damaging cuts, rewritings and alterations.

© Andrew Huth

∾ Piano Concerto No. 3 in E flat major, Op. 75 (1893)

Allegro brillante

In the spring of 1892 Tchaikovsky returned to Russia from a short tour of Western Europe which had included the

Hamburg premiere of *Eugene Onegin*, conducted by Gustav Mahler. In May he moved to his last house at Klin, near Moscow (now preserved as a Tchaikovsky museum), and set to work on a new symphony in E flat major.

Tchaikovsky's evaluation of his own works was often erratic. He had not been particularly satisfied with some recent orchestral compositions; he tended to disparage the newly completed *Nutcracker*, and had even gone so far as to destroy the score of his symphonic ballad *The Voyevode* after conducting its first performance in November 1891. The new symphony, too, was going to prove troublesome. The entire four-movement work was drafted by October and Tchaikovsky then began the orchestration, but broke off towards the end of the first movement's development section. In December he wrote to Vladimir Davidov (his nephew 'Bob'):

> I have gone over attentively and, so to speak, looked
> with an impartial eye at my new symphony, which,
> fortunately, I have not had the time to orchestrate and
> release for performance. The impression it produces is far
> from flattering; in a word, the symphony was written just
> for the sake of writing something, and contains nothing
> interesting or appealing. I have decided to scrap it and
> forget about it. This decision is irrevocable, and it is a
> good thing I have taken it.

He wrote to Bob again two months later: 'You know that I have destroyed the symphony which I wrote and partly orchestrated in the autumn.' But it was not destroyed, merely set aside. Tchaikovsky had been seized with the idea for another symphony – the 'Pathétique' – and became absorbed in it to the exclusion of all other work. In July, however, even before he had completed the orchestration of the 'Pathétique', he returned to the E flat symphony, obviously feeling that its music was far too good to waste. He set to work recasting three of its movements as a piano concerto. By September, when the first movement was finished, his doubts had returned. 'Since it is inordinately long,' he wrote to the pianist Alexander Siloti, 'I have decided to leave only one movement, which I'll call *Allegro de Concert*, or perhaps *Konzertstück*.' (Russian, like English, lacks a satisfactory word for this type of piece.)

We cannot tell how firm Tchaikovsky's decision was, for he died a month after writing this letter. Sergey Taneyev later prepared a version of the Andante and Finale for piano and orchestra from Tchaikovsky's drafts, but these movements (later published under the opus number 79) are too conjectural to carry much authority. Their most satisfactory version is to be found in the reconstruction of the entire four-movement symphony made by the Soviet scholar Semyon Bogatyrev, first performed in Moscow in 1957 under the title 'Symphony No. 7'. Bogatyrev argued convincingly that the *Scherzo-fantaisie* in E flat minor from Tchaikovsky's Eighteen Piano Pieces Op. 72 was originally intended as the symphony's third movement.

Although Tchaikovsky said he found the Allegro brillante 'inordinately long', it is in fact no longer than the opening movements of his previous two piano concertos, and indeed its more tightly knit construction actually makes it seem shorter in performance. Its genesis as the first movement of a symphony means that it is not a lyrically discursive work, but a compact structure which allows little opportunity for anything not strictly related to the symphonic argument. In recasting the piece, Tchaikovsky made only one significant formal change: the insertion of a long solo cadenza between the end of the development and the beginning of the recapitulation. Apart from this extra section, essential to the work's dramatic balance, the differences between symphony and concerto are all ones of texture and instrumentation.

Without knowing the work's history, it would be impossible to deduce that the piano part had been grafted on to an already composed movement. Soloist and orchestra are very finely balanced, sharing and exchanging material on far more equal terms than in any other of Tchaikovsky's concertante works. His ingenuity in devising effective piano figurations and in adapting his themes to the characters of different instruments is never strained or ostentatious, but seems to arise naturally from the progress of the musical argument. Structural and decorative elements cannot be separated; nothing is superfluous, and nothing is overstated.

Composers are not always the best judges of their own works. Tchaikovsky's absorption in the 'Pathétique' Symphony probably accounts for much of his coolness towards the music which eventually became the Third Piano Concerto; perhaps he simply felt that it was not the sort of music he wanted to be composing at that particular time. Be that as it may, the high quality of its invention and construction should earn the concerto a firm place among Tchaikovsky's finest works.

© Andrew Huth

∾ Violin Concerto in D major, Op. 35
(1878)

1   Allegro moderato – Moderato assai
2   Canzonetta: Andante –
3   Finale: Allegro vivacissimo

The Violin Concerto came to Tchaikovsky quite unexpectedly. In March 1878 he was staying with his brother Modest at Clarens on Lake Geneva, and had begun to compose a piano sonata. It was eight months since his ill considered marriage, which had been followed by flight from his wife, mental and physical breakdown, and wretched months of wandering in Western Europe during which he was only slowly able to recover his health. He occupied himself with the scoring of the Fourth Symphony and his opera *Eugene Onegin*, but felt incapable of starting any new project. The piano sonata, undertaken more from a sense of duty than anything else, was exasperating him: 'Am I played out? I have to squeeze out of myself weak and worthless ideas, and ponder every bar.'

Then on 14 March he was joined by the young violinist Josef Kotek, who was then studying with Joachim in Berlin. Kotek had graduated in 1876 from the Moscow Conservatoire, where he had attended Tchaikovsky's theory class. He had been engaged during that year to play for the wealthy widow Nadezhda von Meck, and it was largely as a result of this that there began the extraordinary correspondence between Tchaikovsky and the patroness he never met. There has been much speculation as to the degree of intimacy that existed between the composer and his pupil; but their closeness is attested by the fact that the only two witnesses at Tchaikovsky's wedding were his brother Anatoly and Kotek.

With Kotek's arrival at Clarens, Tchaikovsky's spirits improved enormously. The two musicians indulged in hours of music-making together, and one of the pieces they played was a violin and piano arrangement of the recently published *Symphonie espagnole* by Lalo. 'It has a lot of freshness, lightness, of piquant rhythms, of beautifully and excellently harmonised melodies,' wrote Tchaikovsky to Mme von Meck. 'He, in the same way as Léo Delibes and Bizet, does not strive after profundity, but he carefully avoids routine, seeks out new forms, and thinks more about *musical beauty* than about observing established traditions, as do the Germans.'

Three days after Kotek's arrival, Tchaikovsky laid aside the recalcitrant piano sonata and embarked on a work of his own for violin and orchestra. Within eleven days he had finished the concerto, completing the scoring in a further two weeks. Both Modest and Kotek, however, had reservations about the original slow movement, and Tchaikovsky came to agree with them (the piece survives as *Méditation*, the first of the three violin and piano pieces that make up the *Souvenir d'un lieu cher*, Op. 42). The present Canzonetta was quickly composed in its place.

The concerto's early career was problematic. Although Kotek would have been the obvious choice of dedicatee, Tchaikovsky decided instead to inscribe the work to Leopold Auer. Fear of malicious gossip may have played some part in this (or so Tchaikovsky hinted to his publisher), but it may also have been that Tchaikovsky felt Auer's distinction would enhance the new work's appeal. If so, the dedication misfired, as the composer admitted:

> I do not know whether Auer was flattered by my dedication – only that, despite his sincere friendship for me, he never wanted to master the difficulties of this concerto, deemed it awkward to play – and that a verdict such as this from the authoritative St Petersburg virtuoso cast my poor child for many years into the abyss, it seemed, of eternal oblivion.

It was Adolf Brodsky who eventually gave the work its first performance in December 1881 in Vienna. Public opinion was divided, but generally unenthusiastic, and the critic Eduard Hanslick outdid himself in nastiness by observing that it was one of those pieces of music in which 'you could hear how they stink' (Tchaikovsky could quote the entire review by heart for the rest of his life). Brodsky introduced the concerto to Moscow nine months later, this time to the kind of enthusiastic reception that has greeted the work ever since.

The circumstances of the concerto's composition show Tchaikovsky in a brief period of happiness, turning aside for a moment from his personal worries and, in doing so, rediscovering an aspect of his musical nature that had lain neglected for too long. The Violin Concerto does not aim at the emotional charge and formal daring of *Eugene Onegin* or the Fourth Symphony, works whose creation was inextricably bound up with the personal turmoil of the previous year. Rather, it shows Tchaikovsky's supreme mastery of those qualities he admired so much in Lalo's *Symphonie espagnole*.

The concerto begins with an introduction which foreshadows themes to come and is, unusually, in a slightly quicker tempo than the main body of the first movement. This is a lucid sonata-form design based around three themes, all introduced by the soloist. As in Mendelssohn's Violin

Concerto, the cadenza is placed at the end of the development, leading to a reprise where the main theme reappears, magically, on the flute. Throughout the movement (and indeed the concerto) Tchaikovsky achieves a wonderful balance between statement and development, structure and decoration, sentiment and display.

The Canzonetta, Tchaikovsky's substitute for his original slow movement, is in the key of G minor. Its fragility and remoteness from the brilliance of the flanking movements is enhanced by the fact that it neither begins nor ends in its tonic key: at the opening, wind instruments modulate from D major, cadencing into G minor only with the entry of the soloist and the muted orchestral strings with the melancholy principal theme; at the end of the movement, this music returns to provide another modulating link to the Finale.

It was this roughly vigorous movement that most outraged Hanslick. Beginning with an orchestral flourish and an anticipatory cadenza for the soloist, it develops into one of Tchaikovsky's most rhythmically taut finales. In contrast to the urbane charm of the first movement and the vocal cantilena of the second, both themes are dance-inspired; and throughout, a quick duple metre is resourcefully exploited to provide an exciting demonstration of Tchaikovsky's Russianness at its most extrovert.

© Andrew Huth

Michael Tippett (1905–98)

Tippett studied at the Royal College of Music, but he was unhappy with his early works and withdrew them, seeking a period of further study – of counterpoint with R. O. Morris – which prepared the ground for his first mature works, the String Quartet No. 1 (1935; rev. 1944) and the Piano Sonata No. 1 (1936–7). His moral and political convictions pervaded his life and music: he conducted in Oxted, Surrey, in the 1930s, then organised the South London Orchestra of Unemployed Musicians, and was imprisoned for three months in 1943 for refusing to comply with military exemption requirements. After the war he was a leader of the revival of early music at Morley College. His first public success was the oratorio *A Child of Our Time* (1939–41), a public statement against persecution, which included settings of Negro spirituals. He wrote five operas, also to his own texts, as well as four concertos, four piano sonatas, five string quartets, and two major choral works concerned with Man's relationship to Time, *The Vision of St Augustine* (1965) and the vast, eclectic *The Mask of Time* (1980–2).

∾ Triple Concerto (1978–9)

1 Medium fast – Interlude (Medium slow) –
2 Very slow, calmer still – Interlude (Medium fast) –
3 Medium fast

The peaks in Michael Tippett's musical output are his oratorios *A Child of Our Time* and *The Mask of Time*, and his five operas. These are works of synthesis. They draw together many facets from within his richly diverse creative personality. In among these dramatic pieces are instrumental and vocal compositions which are either offshoots from them or a prefiguration of their stylistic and formal character. Thus, for example, the *Fantasia Concertante on a Theme of Corelli* (1953) and the Piano Concerto (1955) stem directly from Tippett's first opera, *The Midsummer Marriage* (completed in 1952); whereas much of his Symphony No. 2 (1956–7) offers clues to the nature of his second opera, *King Priam*, completed in 1961.

Tippett's Concerto for violin, viola, cello and orchestra (1978–9) was one of a succession of works with a new formal pedigree. Each of them – the Fourth Symphony (1976–7), Fourth String Quartet (1977–8) and this Triple Concerto – comprises a continuous span of music whose component sections are nevertheless distinguishable. The composer described the Fourth Symphony as a 'birth-to-death' piece. The Fourth Quartet and Triple Concerto also begin with a musical 'birth motif' and encompass a whole cycle of experience, though they are quite different in character. Already when writing them, Tippett was preparing himself for *The Mask of Time* (1980–2), which centres upon myths of Creation, Man and Time. Such preparation entailed a change of style from hard-hitting rhetoric to effulgent lyricism, and we can observe this change listening in turn to the Fourth Symphony, Fourth Quartet and Triple Concerto. Significantly, *The Mask of Time* – another work of synthesis – quotes from all three.

Near the end of Tippett's Fourth Quartet, there is a sudden descent from violence into a mood of peace and rapture, suggesting the possibility of a new beginning. This provided Tippett with a specific reference point in the Triple Concerto, bringing together the three soloists for the first time: for, after the work has been launched by an orchestral 'birth motif', the soloists – first viola, then cello, then violin – are introduced as three quite distinct and independent instrumental personalities, and thus their first ensemble passage only just resolves their differences.

Probably influenced by the first movement of Elgar's Violin Concerto, Tippett excludes the standard development section here and writes a first movement (not, though, a separate movement) whose formal shape allows pride of place to its freely burgeoning invention. The orchestral birth motif introduces each part, transposed up a tone on its second appearance. The main focus throughout is the lyricism of the solo writing. The other ingredients – motifs on the brass and the woodwind, an important ritornello idea consisting of exchanges between orchestra and soloists – simply provide a context for the rapturous contributions of the soloists.

Linking the three movements are short interludes, the first setting the scene for the nocturnal slow movement, and the second (featuring timpani, untuned percussion and fanfare-like outbursts on the brass) greeting the dawn and daylight that are manifest in the finale.

The slow movement contains evidence of Tippett's response to Javanese music, which he first heard in the flesh, so to speak, shortly before he began the concerto. Here he has recreated in his own way those textures in gamelan music in which a solo singer, perhaps also a flute or (bowed) string instrument, join together for the same serene flow of endless melody. Surrounding the melody are the softest gong sounds which often (to Tippett's ears) add a 'bluesy' colouring to the inflections of the melody.

Formally, this movement is straightforward, with two orchestral episodes temporarily halting the soloists' flow of ornate melody. Tippett adds further embellishment to the soloists' lines, giving two of them an obbligato orchestral instrument: the cello pairs off with the bass oboe; the violin is partnered by an alto flute. When the violin and viola embark on a duet in canon, the orchestral strings accompany them with fast pizzicatos (another transformation of gamelan texture). Only occasionally does any latent tension come near to the surface: for the most part, the mood is one of ecstasy and rapture.

After the second interlude, there is a slow episode of explicit 'dawn' music (even quoting from the concluding dawn scene in *The Midsummer Marriage*) with the soloists playing music of increasingly decorative character. The finale proper gets under way with the orchestra enunciating a tune which Tippett marks 'singing, rich, golden', the brass supplying punctuation. This tune is extended in three further stages, after the soloists have added their own commentary.

In a succeeding transitional passage, in which the ritornello idea from the first movement is recalled and the soloists contribute a dancing countertheme, we reach once again the original birth motif and the opening cadenzas which are now modified. As if to emphasise that this work is potentially endless, Tippett suddenly fragments his mosaic and leaves us to continue it in our own minds.

The Triple Concerto was premiered at a BBC Proms concert on 22 August 1980, by György Pauk, Nobuko Imai and Ralph Kirshbaum, with the London Symphony Orchestra conducted by Sir Colin Davis.

© Meirion Bowen

Ralph Vaughan Williams (1872–1958)

Unlike Elgar before him, Vaughan Williams received a traditional musical education at the Royal College of Music in London, but he also studied abroad – in Berlin with Bruch and in Paris with Ravel. Soon after his return came the *Fantasia on a Theme by Thomas Tallis* and *A Sea Symphony* (1910); he became active as a collector of folk music and edited *The English Hymnal* (1906). After completing his second symphony, *A London Symphony* (1913), he joined the army. As well as choral works such as *Sancta civitas* (1925) and *Serenade to Music* (1938), he wrote a Mass and made many choral arrangements of English folk songs. Apart from *The Lark Ascending* for violin and orchestra, his concerto-type works – for viola (*Flos campi*), piano, oboe and tuba – remain rarely performed. After the death of his first wife, he remarried aged eighty, and produced two more symphonies before his death.

✦ *The Lark Ascending*: romance for violin and orchestra (1914; rev. 1920)

This idyllic piece – the quintessence of the English pastoral idiom – was sketched out in 1914, on the eve of the Great War, and revised in 1920. By 1914, Vaughan Williams (then aged forty-one) had established himself as a composer of stature, with two symphonies (the *Sea* and the *London*) to his credit. Despite his relatively advanced age, however, he refused to shirk his duty to his country, and in August 1914 he enlisted as an orderly with the Royal Army Medical Corps, with whom he served in France and Salonika. In 1918 he returned to France as an artillery officer.

The war took a terrible toll on British music, as on all art forms. In 1916 Vaughan Williams wrote to his close friend Gustav Holst from France:

I've indeed longed to be home in many ways during the last month – but in other ways I should not like to come home for good till everything is over, or in some other normal way . . . I sometimes dread coming back to normal life with so many gaps – especially of course George Butterworth – he has left most of his MS. to me – and now I hear that Ellis is killed – out of those seven who joined up together in August 1914 only three are left.

Among the musical dead, two years after the start of the war, were the composers Cecil Coles and George Butterworth, the cellist Edward Mason, the concert promoter F. B. Ellis and the pianist Denis Browne – all colleagues of Vaughan Williams. Yet while the unimaginable horror of the Western Front left an immediate mark on English literature – most notably in the savage war poems of Wilfred Owen and Siegfried Sassoon – English music was slow to react. It was as if its revitalisation through the rediscovery of its roots in Tudor music, and the newly pervasive influence of folk song, were too recent to be disturbed by the trauma of war.

As Michael Kennedy has pointed out, there is no musical equivalent of Wilfred Owen: the bitter aftertaste of war lingers mainly in the music of those not directly involved in the fighting – Elgar, Bridge, Ireland and Bax. Those who fought and survived, including Vaughan Williams, Ivor Gurney and Arthur Bliss, seemed to find solace in their newly discovered pastoral idioms: on his demobilisation in 1919, Vaughan Williams turned to the revision of several pre-war works, including the *London* and *Sea* symphonies, the *Tallis Fantasia*, the opera *Hugh the Drover* and *The Lark Ascending*.

The Lark Ascending was completed in an atmosphere of utter rural tranquillity at King's Weston, the lovely West Country home of Philip Napier Miles. Miles was a benefactor of the Glastonbury Festival, the 'English Bayreuth', which ran from 1914 until 1926, and included some 350 staged performances, including six operas by its founder, Rutland Boughton, together with revivals of then unknown works by Gluck, Purcell, Blow, Locke and others. In 1919 Vaughan Williams was among the visitors to the festival, and soon became a regular house guest at King's Weston, a mansion built by Vanbrugh which looked westwards out over the Bristol Channel. There, in December 1920, Vaughan Williams and the violinist Marie Hall put the finishing touches to *The Lark Ascending*. With the pianist Geoffrey Mendham, Hall first played the piece in public at a local choral society concert, prior to giving its London premiere in 1921 at the Queen's Hall, with the British Symphony Orchestra under Adrian Boult.

By then styles were changing, and out of a long programme *The Lark Ascending* was the only piece, as *The Times* remarked, 'which showed serene disregard of the fashions of today or yesterday. It dreams its way along.' And, ever indifferent to the dictates of fashion, Vaughan Williams continued to mine this rich idyllic seam in his next major works – *A Pastoral Symphony* and the Bunyan-inspired 'pastoral episode' *The Shepherds of the Delectable Mountains* (later included in his opera *The Pilgrim's Progress*).

The Lark Ascending was inspired by a poem by the Victorian writer George Meredith, the following lines from which Vaughan Williams quoted as a preface to the score. They offer as succinct a description of the music as one could want:

> He rises and begins to round,
> He drops the silver chain of sound,
> Of many links without a break,
> In chirrup, whistle, slur and shake . . .
> For singing till his heaven fills,
> 'Tis love of earth that he instils,
> And ever winging up and up,
> Our valley is his golden cup,
> And he the wine which overflows

To lift us with him as he goes . . .
Till lost on his aerial rings
In light, and then the fancy sings.

© Wendy Thompson

Antonio Vivaldi (1678–1741)

Vivaldi was born in Venice, where his father gave him violin lessons. At fifteen he began training for the priesthood, and in 1703, the year of his ordination, he began his long association with the Ospedale della Pietà, one of the city's four boarding schools for orphan girls. His first works, the Op. 1 Trio Sonatas and Op. 2 Violin Sonatas, were published in 1705 and 1709, but he won wider repute with his set of twelve concertos *L'estro armonico*, Op. 3, published in Amsterdam. His *Ottone in villa* (1713), premiered in Vicenza, was the first of almost a hundred operas (many now lost), and his sacred oratorio *Juditha triumphans* (1716) is a testament to the musical talents of the girls at the Ospedale. From 1718 to 1720 Vivaldi was in the service of Prince Philip of Hesse-Darmstadt, governor of Mantua; during the 1720s he played for the Pope and was granted several audiences with Emperor Charles VI. However, his career declined in the 1730s, and in 1740 Vivaldi moved to Vienna, where he died in poverty.

The Four Seasons (before 1725)

∿ Violin Concerto in E major, Op. 8 No. 1, 'La primavera' (Spring), RV269

1 Allegro
2 Largo e pianissimo sempre
3 Danza pastorale: Allegro

∿ Violin Concerto in G minor, Op. 8 No. 2, 'L'estate' (Summer), RV315

1 Allegro non molto
2 Adagio – Presto
3 Presto

✍ Violin Concerto in F major, Op. 8 No. 3, 'L'autunno' (Autumn), RV293

1 Allegro
2 Adagio molto
3 Allegro

✍ Violin Concerto in F minor, Op. 8 No. 4, 'L'inverno' (Winter), RV297

1 Allegro non molto
2 Largo
3 Allegro

That the four violin concertos of Vivaldi's *The Four Seasons* are among the best-loved pieces in the entire classical repertory should not blind cynics to their worth. Sometimes works which achieve 'popular classics' status really have earned their position, and *The Four Seasons* – tuneful, skilfully written and upliftingly evocative of their subject – are a prime example. Despite having achieved considerable fame in their own time, they were virtually forgotten from the middle of the eighteenth century until the middle of the twentieth, when they began their rise to ubiquity with the help of the recording industry and the post-war emergence of the chamber orchestra. There have now been well over 150 different recordings, while visitors to Venice can take their pick of costumed *Four Seasons* concerts in the city's churches, testament to this music's lasting freshness. Enduringly attractive, unquenchably vital and genuinely his own, Vivaldi's special magic refuses to stale.

Little is known about these works' origins. They were first published in 1725, as the first four concertos of a set of twelve, Vivaldi's Op. 8. *The Four Seasons*, however, were clearly a few years old by then, since in his dedication of the set Vivaldi begs his Bohemian patron, Count Wenzel von Morzin, 'not to be surprised if among these few and feeble concertos, Your

Illustrious Grace will find the Four Seasons, already long since under the indulgent and generous eye of Your Grace'. But the composer also wrote of his 'great pride' in publishing them, and we can be sure that he considered them to be Op. 8's principal selling point, since the title he gave to the set as a whole – *Il cimento dell'armonia e dell' inventione* (The contest between harmony and invention) – is a perfect description of their dynamic mix of compositional 'correctness' with the wilder demands of musical descriptiveness.

Further evidence of Vivaldi's special regard for *The Four Seasons* rests in the unique inclusion in the original printed score of four sonnets – possibly by the composer himself – which set out the scenes and events described in the music. To make things still clearer, there is even a 'key' in the form of letters indicating the relevant passages in the music. Thus we know that the sinuously chromatic line for the soloist towards the end of the first movement of Summer depicts a shepherd boy crying for fear of an approaching storm, that the caperings of Autumn's first movement are those of drunken peasants at harvest time, and that the bleakly tentative opening to the last movement of Winter evokes the uncertainties of walking on ice. Such representations require elucidation, perhaps, but there are numerous others in which the intended effect is clear enough; for instance the birdsong in the first movements of Spring and Summer, or the various storms which seem to afflict Vivaldi's countryside so regularly. Others still would have been readily apparent to an audience of the composer's time, among whom opera-goers in particular would have recognised such standard stage devices as the undulating violin lines for streams in the first movement of Spring, the prancing music of the hunt in the last movement of Autumn, or the 'teeth-chattering' tremolos in the first movement of Winter.

It would be a mistake, however, to see these concertos as mere identikit constructions. Vivaldi's use of stock elements is not only unfailingly effective but utterly true to his own distinctive musical voice. And he can be startlingly original, for instance in the second movement of Spring, where the shepherd (represented by the soloist) slumbers among rustling leaves (orchestral violins) while his faithful dog barks (violas), or the extraordinary, dream-like 'sleep' movement of Autumn. Finally there are fleeting moments of pictorial genius, like a well-placed brushstroke, such as the first stirrings of the breeze which disturb the dog-day torpor in the first movement of Summer (conjured by nothing more than high violin triplets), the sudden whiplash of the corn in the storm which follows, or the almost tangible cosiness of the fireside scene in the slow movement of Winter, where pizzicato violins imitate rain hitting the window outside.

Within a few decades of his death, Vivaldi was remembered solely as a fine violinist; his music was dismissed as wilfully bizarre, more concerned with achieving effect than pleasing the ear. Yet the rehabilitation of *The Four Seasons* is a perfect example of how music can do both, making it possible to enjoy it just as well with a knowledge of its descriptive subtext as without. Either way, these four concertos are masterpieces of the Baroque age.

© Lindsay Kemp

William Walton (1902–83)

Born in industrial Lancashire, Walton made an early escape to Oxford, becoming a chorister at Christ Church Cathedral, then staying on at Christ Church as an undergraduate. Here he had the good fortune to fall in with the literary Sitwell family (Edith, Sacheverell and Osbert), who supported him for ten years as well as introducing him to leading artists of the day. His *Façade* (1922) – a chic, jazzy entertainment for reciter and ensemble, to texts by Edith – caused a stir. The Viola Concerto (1928–9) soon followed, as did the cantata *Belshazzar's Feast* (1929–31), which quickly became a staple of British choral societies. During the 1940s he produced film scores for, among others, Olivier's *Henry V* and *Hamlet*. Following his marriage in 1949 he and his wife Susana moved to Ischia, off the Naples coast. He also wrote concertos for violin (1938–9) and cello (1956–7), and showed a flair for occasional music, displayed in the marches *Crown Imperial* and *Orb and Sceptre* written for the coronations of George VI and Elizabeth II respectively.

∾ Cello Concerto (1956–7)

1 Moderato
2 Allegro appassionato
3 Lento – Allegro molto – Adagio

Every composer's work can be perceived as a blend of action and reflection, and compositions in which reflection is primary are more likely to earn the label 'Romantic' than those in which the active elements are uppermost. For Walton, however, like Elgar, the terms action and reflection seem too neutral. 'Celebration' and 'reverie' are perhaps more appropriate to the public and private poles of styles which have such close associations with facets of national identity. After

Elgar, Walton was our foremost exponent of the ceremonial march, the memorable *pièce d'occasion*. Yet, like Delius rather than Elgar, he spent many years living abroad, and his later music, showing little nostalgia for English pastoral calm or jazz-age perkiness, has an inner warmth which suggests a complete and enviable contentment.

With Elgar's example still in mind, one can easily come to assume that the only successful British cello concerto will be one which is essentially a self-communing swansong, with only rare moments of more active exhibitionism. Walton, whose earlier concertos for viola (1928–9) and violin (1938–9) were replete with a rich lyricism then by no means the predominant feature of his style (as the dramatic force of *Belshazzar's Feast* and the First Symphony confirms), nevertheless had no difficulty in avoiding the imitation of Elgar. His work shuns the elegiac, even at its most expressive. It is at times contemplative, but never bitter. It accepts and celebrates what is, rather than what has been, or might have been.

The concerto was commissioned by Piatigorsky and composed in 1956, two years after Walton's most substantial postwar work, the opera *Troilus and Cressida*. It was written on the island of Ischia, Walton's Italian home, and while a Mediterranean warmth and colour can certainly be sensed throughout, there is an even more basic Waltonian allusiveness of form and style whose qualities have nothing to do with geographical location.

Like the viola and violin concertos, this work is in three movements with the fastest – a garrulous, febrile scherzo – in the middle. The forms of the first two movements evade the more obvious elements of classical precedent, but the third is a clearly defined set of variations – four in all, the second and fourth for cello alone – with an extended coda which reaches beyond recollection of the eloquent theme of the finale and brings the work back to its point of origin in the expansive cadences of the Moderato.

The balance of complex and simple structures is matched by a style whose chief delight is that, though tonal, one is never very sure when a common chord will appear or how long it will last. Equally, the listener is kept guessing about the degree to which a melodic phrase may be prolonged or how many of its accents displaced. *Façade* revealed Walton to be a notably witty composer, and comedy of the most refined variety is present in all but the most overtly serious moments of this work. As in Debussy's late cello sonata, the soloist is a Harlequin rather than a Lear, a Columbine rather than an Electra. The composer's Romanticism cannot even be called 'defiant': it is uninhibited, elegant, supremely entertaining.

© Arnold Whittall

∿ Viola Concerto (1928–9; rev. 1961)

1   Andante comodo – Con spirito – A tempo primo ma
    più lento
2   Vivo, e molto preciso
3   Allegro moderato

We owe the existence of Walton's Viola Concerto to two of the leading lights on England's musical scene in the 1920s. Sir Thomas Beecham suggested to the rising young composer the idea of a concerto for Lionel Tertis. And Tertis himself had already done much to establish the viola as a solo instrument, despite the scant repertory then available.

Walton wrote most of the concerto during a working winter spent with the Sitwell family in Amalfi. Tertis, however, reacted with startled hostility when Walton sent him the completed score, and sent it back by return of post. Fortunately the composer–violist Paul Hindemith agreed to give the premiere instead, and this took place on 3 October 1929 at a Henry Wood Prom in London's Queen's Hall, with Walton conducting. Walton never forgot the older composer's gesture of support; his own *Variations on a Theme by Hindemith* for orchestra, completed in 1963, were a long-promised creative 'thank you'. And Tertis, to his credit, quickly admitted his misjudgement of the new concerto, giving the first of many performances of it in 1930.

Compared to Walton's earlier works, the Viola Concerto announced a deeper, suddenly much more mature musical spirit – one whose wistful Romanticism was now perfectly integrated with the composer's incisive technical skills. Part of the transformation, at least, can be traced in the concerto's dedication: 'To Christabel'. The Hon. Mrs Christabel McLaren (later Lady Aberconway) was a beautiful, intelligent society hostess and unofficial patroness of artists, by whom Walton was deeply smitten. In fact he and Christabel never became lovers, rather to their mutual relief, and they always remained friends. But their relationship played an unmistakable part in the concerto's creation.

In 1961 Walton revised his original score, reducing its triple woodwind to double, omitting the tuba and third trumpet, and adding a harp. Much of the accompanying figuration is quite radically altered in this less astringent later version, and there are also major changes of scoring and tempo: the second movement, for instance, is marked to be played much faster in the revised version. Intriguingly, however, Walton did not withdraw the original score, while making it clear that he preferred his later revision.

The loveliness of the concerto's opening theme, announced by the soloist, is underpinned by the not-quite-clash of harmony with its accompaniment: the viola's second note is C natural, while the bassoon plays C sharp. This harmonic 'false relation' highlights two very different influences on Walton's style – 1920s jazz, and the Tudor church composers whose music he had often sung as a chorister at Oxford's Christ Church Cathedral – and its bitter-sweet sound suffuses the whole work. A second, brisker theme in the viola's low register and its gentler, upper-register pendant (softly accompanied by flute and clarinets) leads into some busy development. Then the first tune's restatement (on high oboe and flute) moves towards a quiet conclusion.

The speedy, tangily scored second movement is driven along by the soloist's non-stop activity; however, this never strays too far from its opening theme, for all the canny and unexpected cross-rhythms that try to catch it out.

The finale grows out of two main tunes: a perky first one stated by solo bassoon; and a graceful, lilting second, introduced a little later by the solo viola above the harp's accompaniment. The movement develops through a passionately sustained climax (where the soloist is silent) towards its haunting conclusion. The finale's main bassoon theme, now on low clarinet and harp, combines with the soloist's recall of the first movement's opening tune; other themes, too, are wistfully restated; and the C natural/C sharp 'false relation' endures to the very final bars.

© Malcolm Hayes

ಊ Violin Concerto (1938–9; rev. 1943)

1   Andante tranquillo
2   Presto capriccioso alla napolitana – Trio (Canzonetta)
    – Tempo I
3   Vivace

Walton composed four concertos: for piano (1926–7; rev. 1943), for viola (1928–9; rev. 1961), for violin (1936; rev. 1943) and for cello (1955–6; rev. 1975). He called the earliest a *Sinfonia concertante* for orchestra with piano; it is a lightweight work in which, as the title suggests, the soloist is as much part of the orchestra as in contest against it. Then came the Viola Concerto of 1929, composed at Beecham's suggestion for Lionel Tertis, whose instrument – with its veiled, middle-register tones – demanded more intimacy than brilliance. Serious, poetic, passionate and committed, it remains one of the great concertos for any instrument of the twentieth century. So, by the time Walton came to write his Violin Concerto, he had had the experience of composing concertante and lyrical works, but not one in which virtuosity was the prime consideration.

William Primrose, who had played the Viola Concerto, suggested to Jascha Heifetz that he ask Walton for a concerto. Heifetz had made his London debut in 1920, and in 1938 was at the height of his powers, his technical perfection serving a rigorous intellect. For Walton it was a challenge, and he had some qualms at undertaking the commission. He had to turn down a lucrative offer for film music, which came at the same time. Then the concerto began to develop 'in an extremely intimate way, not much show, bravura', and Walton wondered whether the 'still small voice' would get over in a vast American concert hall. (This, after the barbaric choruses of *Belshazzar's Feast* and the thrust of the First Symphony! But it was perhaps the relationship of the solo instrument to the orchestra that concerned him.) He worried lest the violin part would not be elaborate enough for Heifetz.

He need not have worried. One distinctive feature of the concerto is that it develops from a gentle, reflective opening to become a vigorous work encompassing extremes of emotion: the soloist enters, *piano*, at the second bar; there is no exposition for orchestra alone. The colouring of clarinets and horns, the soaring solo violin, the rather lush harmonies, all are Romantic. Another feature is that many of the themes are multi-voiced. The generous, dreamy violin melody has a tune under it (cellos with bassoon and clarinet); this 'undertune' is important in the development, and in the recapitulation it is actually played by the soloist, the flute having the main melody. Hammering rhythmic transformations begin the development; the cadenza comes unexpectedly halfway through it, before the second subject is lyrically extended. At the return to the original metre and tempo, there are tender chromatic caresses added in woodwind.

'Alla napolitana' is given as a direction to the second movement. The main theme is a tarantella, composed after Walton had in fact been bitten by a tarantula. It is a brilliant, showy scherzo, insolent in its accent-shifts, precarious tonality and fiendishly difficult harmonics and pizzicatos for the soloist.

Frank Howes described it as an example of that 'sharp, bright, dangerous, and flickering tone' characteristic of Walton. There is a seductive waltz tune, but whereas the first movement was marked by expansive wide-compassed melodies and rich harmony, in this there are some blunt unisons, and the trio-canzonetta tune (solo horn) is compact and conjunct.

The last movement begins with a discreet theme in the bass. The second subject, long, sinuous and flowing over a shimmering accompaniment, is said to reflect the light on the sea from the Villa Cimbrone above Ravello, where Walton composed much of the concerto. His love for Italy was lifelong, from his first visit with the Sitwells in the 1920s, to his eventual home-building on Ischia. His companion in 1938 was Viscountess Wimborne – 'beautiful, intelligent Alice' – who, he later let it be known, inspired this music.

So, like Elgar, Walton enshrined a 'soul' in his Violin Concerto. This, together with the facts that both concertos are in B minor, and both combine a rare intimacy within a virtuoso-style brilliance, has led to comparisons between them. A difference between the two men's composing processes is that Elgar was a master of gradual, subtle transitions, while Walton favours sudden, dramatic mood changes. Also, Elgar's developments seem to arise out of the character of his themes; Walton's suggest the force of circumstances acting on his. Neither method is better than the other, but noting them allows a deeper appreciation of each work.

As in the Viola Concerto, the emotional weight of Walton's Violin Concerto comes towards the end. He turns the opening theme of the finale into a repeated bass, and over this he floats a double-stopped 'memory' of the concerto's opening theme, then runs this into the 'shimmering sea' theme. This bringing together of past and present, as it were, probes deeply and thoughtfully into the experience of this rich music.

The concerto is dedicated to Jascha Heifetz, who gave the first performance with the Cleveland Orchestra under Artur Rodzinski on 7 December 1939. He recorded it twice – under Eugene Goossens in 1941, and then again, in the revised version, with Walton himself in 1950.

© Diana McVeagh

Chronology of works

1717–23	J. S. Bach	Violin Concerto in E Major, BWV 1042
pre-1723	J. S. Bach	Concerto for Two Violins in D minor, BWV 1043
pre-1725	Vivaldi	*The Four Seasons*
1730	J. S. Bach	Violin Concerto in A minor, BWV 1041
c.1730	J. S. Bach	Harpsichord Concerto in D minor, BWV 1052
c.1765	Haydn	Cello Concerto No. 1 in C major
1775	Mozart	Violin Concerto No. 4 in D major, K218
	Mozart	Violin Concerto No. 5 in A major, K219
1779	Mozart	Sinfonia Concertante in F flat major, K364
1784	Mozart	Piano Concerto No. 17 in G major, K453
	Mozart	Piano Concerto No. 19 in F major, K459
1785	Mozart	Piano Concerto No. 20 in D minor, K466
	Mozart	Piano Concerto No. 21 in C major, K467
1785–6	Mozart	Piano Concerto No. 22 in E flat major, K482
1786	Mozart	Piano Concerto No. 23 in A major, K488
	Mozart	Piano Concerto No. 24 in C minor, K491
	Mozart	Piano Concerto No. 25 in C major, K503
	Mozart	Horn Concerto No. 4 in E flat major, K495
1787	Mozart	Horn Concerto No. 3 in E flat major, K447
1788–91	Mozart	Piano Concerto No. 27 in B flat major, K595
c.1788–1801	Beethoven	Piano Concerto No. 2 in B flat major, Op. 19
1791	Mozart	Clarinet Concerto in A major, K622
1795	Beethoven	Piano Concerto No. 1 in C major, Op. 15 (revised 1800–1)
1797–1800	Beethoven	Piano Concerto No. 3 in C minor, Op. 37
1804–6	Beethoven	Piano Concerto No. 4 in G major, Op. 58
1806	Beethoven	Violin Concerto in D major, Op. 61
1809	Beethoven	Piano Concerto No. 5 in E flat major, Op. 73, 'Emperor'
1829–31	Chopin	Piano Concerto No. 2 in F minor, Op. 21
1830	Chopin	Piano Concerto No. 1 in E minor, Op. 11
1832	Mendelssohn	Piano Concerto No. 1 in G minor, Op. 25
1834	Berlioz	*Harold in Italy*, Op. 16
1839	Liszt	Piano Concerto No. 2 in A major (revised 1849–61)
1841–5	Schumann	Piano Concerto in A minor, Op. 54
1844	Mendelssohn	Violin Concerto in E minor, Op. 64
1849	Liszt	Piano Concerto No. 1 in E flat major (revised 1853, 1856)
1849	Liszt	*Totentanz* (revised 1853, 1859)

1850	Schumann	Cello Concerto in A minor, Op. 129
1854–8	Brahms	Piano Concerto No. 1 in D minor, Op. 15
1863	Saint-Saëns	*Introduction and Rondo Capriccioso*, Op. 28
1864–8	Bruch	Violin Concerto No. 1 in G minor
1868	Saint-Saëns	Piano Concerto No. 2 in G minor, Op. 22
	Grieg	Piano Concerto in A Minor, Op. 16 (revised 1907)
1872	Saint-Saëns	Cello Concerto No. 1 in A minor, Op. 33
1874–5	Tchaikovsky	Piano Concerto No. 1 in B flat minor, Op. 23
1878	Tchaikovsky	Violin Concerto in D major, Op. 35
	Brahms	Violin Concerto in D major, Op. 77
1878–81	Brahms	Piano Concerto No. 2 in B flat major, Op. 83
1879–80	Tchaikovsky	Piano Concerto No. 2 in G major, Op. 44
1879–82	Dvořák	Violin Concerto in A minor, Op. 53
1885	Franck	*Symphonic Variations*: for piano and orchestra
1887	Brahms	Concerto for Violin, Cello and Orchestra, Op. 102
1890–1	Rakhmaninov	Piano Concerto No. 1 in F sharp minor, Op. 1 (revised 1917)
1893	Tchaikovsky	Piano Concerto No. 3 in E flat major, Op. 75
1894–5	Dvořák	Cello Concerto in B minor
1900–1	Rakhmaninov	Piano Concerto No. 2 in C minor, Op. 18
1903	Sibelius	Violin Concerto in D minor, Op. 47 (revised 1905)
1907–10	Elgar	Violin Concerto in B minor, Op. 61
1909	Rakhmaninov	Piano Concerto No. 3 in D minor, Op. 30
1909–10	Skryabin	*Prometheus: The Poem of Fire*, Op. 60
1911–15	de Falla	*Nights in the Gardens of Spain*: symphonic impressions for piano and orchestra
1911–12	Prokofiev	Piano Concerto No. 1 in D flat major, Op. 10
1913	Prokofiev	Piano Concerto No. 2 in G minor, Op. 16 (revised 1923)
1914	Dohnányi	*Variations on a Nursery Song*, Op. 25
	V. Williams	*The Lark Ascending*: romance for violin and orchestra (revised 1920)
1916	Szymanowski	Violin Concerto No. 1, Op. 35
1916–17	Prokofiev	Violin Concerto No. 1 in D major, Op. 19
1917–21	Prokofiev	Piano Concerto No. 3 in C major, Op. 26
1919	Elgar	Cello Concerto in E minor, Op. 85
1923–4	Stravinsky	Concerto for Piano and Wind Instruments
1924	Gershwin	*Rhapsody in Blue*
1925	Gershwin	Piano Concerto in F
1926	Bartók	Piano Concerto No. 1
1926	Rakhmaninov	Piano Concerto No. 4 in G minor, Op. 40 (revised 1941)
1928–9	Walton	Viola Concerto (revised 1961)

1929–30	Ravel	Piano Concerto for the Left Hand
1929–31	Ravel	Piano Concerto in G major
1930–1	Bartók	Piano Concerto No. 2
1930	Ireland	Piano Concerto in E flat major
1931	Stravinsky	Violin Concerto in D
1932	Poulenc	Concerto for Two Pianos
	Szymanowski	Symphony No. 4 (*Sinfonia concertante*) for Piano and Orchestra, Op. 60
1933	Shostakovich	Piano Concerto No. 1 in C minor, Op. 35
	Szymanowski	Violin Concerto No. 2, Op. 61
1934	Rakhmaninov	*Rhapsody on a Theme of Paganini*, Op. 43
1934–5	Prokofiev	Violin Concerto No. 2 in G minor, Op. 63
1935	Berg	Violin Concerto
1936	Hindemith	*Trauermusik*
1937–8	Bartók	Violin Concerto No. 2
1938	Britten	Piano Concerto, Op. 13
	Poulenc	Concerto for Organ, Strings and Timpani in G minor
1938–9	Walton	Violin Concerto (revised 1943)
1939	Barber	Violin Concerto, Op. 14
	Britten	Violin Concerto, Op. 15 (revised 1958)
	Rodrigo	*Concierto de Aranjuez*: for Guitar and Orchestra
1942	Strauss	Horn Concerto No. 2 in E flat major
1945	Bartók	Piano Concerto No. 3
1945	Strauss	Concerto for Oboe and Small Orchestra
1947–8	Shostakovich	Violin Concerto No. 1 in A minor, Op. 77 (revised 1955)
1948	Copland	Clarinet Concerto
1956–7	Shostakovich	Piano Concerto No. 2 in F, Op. 102
1956–7	Walton	Cello Concerto
1959	Shostakovich	Cello Concerto No. 1 in E flat major, Op. 107
1970	Lutosławski	Cello Concerto
1978–9	Tippett	Triple Concerto
1974	Arnold	Clarinet Concerto No. 2, Op. 115
1979–85	Dutilleux	Violin Concerto: *L'arbre des songes*
1985–8	Ligeti	Piano Concerto
1985	Schnittke	Viola Concerto
1987	Tavener	*The Protecting Veil*
1988	Lutosławski	Piano Concerto
1991–2	MacMillan	*Veni, Veni, Emmanuel*
1993	Adams	Violin Concerto
1994	Knussen	Horn Concerto (revised 1995)
1996	Gubaidulina	Viola Concerto